PAINT EVERY LITTLE THING

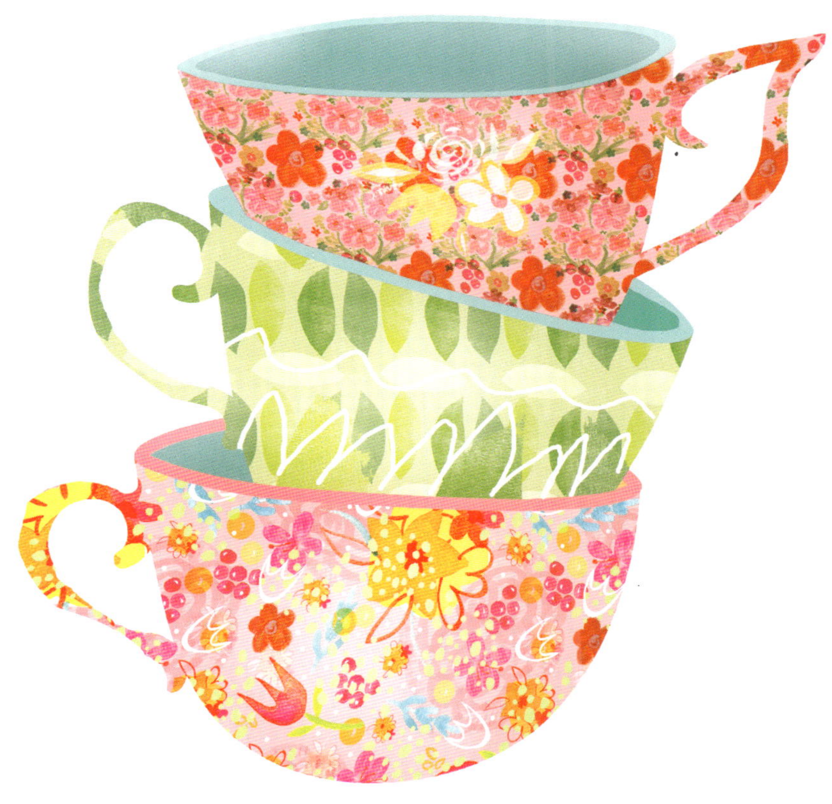

Kristine A. Lombardi

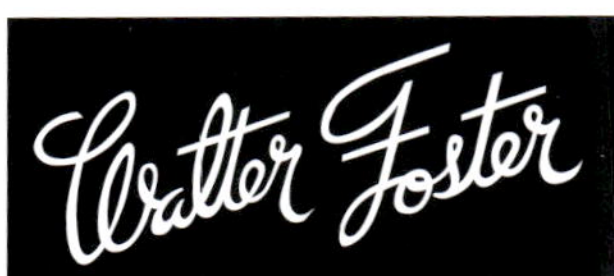

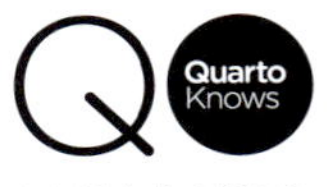

Brimming with creative inspiration, how-to projects, and useful information to enrich your everyday life, Quarto Knows is a favorite destination for those pursuing their interests and passions. Visit our site and dig deeper with our books into your area of interest: Quarto Creates, Quarto Cooks, Quarto Homes, Quarto Lives, Quarto Drives, Quarto Explores, Quarto Gifts, or Quarto Kids.

First published in 2021 by Walter Foster Publishing, an imprint of The Quarto Group.
26391 Crown Valley Parkway, Suite 220, Mission Viejo, CA 92691, USA.
T (949) 380-7510 **F** (949) 380-7575 **www.QuartoKnows.com**

ISBN: 978-1-60058-911-9

Digital edition published in 2021
eISBN: 978-1-60058-912-6

Copyediting by Antara Dutt, Tessera Editorial

Printed in China
10 9 8 7 6 5 4 3 2 1

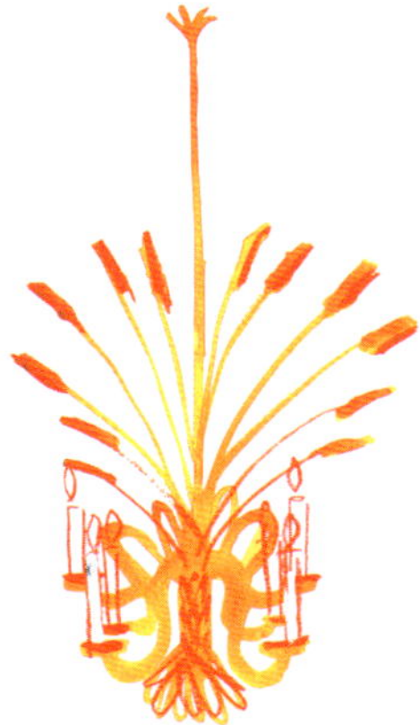

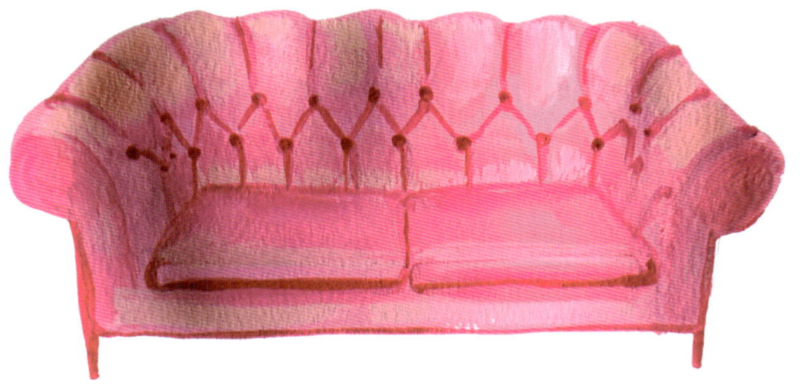

TABLE OF CONTENTS

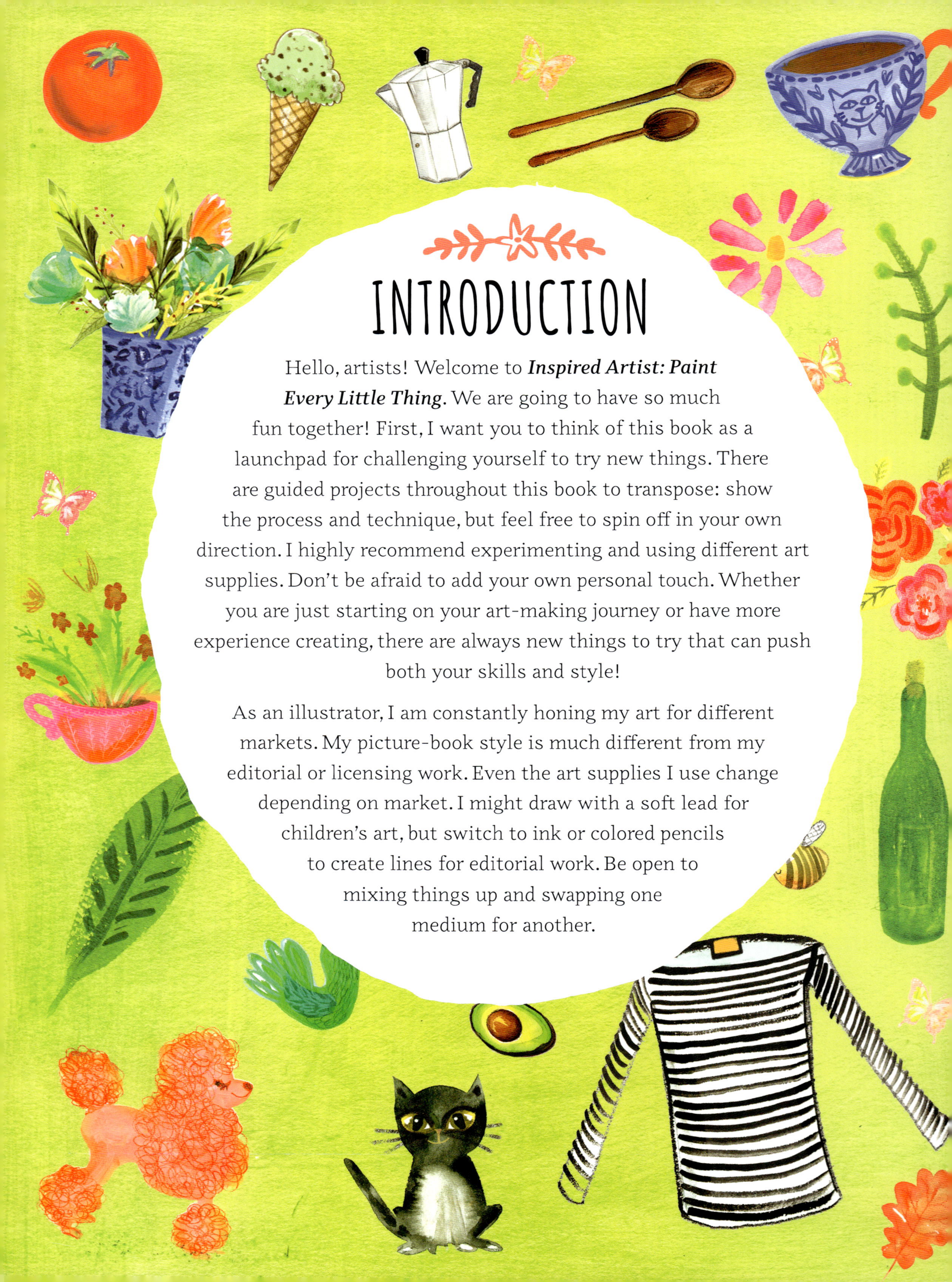

INTRODUCTION

Hello, artists! Welcome to ***Inspired Artist: Paint Every Little Thing***. We are going to have so much fun together! First, I want you to think of this book as a launchpad for challenging yourself to try new things. There are guided projects throughout this book to transpose: show the process and technique, but feel free to spin off in your own direction. I highly recommend experimenting and using different art supplies. Don't be afraid to add your own personal touch. Whether you are just starting on your art-making journey or have more experience creating, there are always new things to try that can push both your skills and style!

As an illustrator, I am constantly honing my art for different markets. My picture-book style is much different from my editorial or licensing work. Even the art supplies I use change depending on market. I might draw with a soft lead for children's art, but switch to ink or colored pencils to create lines for editorial work. Be open to mixing things up and swapping one medium for another.

Nine Different Ways

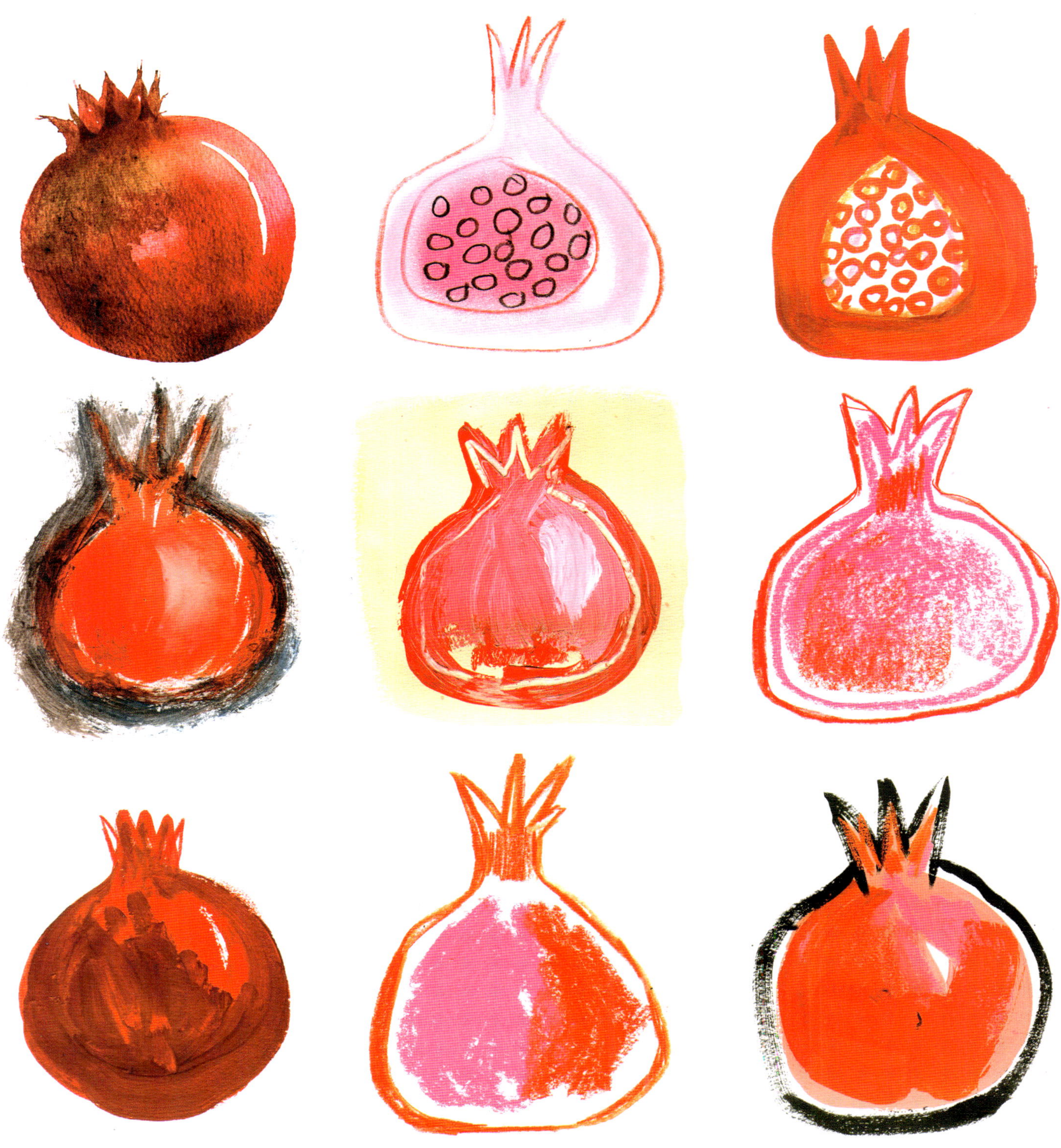

Something fun to explore in this book is what I'm calling "Nine Different Ways," in which I've taken a subject and rendered it in various art mediums, angles, lines, and so on. For example, let's take a look at this pomegranate. This is a gorgeous fruit in terms of color and shape, and its intricate inner pattern of seeds. Your first inclination may be to draw the outer shape, but look further—you could split it open, focus on the textural crown or the juiciness, or capture the myriad colors besides the more obvious red of the fruit. The more you push yourself, the more fun it gets—I promise!

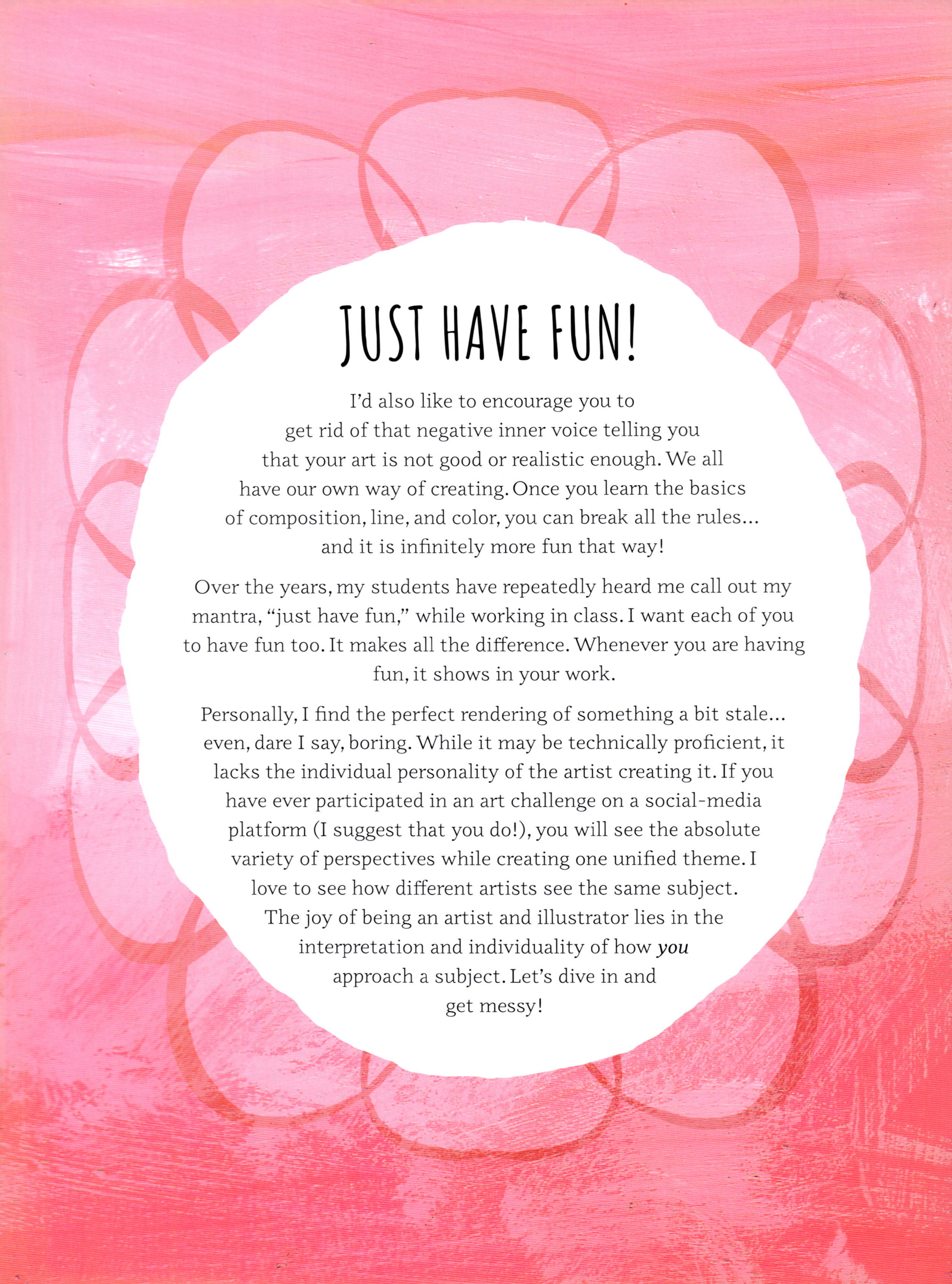

JUST HAVE FUN!

I'd also like to encourage you to get rid of that negative inner voice telling you that your art is not good or realistic enough. We all have our own way of creating. Once you learn the basics of composition, line, and color, you can break all the rules... and it is infinitely more fun that way!

Over the years, my students have repeatedly heard me call out my mantra, "just have fun," while working in class. I want each of you to have fun too. It makes all the difference. Whenever you are having fun, it shows in your work.

Personally, I find the perfect rendering of something a bit stale... even, dare I say, boring. While it may be technically proficient, it lacks the individual personality of the artist creating it. If you have ever participated in an art challenge on a social-media platform (I suggest that you do!), you will see the absolute variety of perspectives while creating one unified theme. I love to see how different artists see the same subject. The joy of being an artist and illustrator lies in the interpretation and individuality of how *you* approach a subject. Let's dive in and get messy!

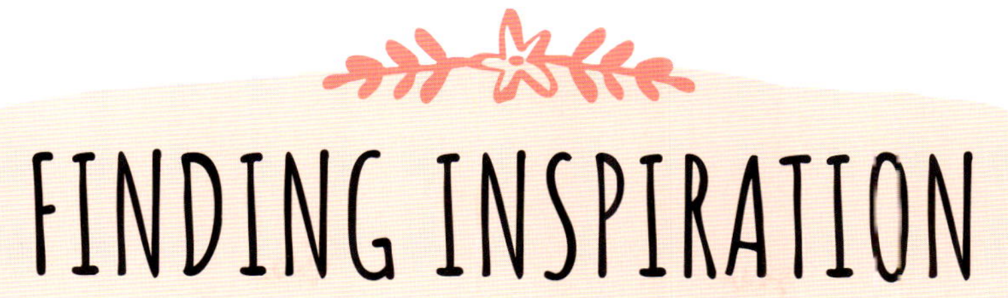

FINDING INSPIRATION

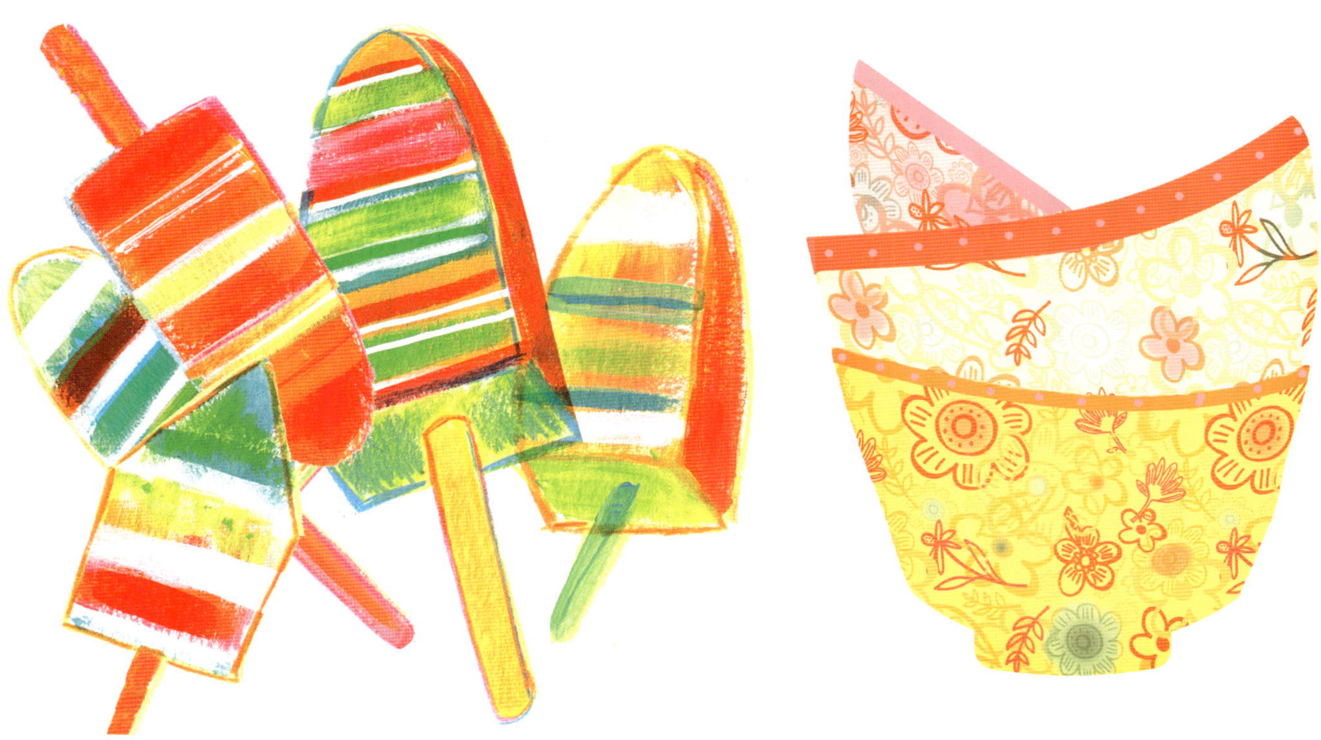

When I'm asked where I find my inspiration, I immediately rattle off at least half a dozen things that come to mind: nature, walking around New York City, vintage picture books, typography, old paper ephemera, and architecture. But my sources extend well beyond those! I find inspiration in just about everything around me.

One of the practices I have kept over the years is culling all those magazines that collect at home and tearing out the pages with images that inspire me. I file the images into colorful themed binders, get a giant box of plastic sleeves from the office-supply store, and slip in two pages back to back. I suppose this is sort of an analog version of Pinterest, but I really like having these binders at my fingertips. I keep them sorted under the following categories: culinary, fashion, home and garden, people and faces, flowers and seasons, and travel.

I've dubbed these my "Eye Candy Binders," and I often flip through them to find inspiration for subject matter, composition, color, and textures. Even if I'm working on a food illustration, I might flip through the fashion binder, often viewing it upside down. I find that after years of illustrating, I tend to gravitate toward the same color palette again and again. By looking at imagery with an objective eye, I can see how other color combinations work successfully in an image. This keeps my work fresh and pushes me to try new things.

It's important that we evolve as artists and makers. There is so much to learn about image making by taking in all the visual data around us. It isn't always a direct path, but there's a reason that certain images resonate with us. If we study them in their totality, we can spot why they work. A bright pop of color looks great paired with a more neutral background, and colors are often comprised of many different hues. For example, a dominant color like the yellow on an autumn leaf actually consists of ochres, umbers, siennas, and caramels.

I love looking at various images to find inspiration, no matter what subject I am working on. I might be looking at the interior of a Cuban restaurant, but find that the bright minty-green wall color, terra-cotta pots, and earthy wooden tables would make a great color combination for a decorative lettering project. Anything is possible! So if you ever feel like you need a creative jolt, reach for those binders! And if that isn't your thing, create folders on Pinterest so that you can keep all the things you love in one place. I can't tell you just how many times I have gone back to look at these binders, and each time I notice something completely different.

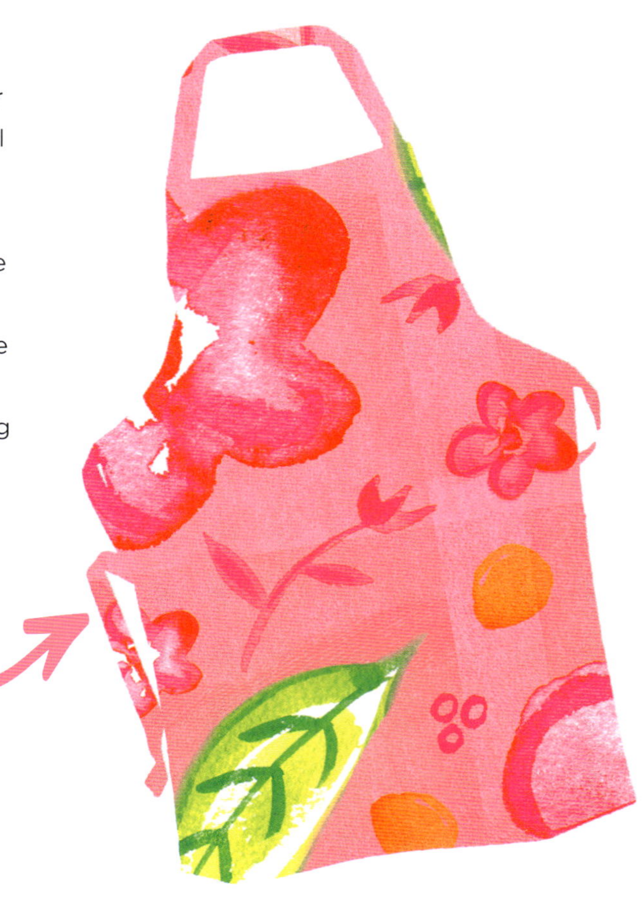

Sometimes inspiration comes from more random places, like a row of colorful nail polish bottles or the chevron arrangement of bricks on a walkway. It could come from the floral fabric on an apron, the stripes on a fishing buoy, or the packaging on a mustard bottle. Be open to all of it! I am constantly taking pictures of things. Some of my favorites are signage and old buildings, but I am also incredibly drawn to vintage and kitsch!

ARTISTIC INSPIRATION

For those of you who might still need some ideas to find your own spark, I have compiled a list possibilities.

- Estate sales
- Antique stores
- Farmer's markets
- Daily walks
- Architecture
- Cafés, bars, and restaurants
- Parks and nature trails
- Cab rides
- Travel
- Gardens
- Cities
- Galleries and museums
- The countryside
- Farms and farm stands
- Magazines
- Old movies
- Baskets and bins
- Fashion
- Fine art
- Records
- Stationery and greeting cards
- Cosmetics
- Perfume bottles
- Interior design
- Industrial design
- Jewelry
- Dishes and ceramics
- Patterns
- Old stamps
- Fabrics
- Furniture
- Food
- Music
- Toys
- Toiletries
- Your closet
- Your cupboards
- Your junk drawer
- Shoes
- Tiles
- Old ledgers
- Pottery
- Glass
- Ceramics
- The beach

Almost anything can provide artistic inspiration if you look hard enough!

A change of your daily scenery may be all you need for a spark of inspiration. I find myself going to ethnic food markets, quirky places like specialty tool shops, restaurant-supply stores, or a crowded cobbler storefront. Sitting in a café is a nice way to be immersed in an environment. The din of the place with all those chattering cups and saucers, the lighting, the music—it's so conducive to creativity. I've done a lot of writing and brainstorming in cafés and find the atmosphere both soothing and stimulating.

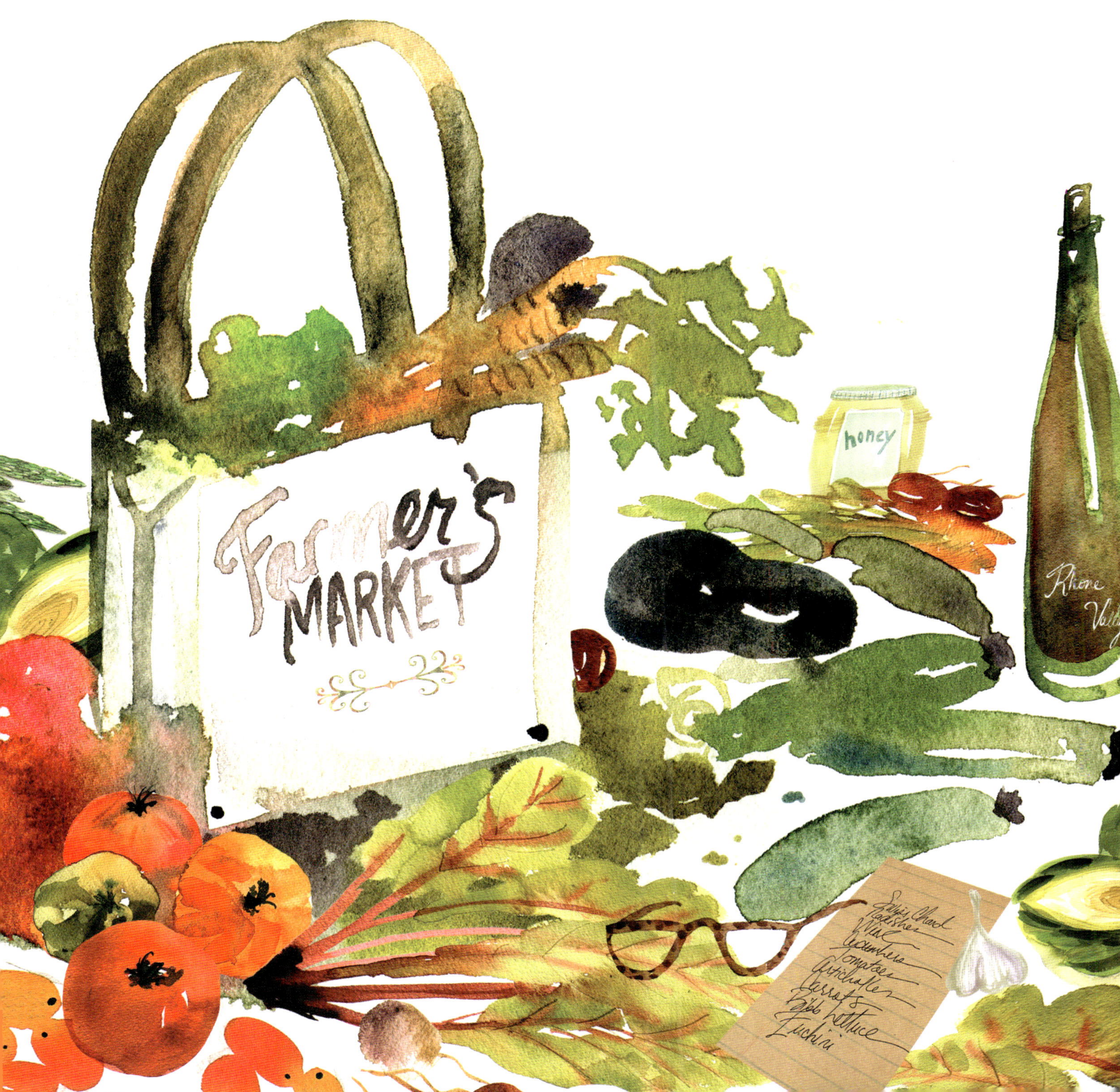

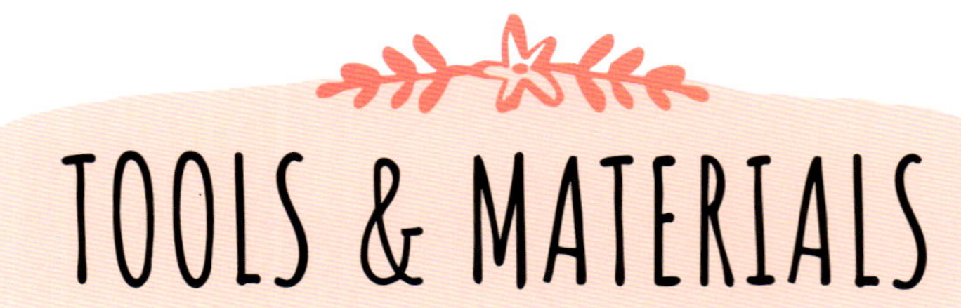

TOOLS & MATERIALS

Experimenting with different mediums can lead to more creativity and discovery. That said, I've focused on watercolor, gouache, colored pencils, pastels, and ink in this book. Feel free to spin off in any direction while trying the projects. Consider them your "base camp," and take them further and add your own touch to them—including different supplies—as you like!

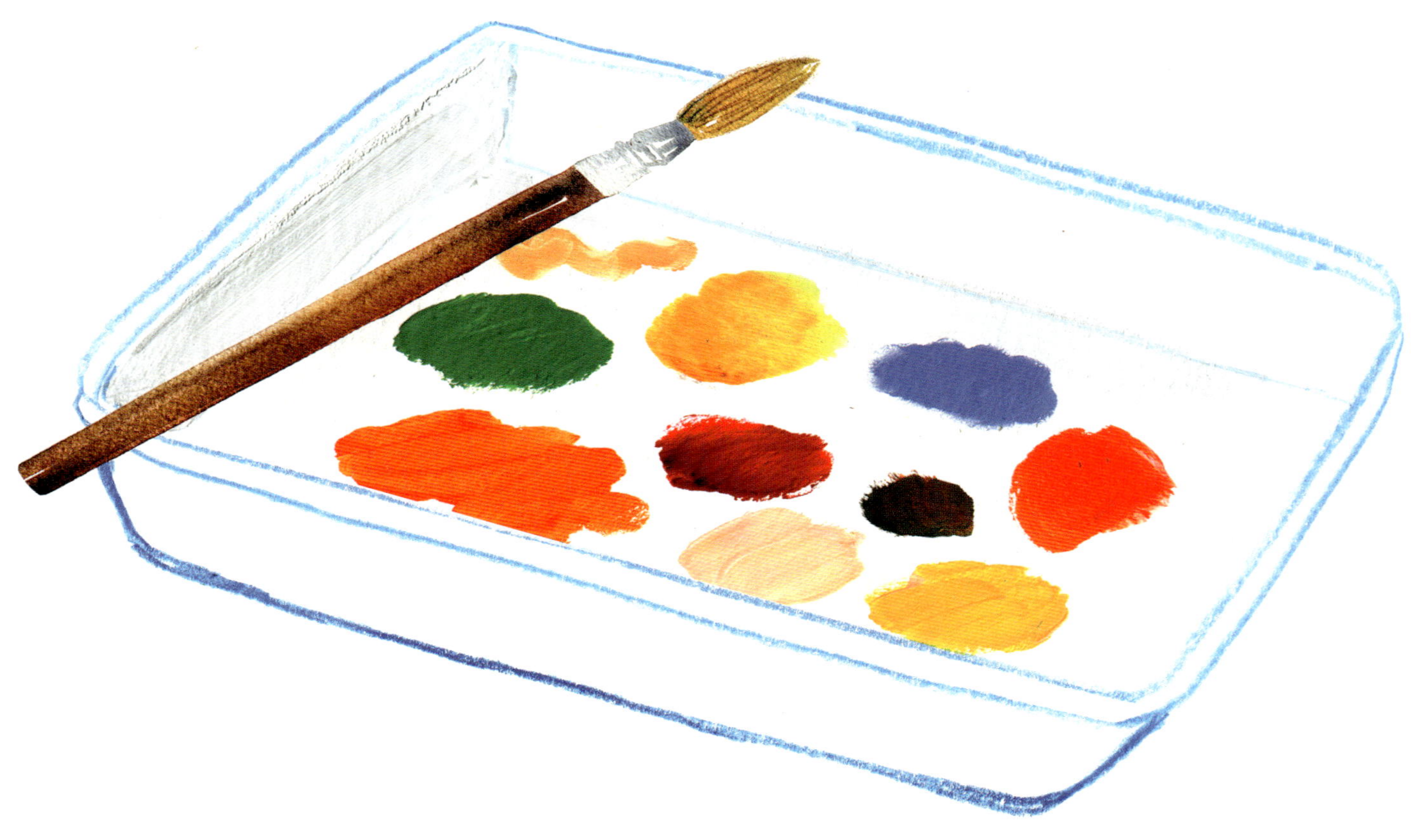

Watercolor

Watercolor is an amazing medium known for its luminosity and overlapping color washes. It can take some time to master, but it has great versatility in its application, and there are many techniques available to the artist.

I prefer Winsor & Newton® tubes, but there are plenty of student-grade options and ready-made kits for those who want to experiment before committing to expensive watercolors. It is a matter of personal choice that I favor tubes, and some artists like pans more. Experiment with both and see which you prefer!

For watercolors, I like a tin with segmented areas that have tilted wells and a center area for mixing. I've also used a much larger plastic palette with additional wells in the studio.

Gouache

Gouache is watercolor's opaque cousin. Its rich, matte color dries quickly, which makes this medium a favorite among illustrators. It comes in both pans and tubes, depending on your preference. For a palette, I find that a large, white, porcelain dinner plate or butcher tray works best. I squeeze out small amounts of pigment and keep a larger dose of white in the center for mixing tints.

For this medium, I favor Holbein Artist Materials® gouache in tubes. The colors are incredibly vibrant and velvety. Of course, they tend to be a bit expensive, so I will often use less expensive brands and save these for special projects. There are student-grade options, which can be purchased in sets at arts-and-crafts stores. You can piggyback special colors onto a basic collection. Always be sure to buy additional white, as you will find that you go through it faster. Since I make many tints in gouache, I always stock up on larger tubes of white (any brand will do) to have on hand. And with pink being one of my favorite colors, I need plenty of white at the ready to mix with red!

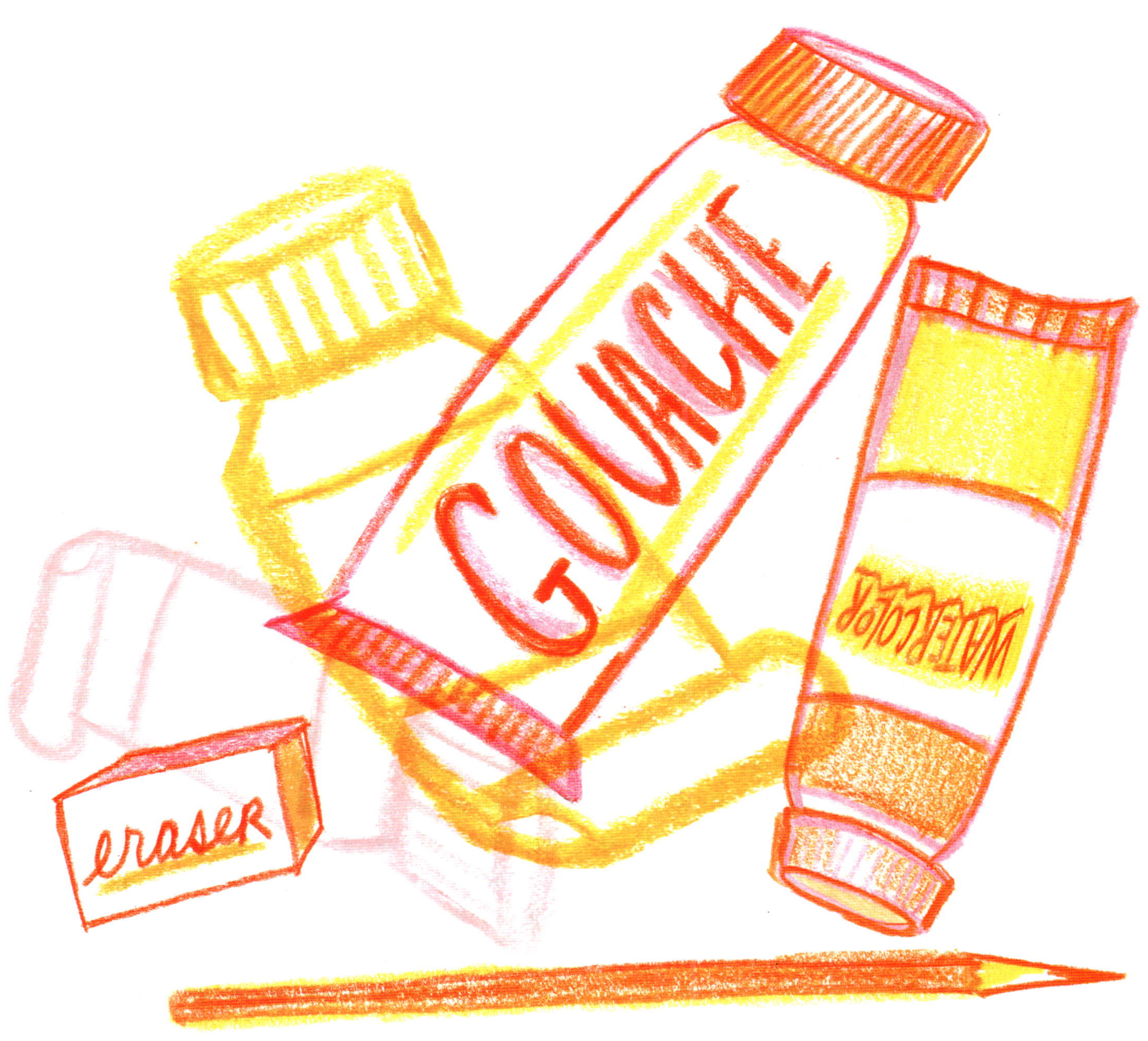

Brushes

There are tons—and I mean tons—of artist brushes out there. But don't be fooled: You can do a lot with very few brushes. And while I like to mix it up and add new brushes to my collection, I find myself returning again and again to the same six brushes. With that in mind, here's a list of those brushes so that you too can keep it simple.

The lineup below is meant more for watercolor projects, but these basic brush types work equally fine for gouache and acrylic. Just be sure to buy stiffer versions with synthetic/nylon bristles. There are plenty of inexpensive options out there, including variety packs. Most of the projects in this book use the same simple brushes.

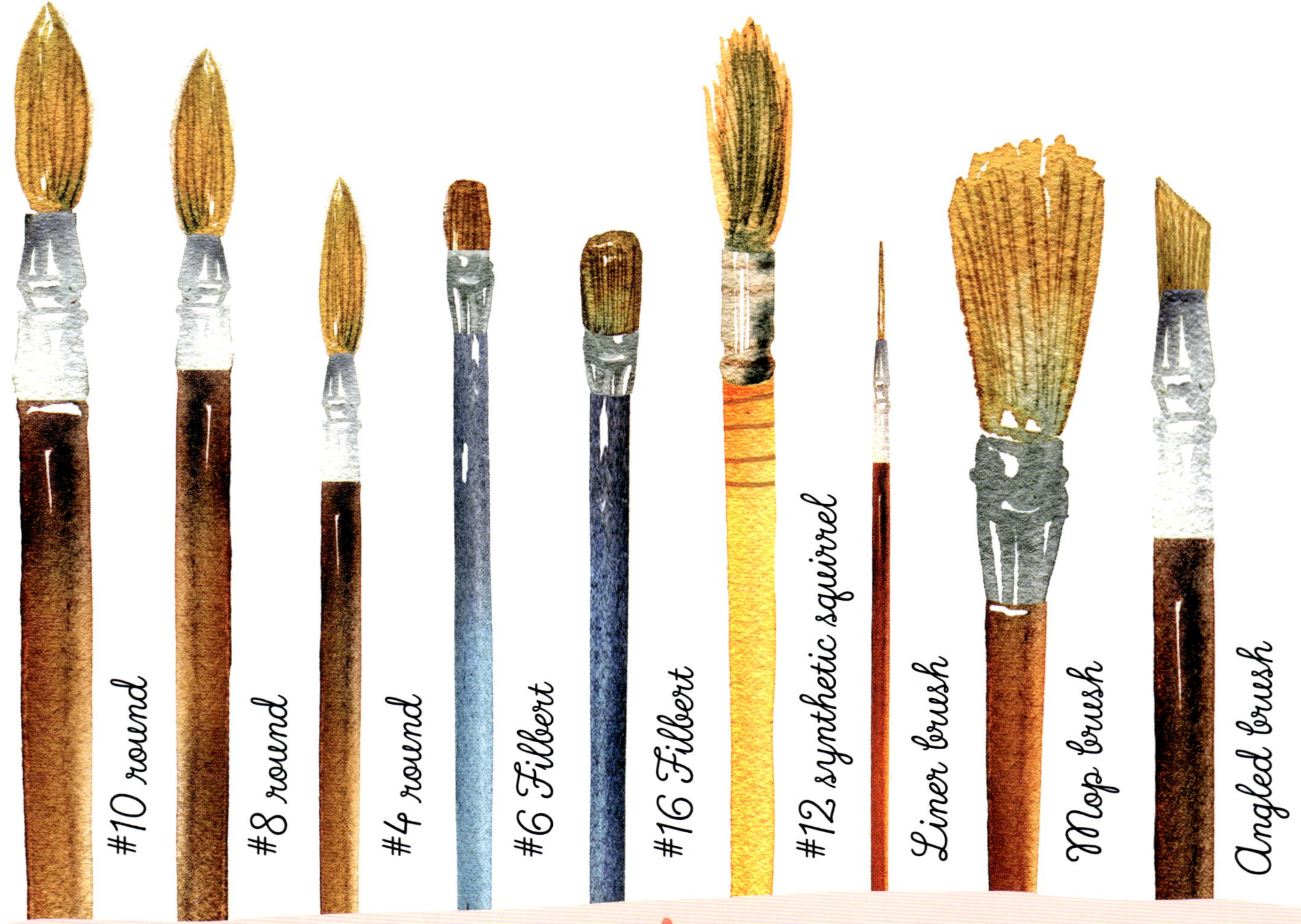

MUST-HAVE BRUSHES

- The **LINER BRUSH** allows you to paint small details.
- The **ROUND BRUSHES** will prove helpful for various blooms, foliage, and shrubs.
- The **FILBERT** has a rounded rectangular shape that's great for broader subjects, such as barks and stones.
- I use the **MOP BRUSH** to lay in background colors for skies, tree trunks, and other large objects. You can soak up a lot of water and pigment with mop brushes, so they come in handy.
- The **ANGLED BRUSH** gives you more control over the lines you make and works well for details.

Paper

Paper can make a major difference in any medium. With watercolors, I consider a good, heavyweight paper almost more important than the pigment (almost!). I tend to apply really wet washes while working in watercolors, so an inexpensive paper would never hold up. There's nothing worse than buckling paper when you are working. Save yourself the headache and invest in thicker paper, whether hot- or cold-pressed. I am brand loyal to Arches® 140-lb

When working in gouache, you can choose a less expensive, 140-lb. pad of watercolor paper. Canson® XL pads are great for this medium. Gouache generally does not require the amount of water that watercolor does, so a student-grade paper works wonderfully.

Colored Pencils

Colored pencils have gained popularity in recent years, but artist-quality pencils are a far cry from the pencils you may have used as a kid. Professional artist-quality colored pencils contain a higher degree of wax and pigment, which allows for a rich, deep, and luminescent color. They are portable and lightweight, and they come in a wide array of colors. For this book, I've limited my use of colored pencils to preliminary drawings and layering over painting, but you can always use them more extensively if you'd like.

My favorite colored pencils are Bruynzeel®, Sakura®, Derwent Coloursoft®, and Prismacolor Premier®. I love using these creamy pencils for layering color and line work over my gouache illustrations. They can lend a depth of color, and I have enjoyed using them in recent years.

Ink

You are also welcome to experiment with a variety of ink pens, as well as bottled ink. One fun alternative you may want to try is "walnut ink," which is a beautiful and rich brown ink made from the inner husks of a walnut. It has a wonderful transparent quality which looks a bit like the aged ink drawings of masters like Rembrandt and da Vinci.

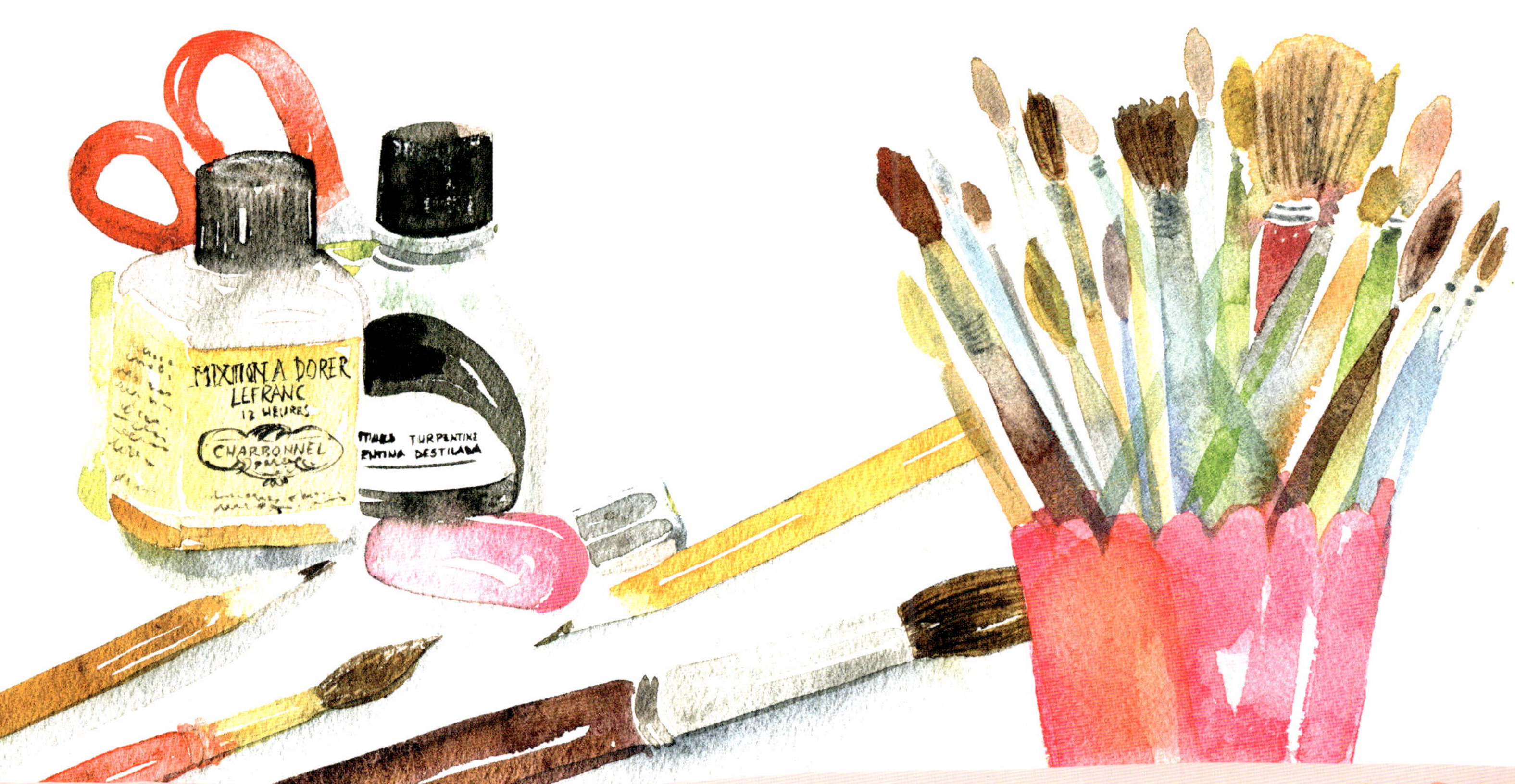

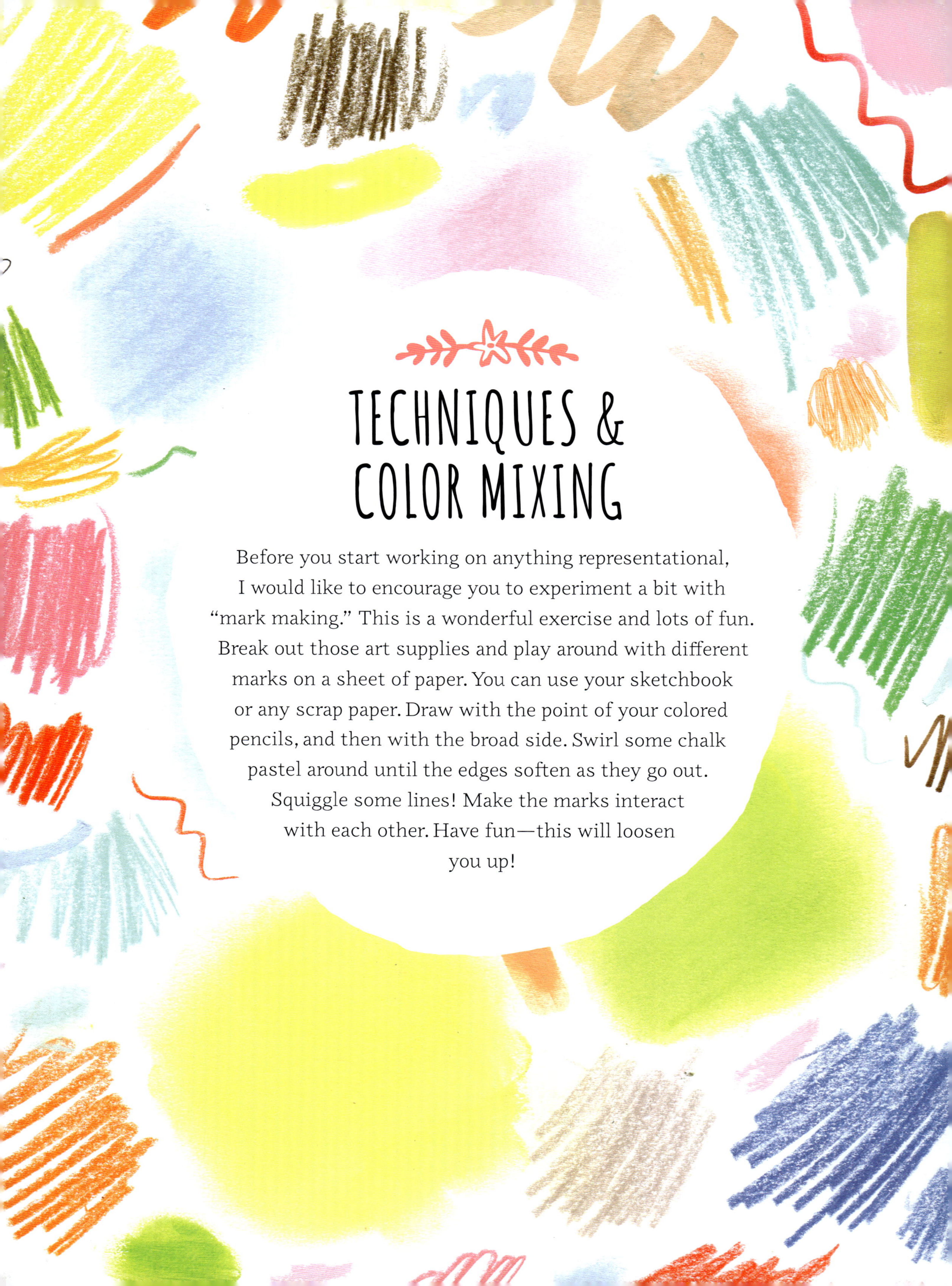

TECHNIQUES & COLOR MIXING

Before you start working on anything representational, I would like to encourage you to experiment a bit with "mark making." This is a wonderful exercise and lots of fun. Break out those art supplies and play around with different marks on a sheet of paper. You can use your sketchbook or any scrap paper. Draw with the point of your colored pencils, and then with the broad side. Swirl some chalk pastel around until the edges soften as they go out. Squiggle some lines! Make the marks interact with each other. Have fun—this will loosen you up!

MY FAVORITE PAINTING TECHNIQUES

Throughout the book, I've touched on numerous techniques, including:

- Wet-into-wet with watercolor (painting on top of wet paint)
- Wet-on-dry with watercolor (painting with wet paint on dry paper or wet paint on dry paint)
- Making simple shapes, and then adding detail
- Laying in washes, and then more opaque painting
- Dark-on-light background
- Light-on-dark background
- Drybrushing for texture: Use a mostly dry brush loaded with paint on a dry surface.
- Leaving white space
- Limited palette
- Tone-on-tone: hues within a similar color family
- Mark making
- Neutrals paired with brights
- Negative painting
- Using a white chalk pencil for drawing on dark backgrounds

Here is an example of different techniques that can be used to paint a simple orange.

1: Creating a preliminary drawing using similar-hued colored pencils.

2: Using a white charcoal pencil to draw on a matte, black-painted background.

3: Filling in drawn shapes with gouache.

4: Painting over the background, allowing the background to dry completely before adding a second layer. Note: Be sure to use very little water in this step to avoid disturbing the background and reactivating pigment.

1

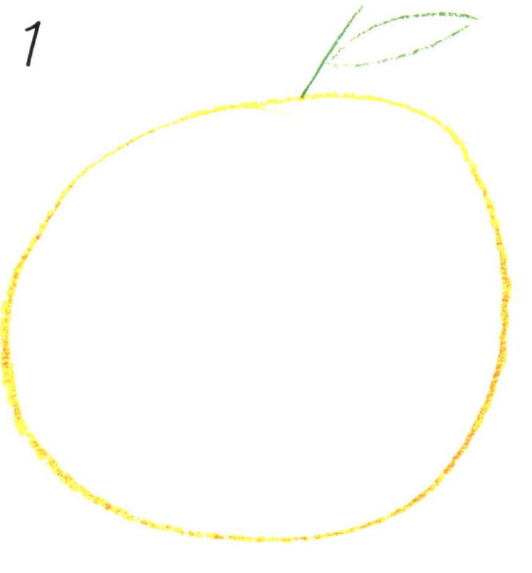

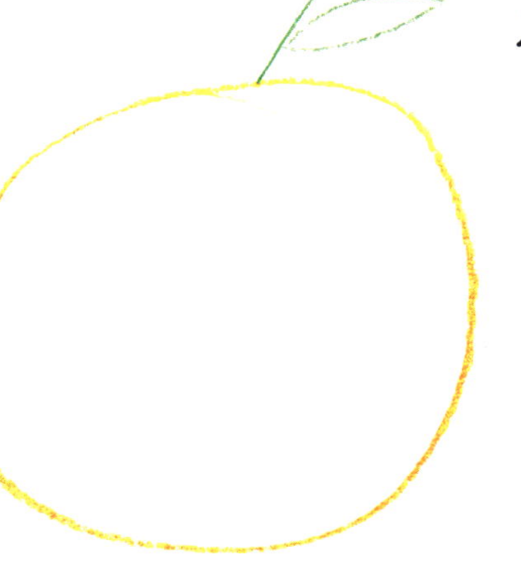

2

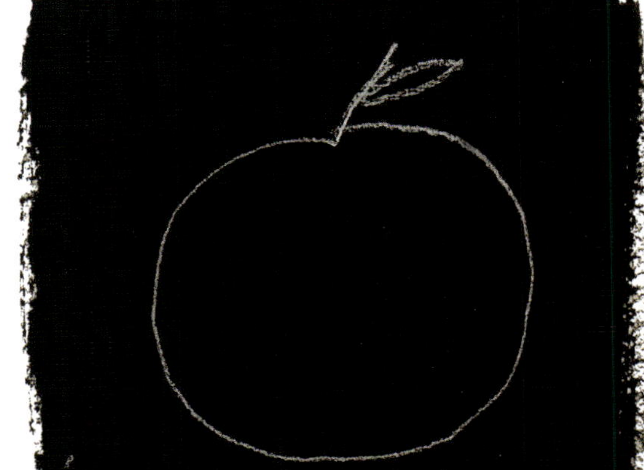

3

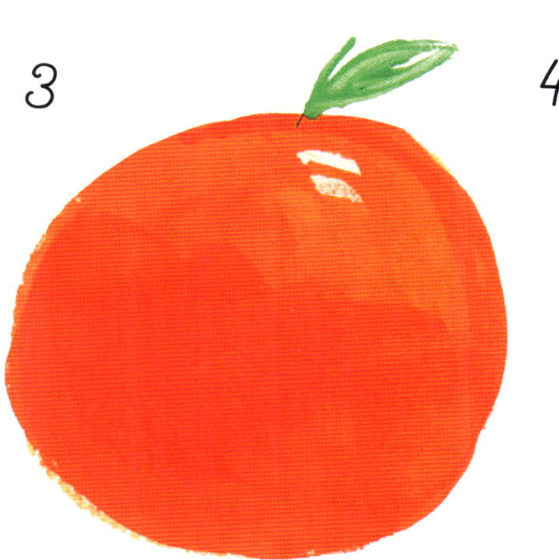

4

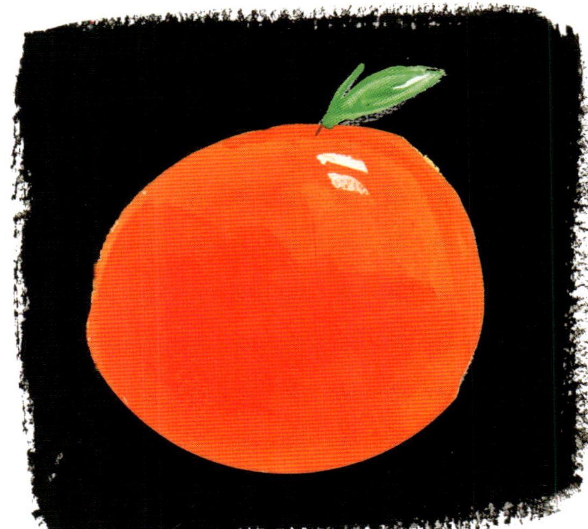

Color Theory

The primary colors—red, yellow, and blue—are the building blocks of other colors. You can mix secondary colors by combining red and yellow to make orange, yellow and blue to make green, and blue and red to make purple. Tertiary colors are created by mixing a secondary color with one of its primary components (i.e., orange with red or green with blue). You can get the most amazing colors by experimenting with different percentages of these colors. By mixing more or less of a primary with a secondary, you will get completely different results. Analogous colors are colors that sit next to each other on the color wheel. They work in harmony with each other. An example is red, orange, and red-orange.

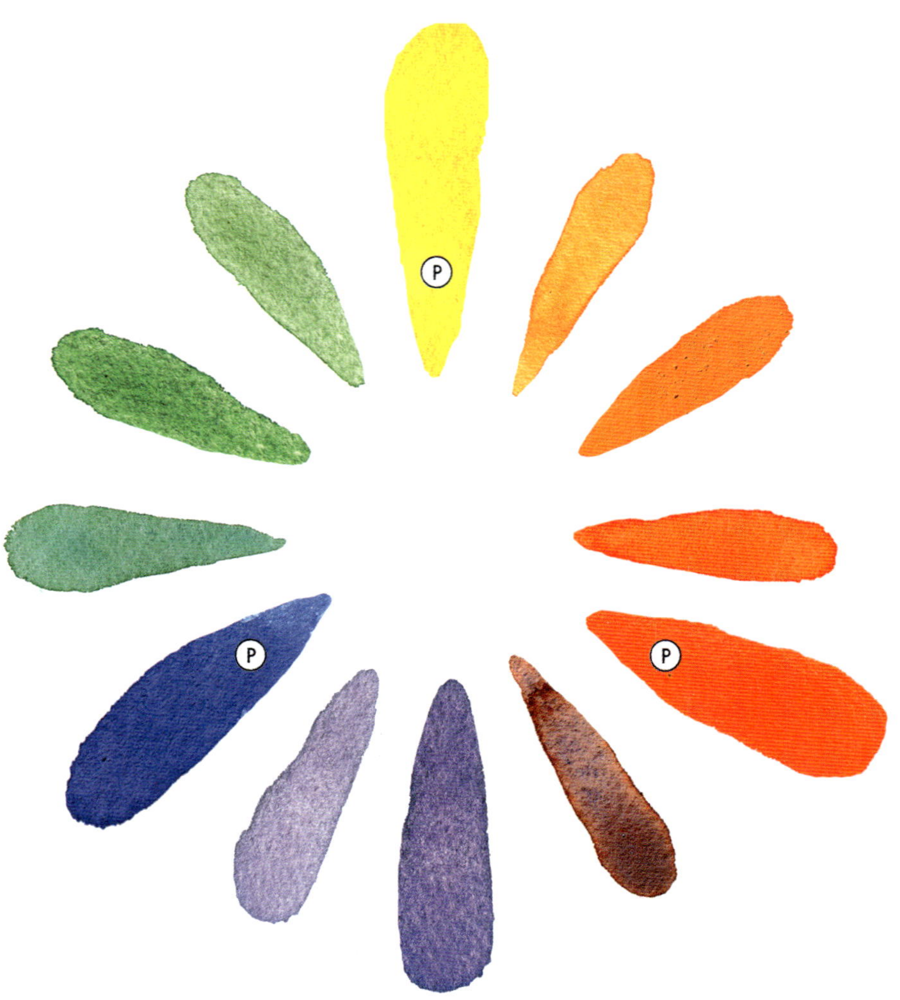

BASIC COLOR TERMS

HUE refers to one of the pure colors on the color wheel, such as red, blue, or green.

SATURATION is a measure of the purity of a color.

TONE is the relative lightness or darkness of a color.

VALUE is a range of tones that span from pure black to pure white.

TINT means adding white to a color to create a high value. (I use this a lot!)

SHADE means adding black to a color to create a low value.

In gouache illustration, I am constantly mixing tints. By mixing in even just a little white, you can really make your colors pop! This chart shows how adding white to the most basic colors in your palette can create beautiful variations.

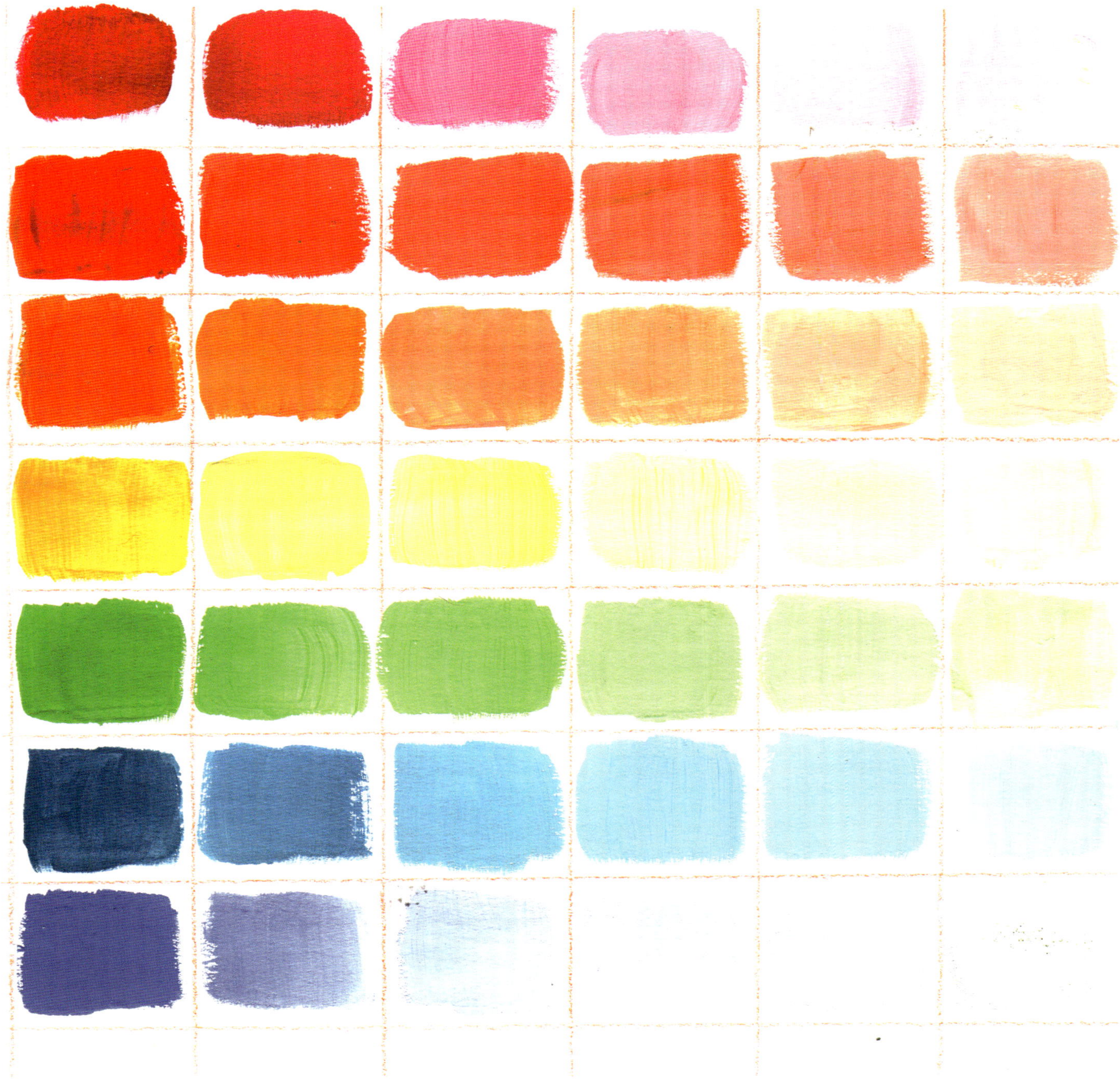

We will play with color in numerous ways in this book. There are infinite possibilities, and contrasting a color beside an opposite, analogous, dark, or light color can yield different results.

I like to create custom palettes when I am working on a particular project. For example, I may swatch some melon colors for a warm-weather travel illustration or harvest colors for an autumnal lettering project.

Each project in the book uses plenty of color, so you can see which ones you like best and begin building your own color stories.

Let's get started!

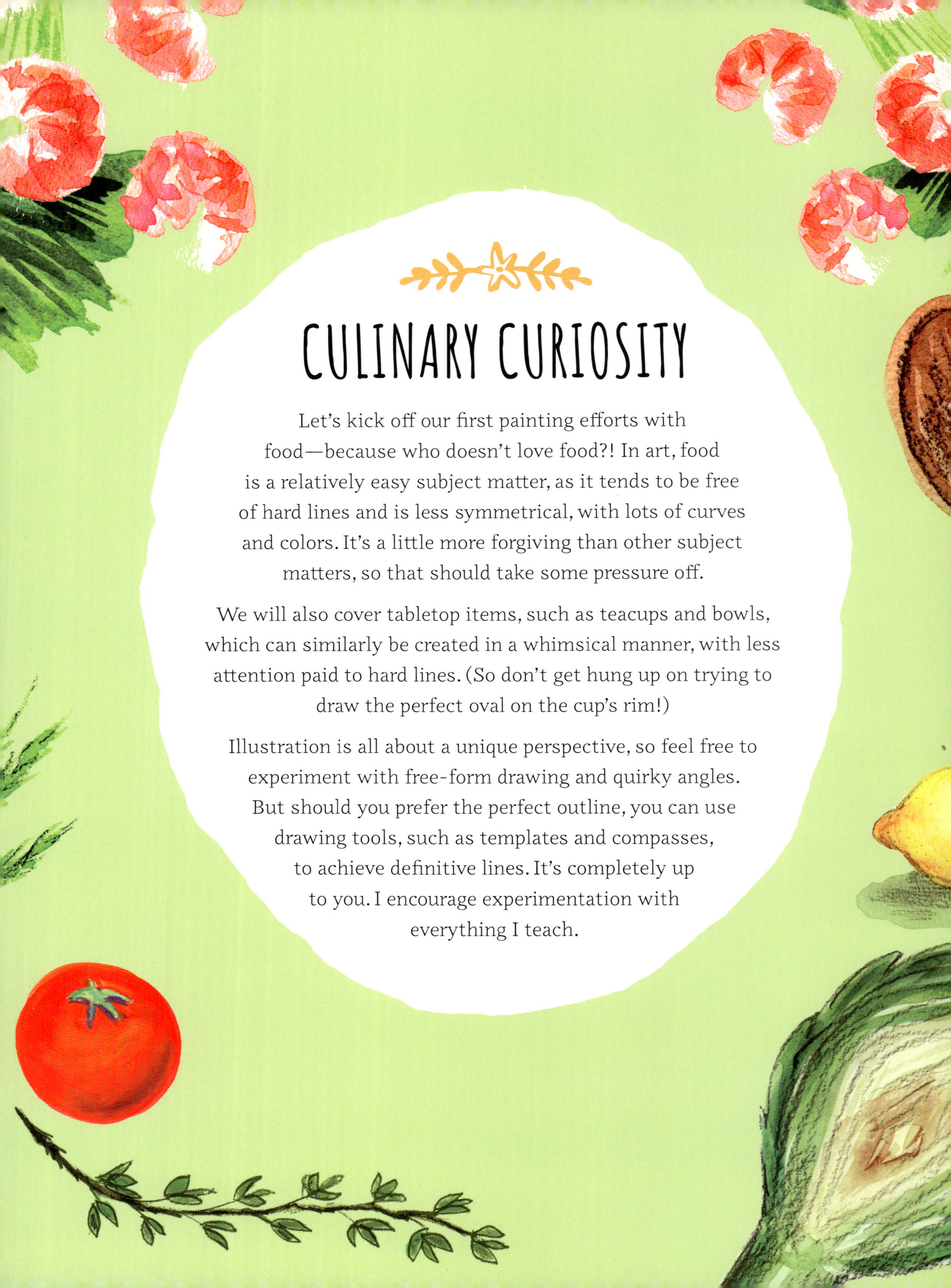

CULINARY CURIOSITY

Let's kick off our first painting efforts with food—because who doesn't love food?! In art, food is a relatively easy subject matter, as it tends to be free of hard lines and is less symmetrical, with lots of curves and colors. It's a little more forgiving than other subject matters, so that should take some pressure off.

We will also cover tabletop items, such as teacups and bowls, which can similarly be created in a whimsical manner, with less attention paid to hard lines. (So don't get hung up on trying to draw the perfect oval on the cup's rim!)

Illustration is all about a unique perspective, so feel free to experiment with free-form drawing and quirky angles. But should you prefer the perfect outline, you can use drawing tools, such as templates and compasses, to achieve definitive lines. It's completely up to you. I encourage experimentation with everything I teach.

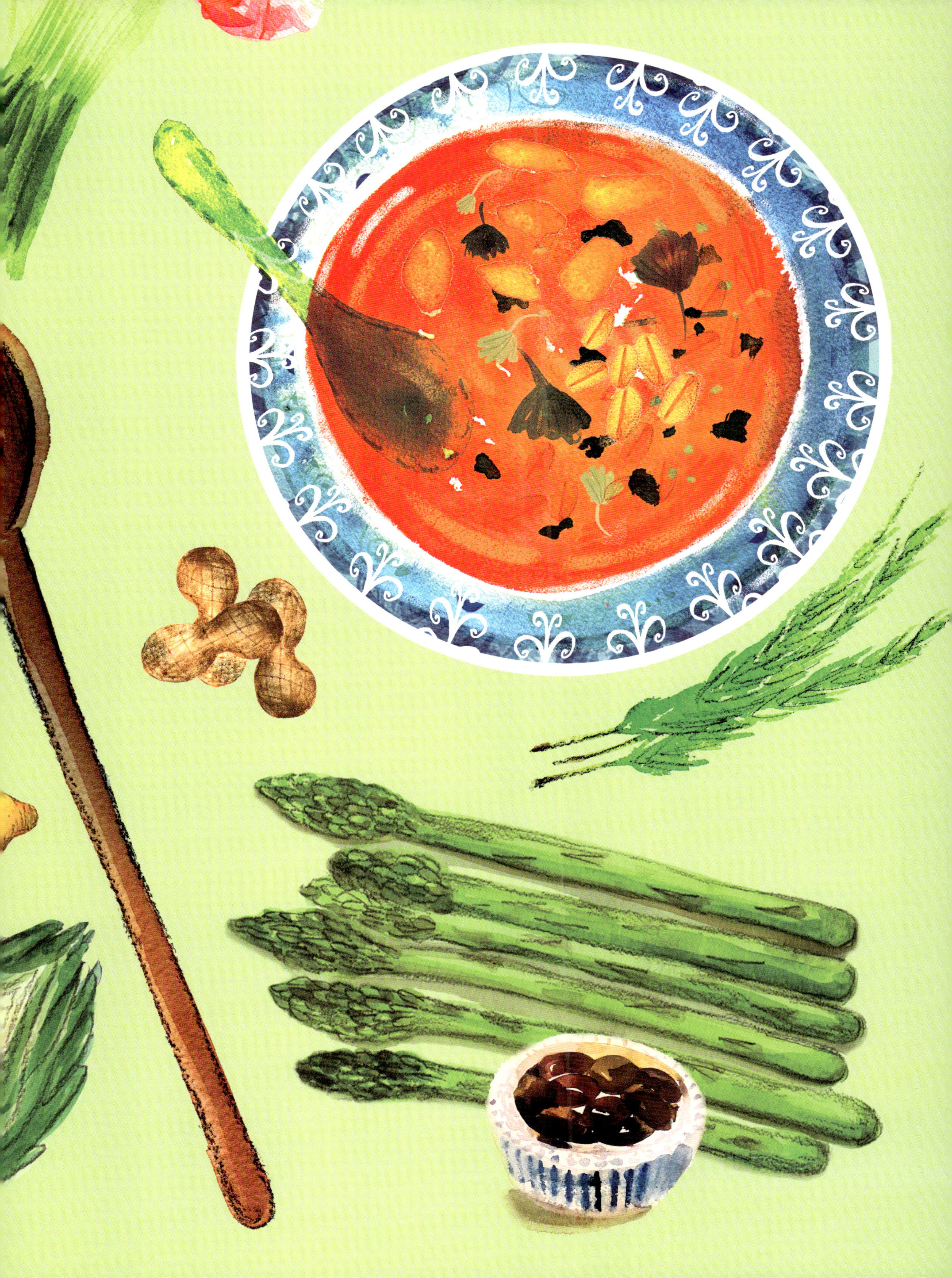

TEA & TOAST

What is more "everyday" than my favorite breakfast of tea and toast? Mix it up and paint your morning cup of coffee if you aren't a tea drinker!

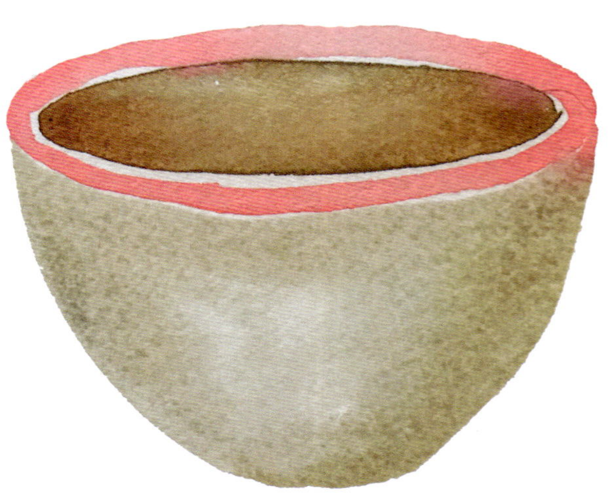

Step 1

Here I've used a neutral watercolor hue and colored pencils as my main mediums. Creating the cup is the first step; add a decorative ring to the rim and some dark brown for the tea.

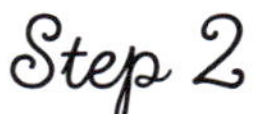

Make the scalloped shape using the same neutral wash.

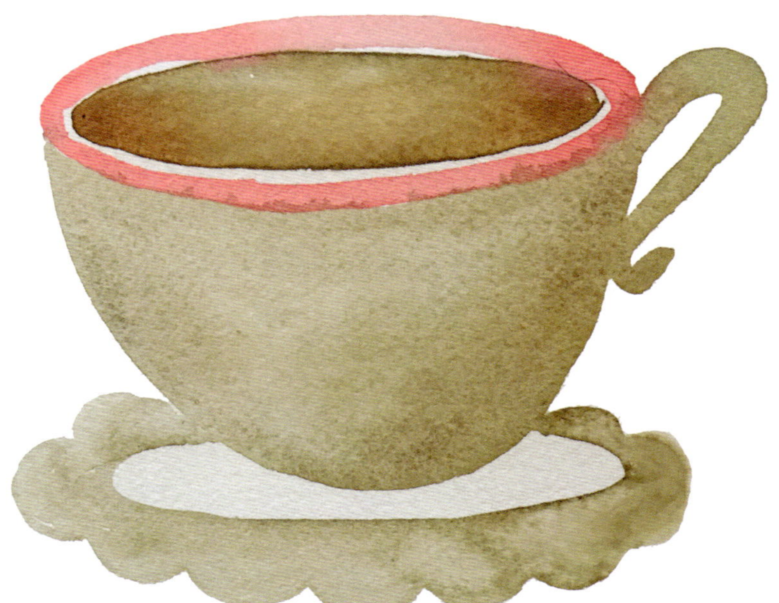

Step 3

The next steps involve various uses of colored pencils. Draw a ring over the initial tea area; add decorative flowers, dots, and stripes; and paint small patterns with a liner brush.

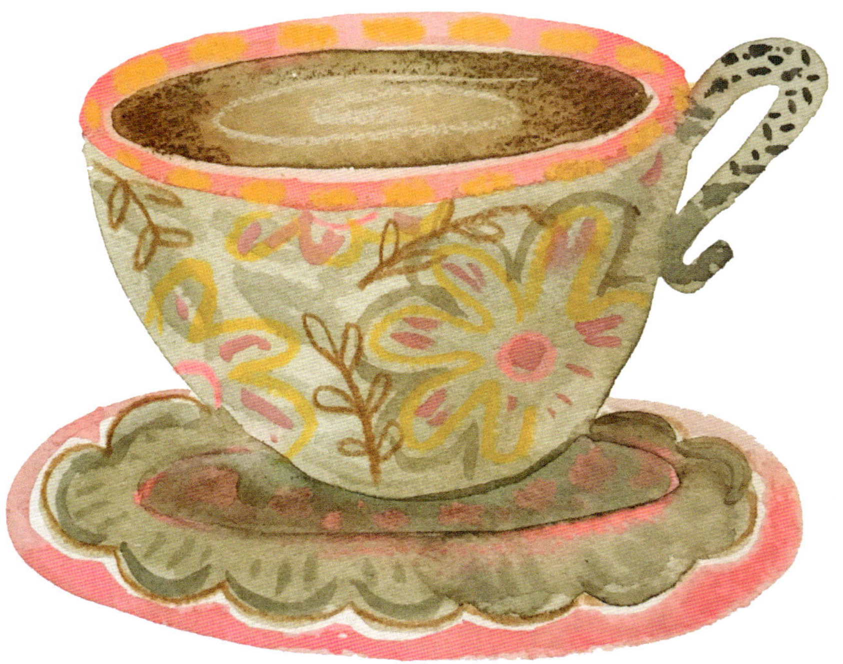

Step 4

Add a matching pink rim to the saucer, as well as additional decorative elements in dark-brown colored pencil. Darken the corners of the tea a bit to create more depth.

Step 5

Add more details with colored pencils and a liner brush, if you wish!

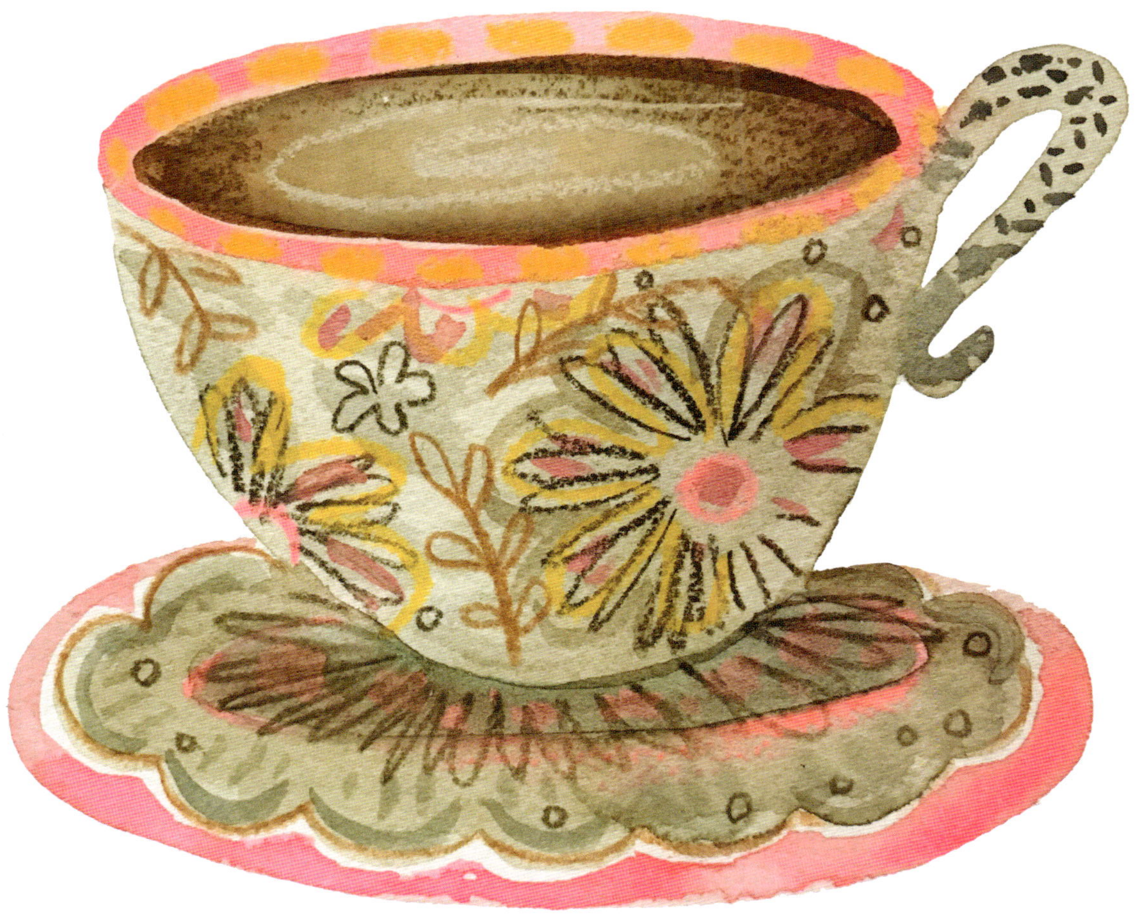

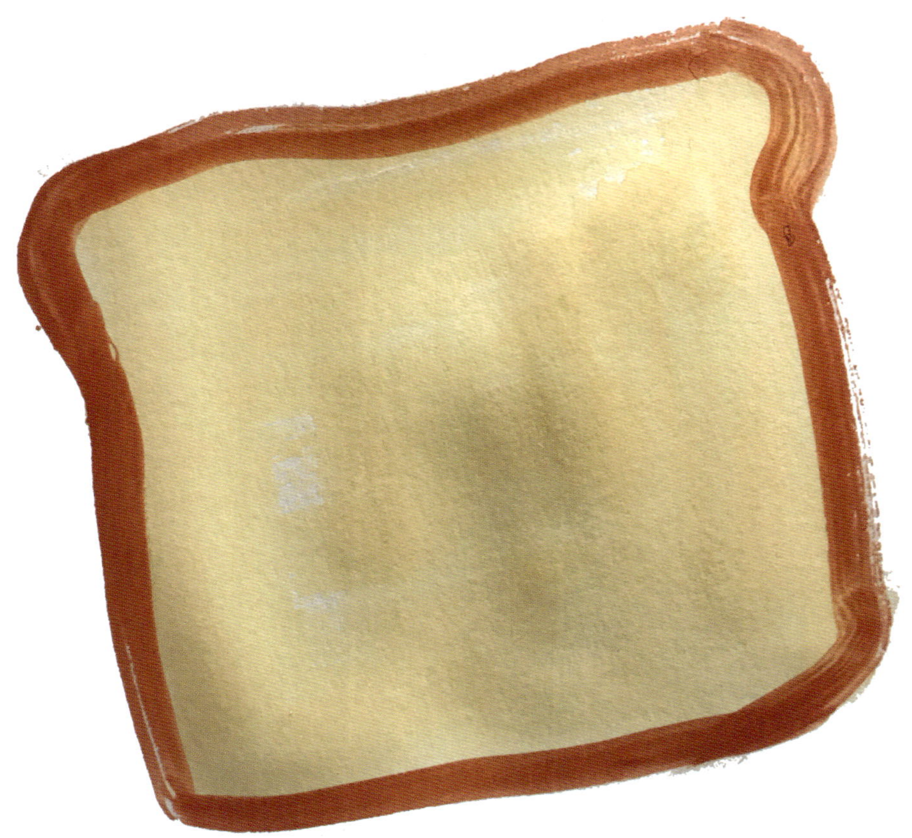

Step 1

To illustrate toast, start with a wash of warm, buttery-yellow gouache, and then add a simple crust. After letting this dry, use masking fluid to mask off the little nooks and crannies of the bread, saving this buttery-yellow for prominence later.

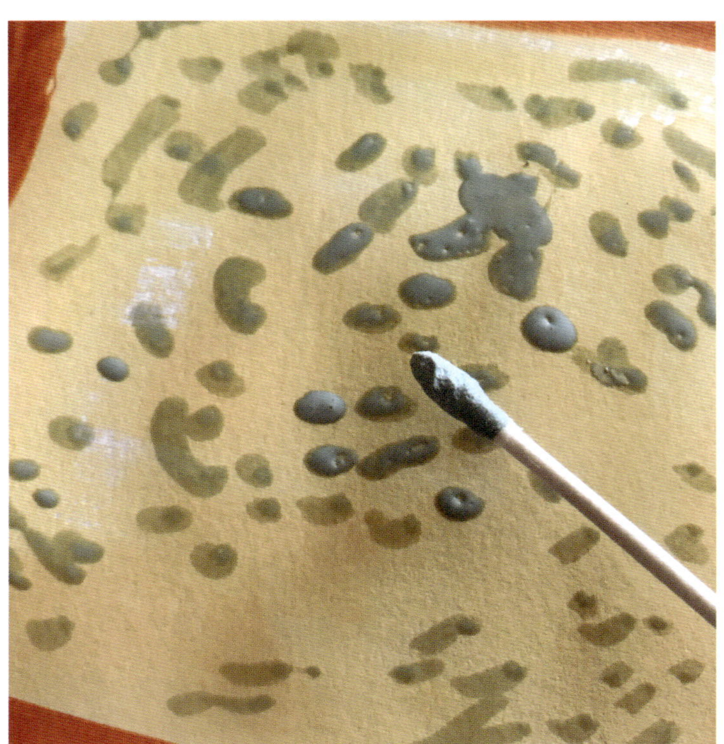

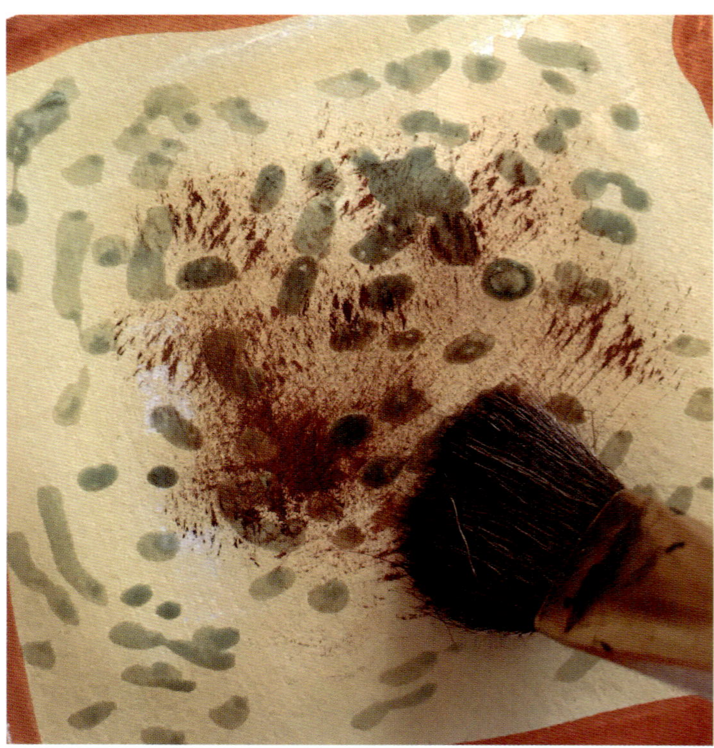

Step 2

Let the masking fluid dry, and then use a large, dry brush to scrape brown gouache across the surface, letting the bristles do the work.

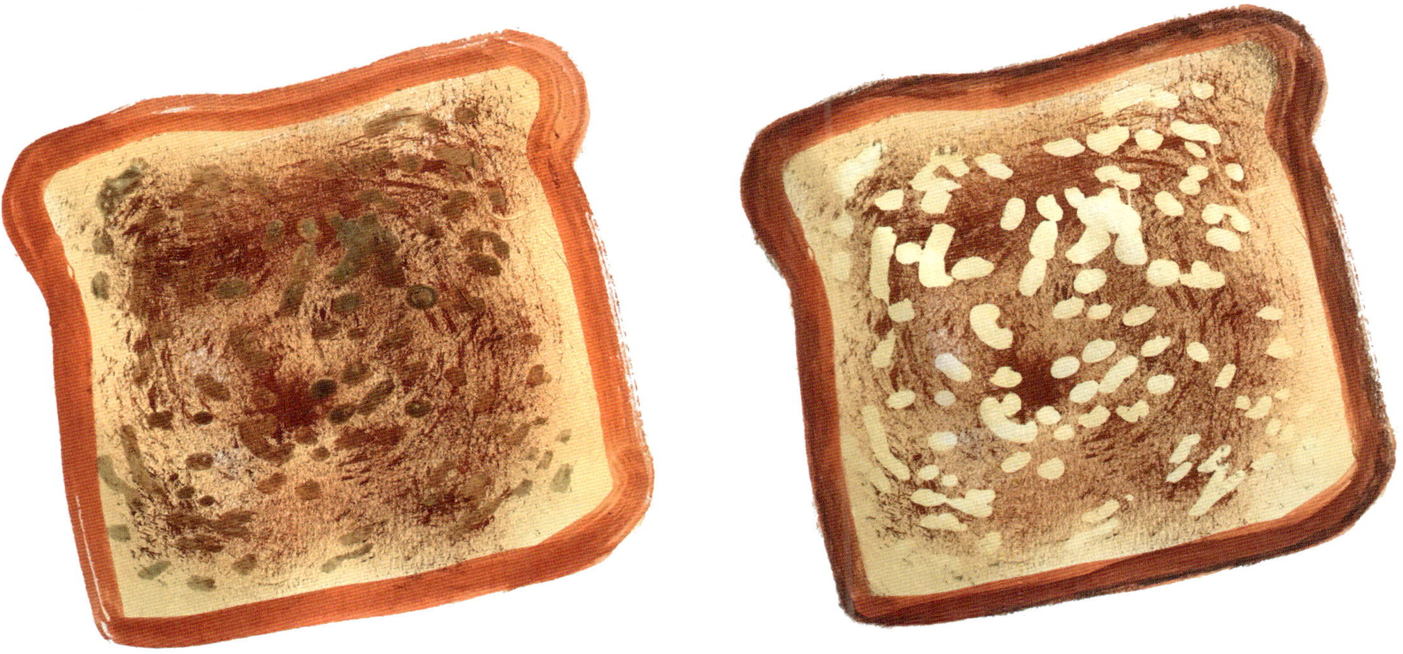

Step 3 Continue to swirl the brown paint around, blotting the brush each time before touching down on the illustration. Once you are satisfied, let it dry, and then use a rubber cement eraser to remove the masking fluid. To bridge the contrast of the nooks and texture of bread, add a light wash of watered-down brown over the top. Let the wash dry, and then refine the illustration using some colored pencils to give the edge of the bread additional texture. Voilà! You now have toast.

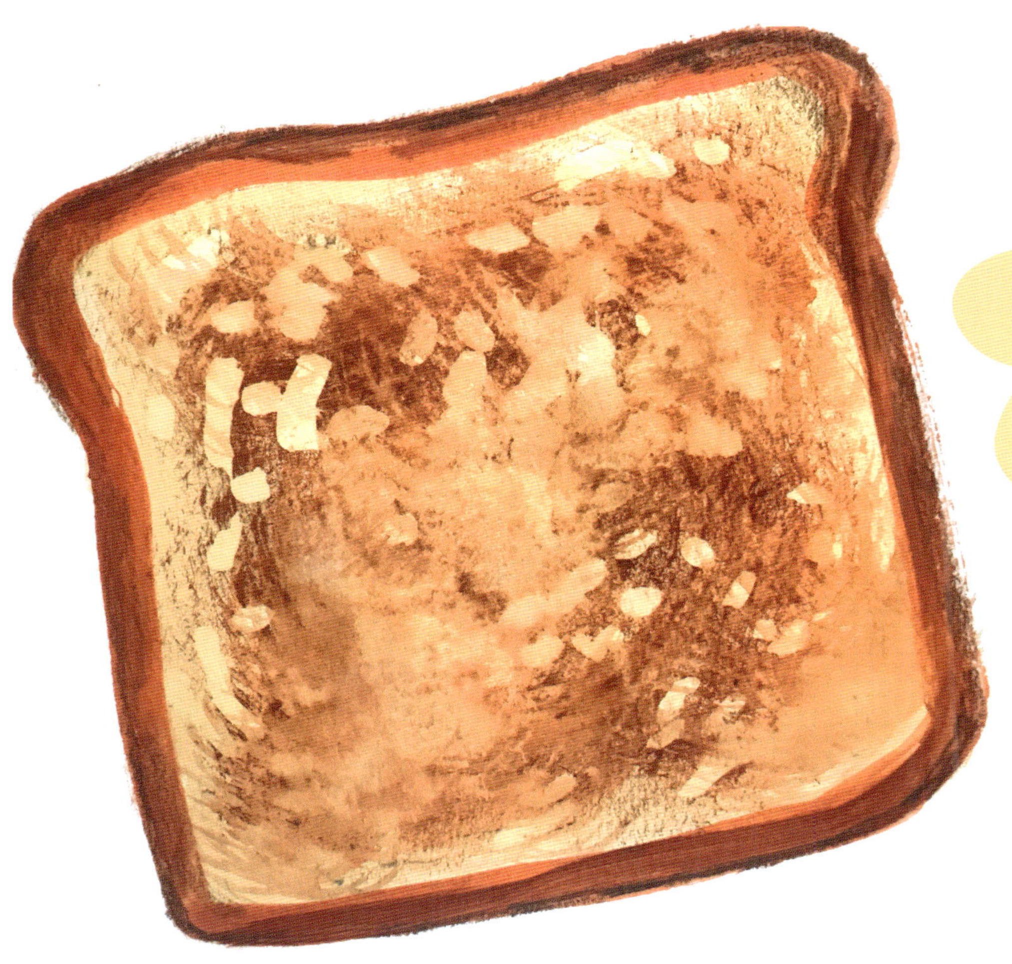

Tip

The drybrushing technique is perfect for creating the unique texture of toast.

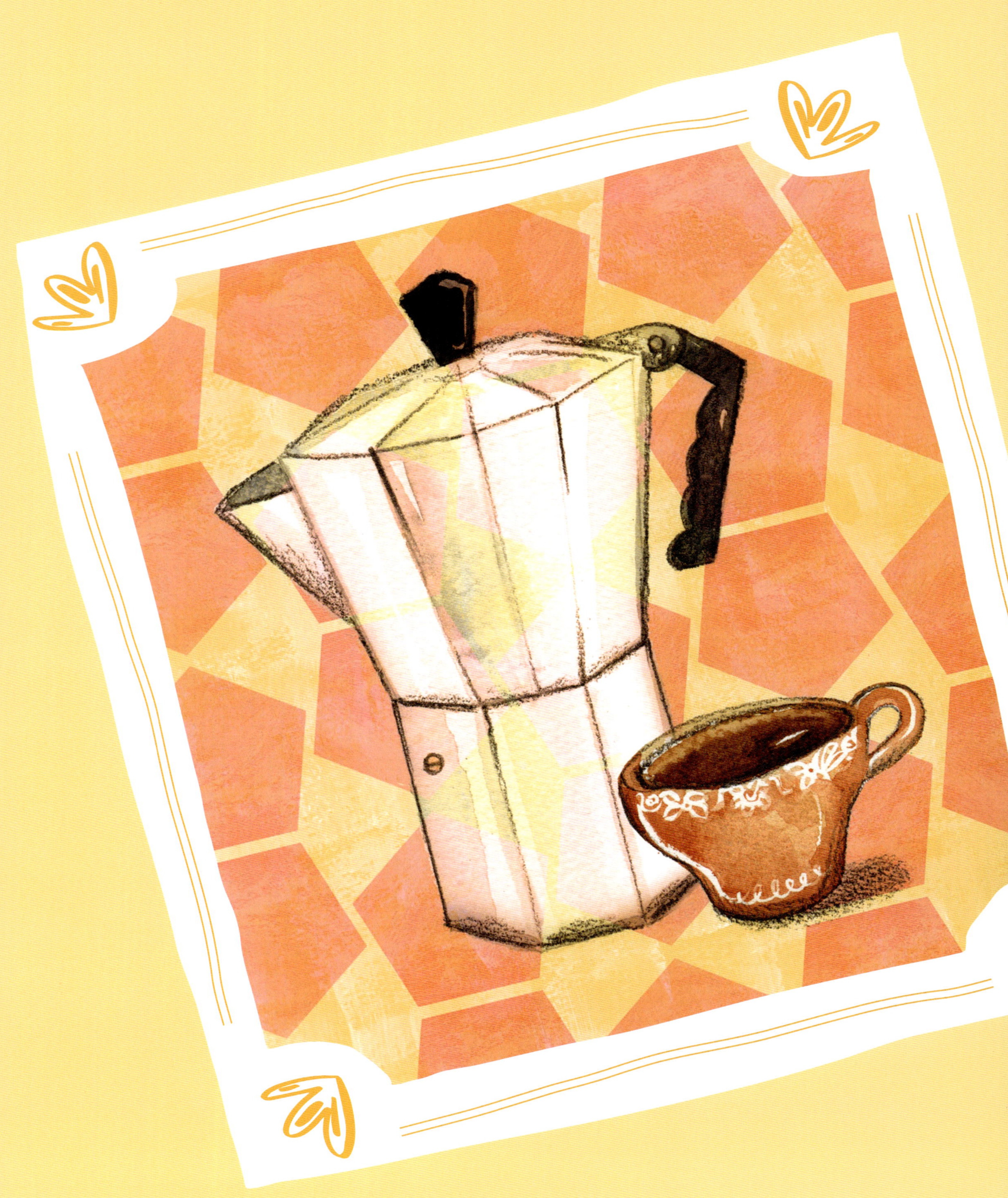

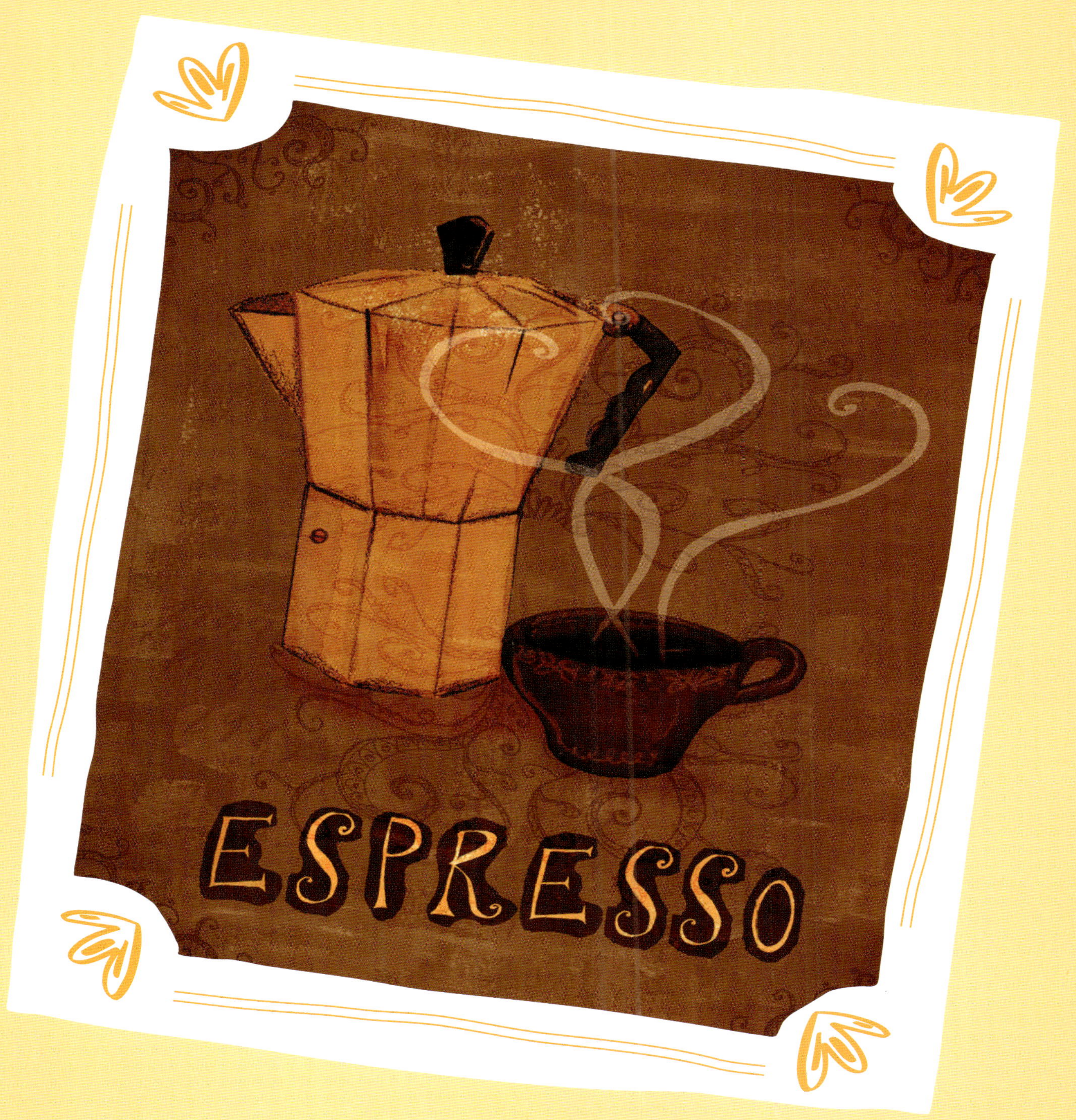

TASTE OF ITALY

This little espresso maker is called a moka pot, as coffee drinkers may already know! It brings back memories of drinking strong coffee in Italy, and it could be painted in any color you like—maybe you prefer red or blue, with complementary background colors? See the color wheel on page 16 for ideas!

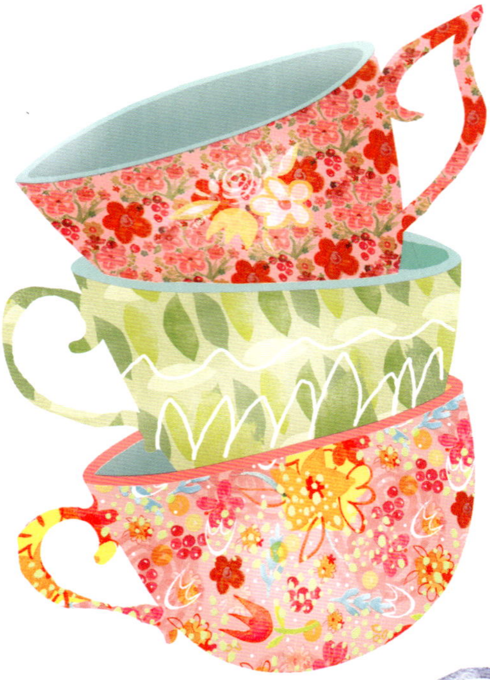

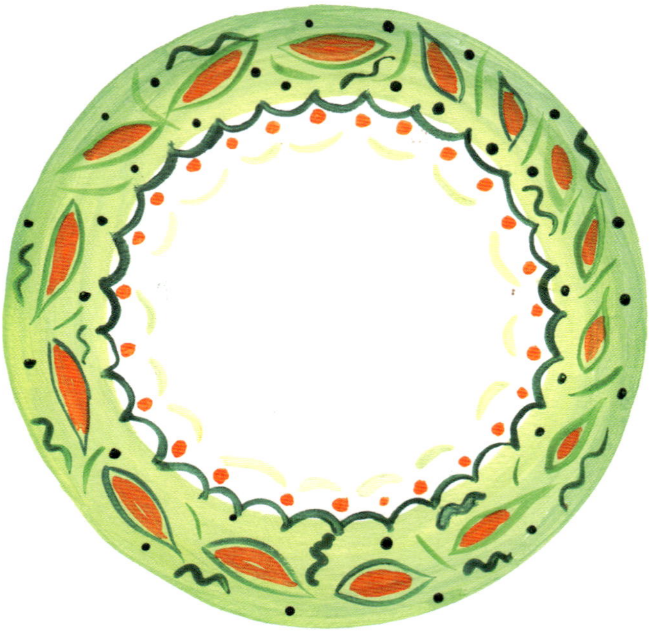

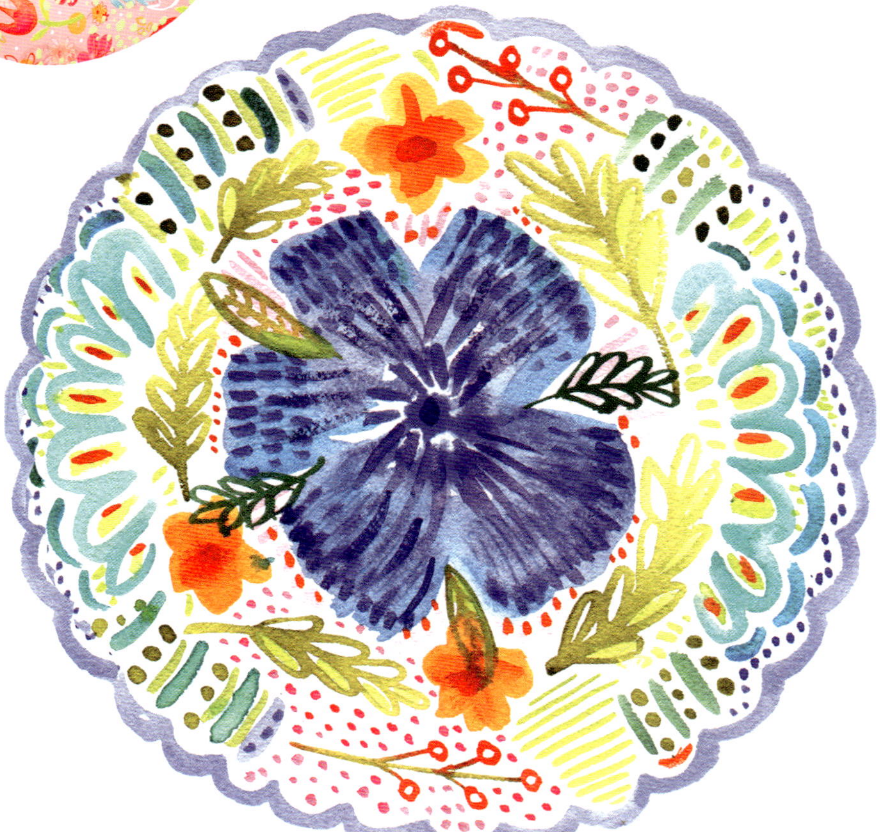

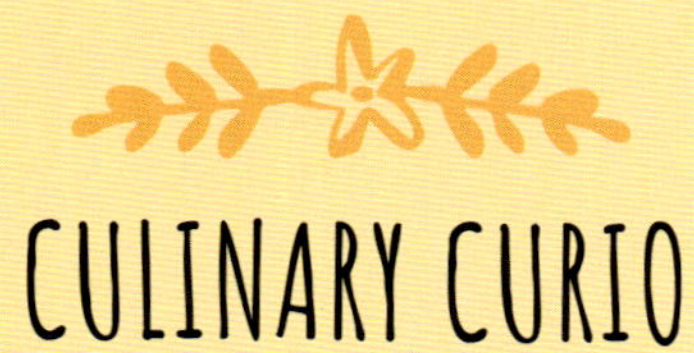

CULINARY CURIO

Take inspiration from patterns and colors seen around the world when creating the dishes for your food.

Nine Different Ways

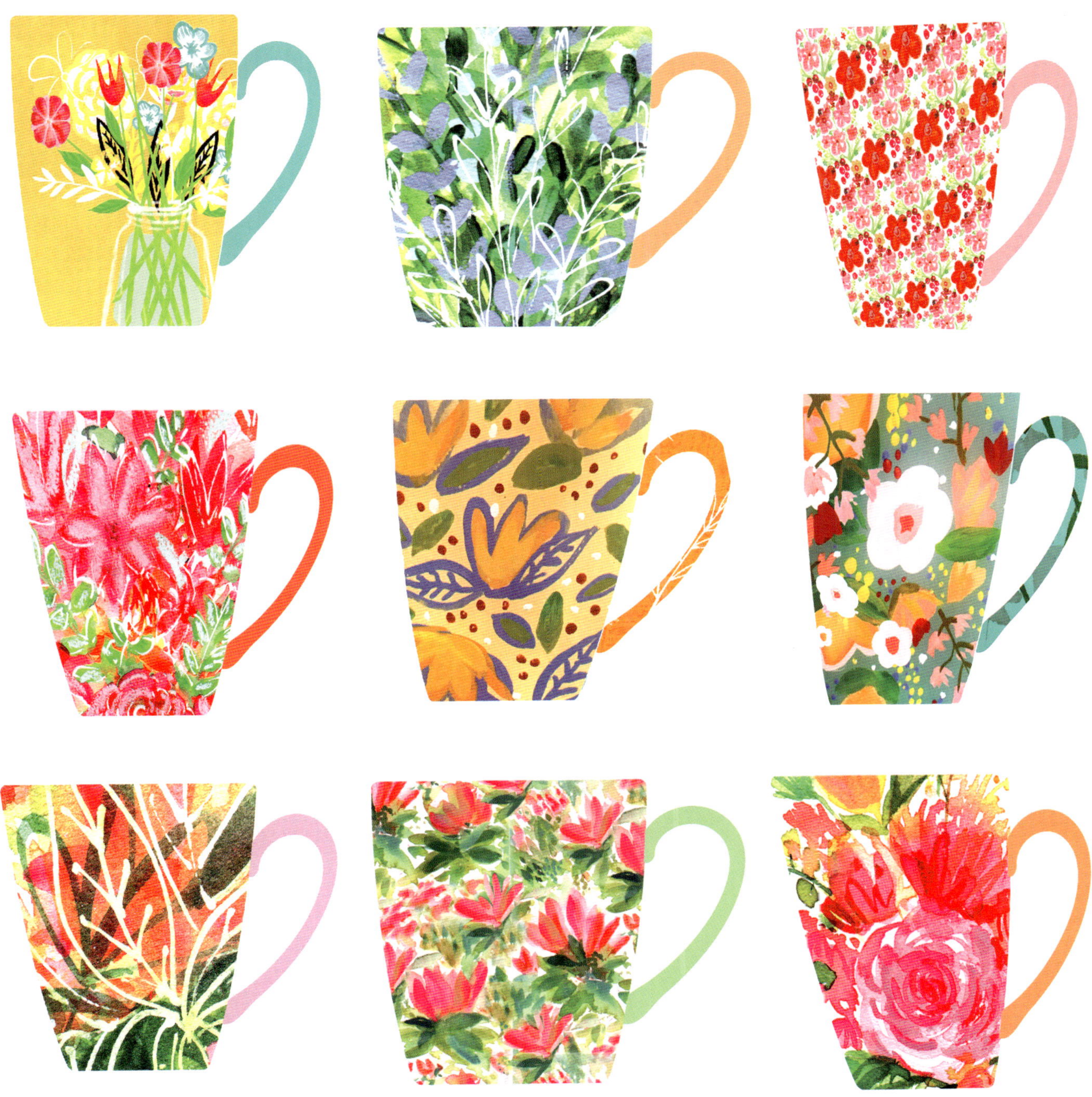

To illustrate quirky angles, take a look at this collection of mugs. Many are skewed or distorted in form, and this gives the art a fun little spin. When working on dishes, mugs, or bowls, play with drawing unusual forms, as well as colorful patterns. I love to create patterns using flowers, ferns, leaves, and other organic material. But feel free to use iconic imagery that is unique to your own aesthetic, whether that is pets, nature, or something else! Again, experiment! These projects are really idea starters to send you exploring.

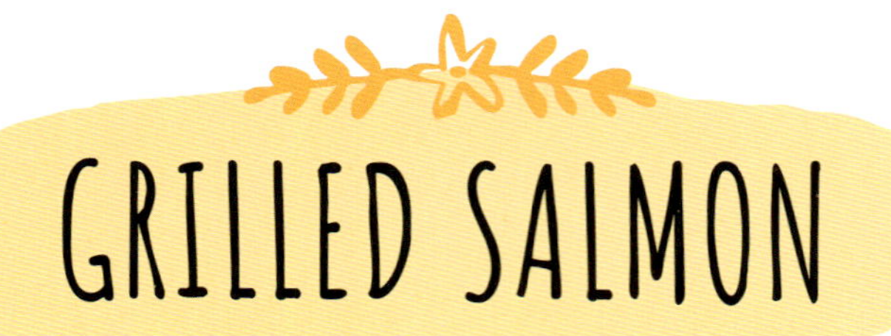

GRILLED SALMON

A piece of grilled salmon is easy and fun to paint. Here I've covered my general steps for painting this without giving as many details as in some of the projects. I want you to feel free to create your own colors and add your own twists.

Step 1

Use colored pencil to draw the basic shape of the salmon. I've used gouache to create the mass of the fish. If you study the subject, you will see that what gives it dimension is the different values between the top of the cut and the side. The side is a bit darker, as it is more in shadow. Once this is mapped out, you can refine the fish by adding lighter tints (coral hue plus white) over the initial color.

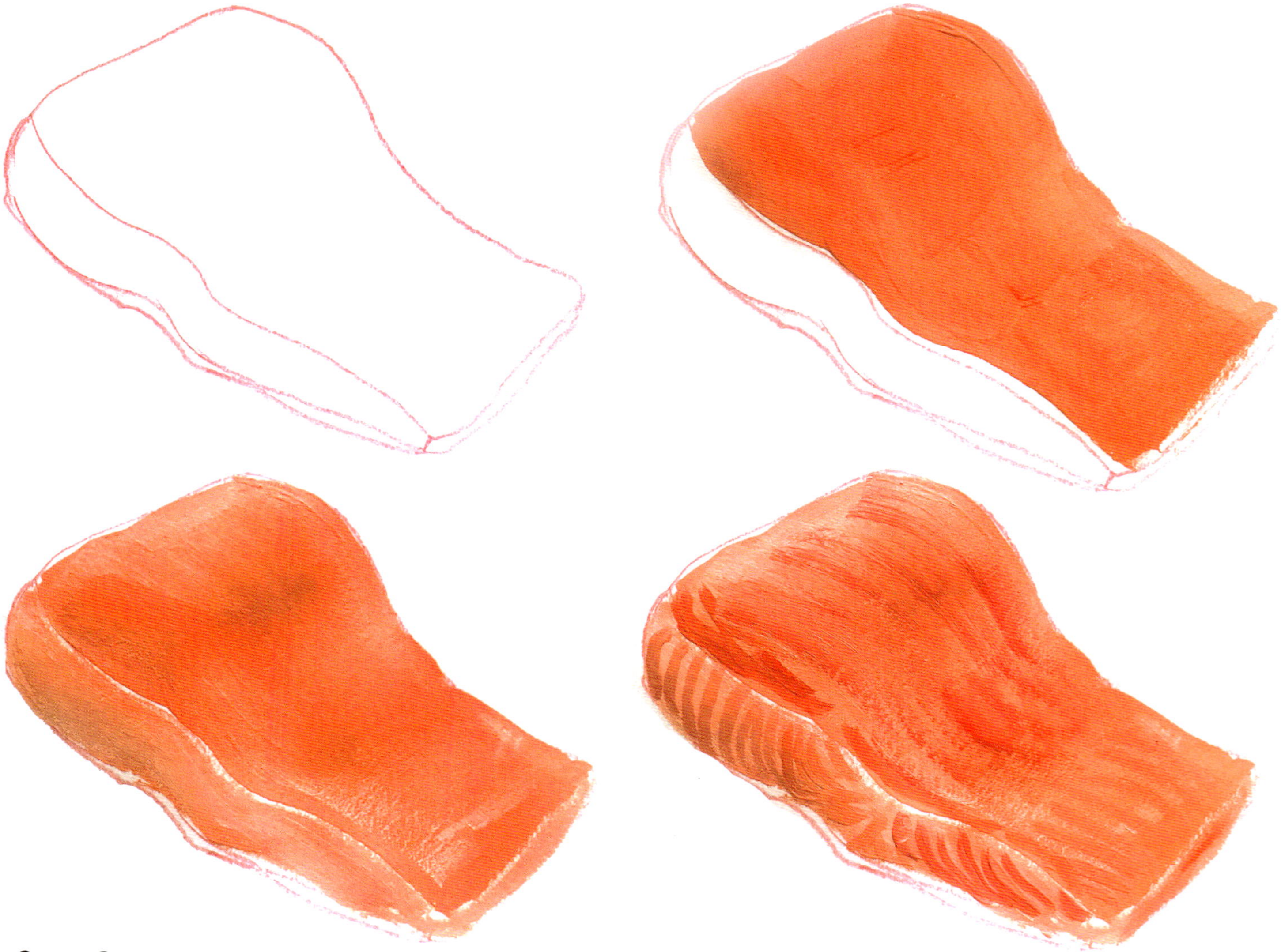

Step 2

Let the base layer dry, and then use a dry brush to add more texture to the top of the fish. For the side, use a small, pointed brush to add the fatty threads. Use sepia for the bottom of the skin, as well as the char lines on top of the cut. Simply paint lines on a diagonal, and then go in the opposite direction, paying attention to the peaks and valleys in the fish so that these marks are in line with the overall dimension.

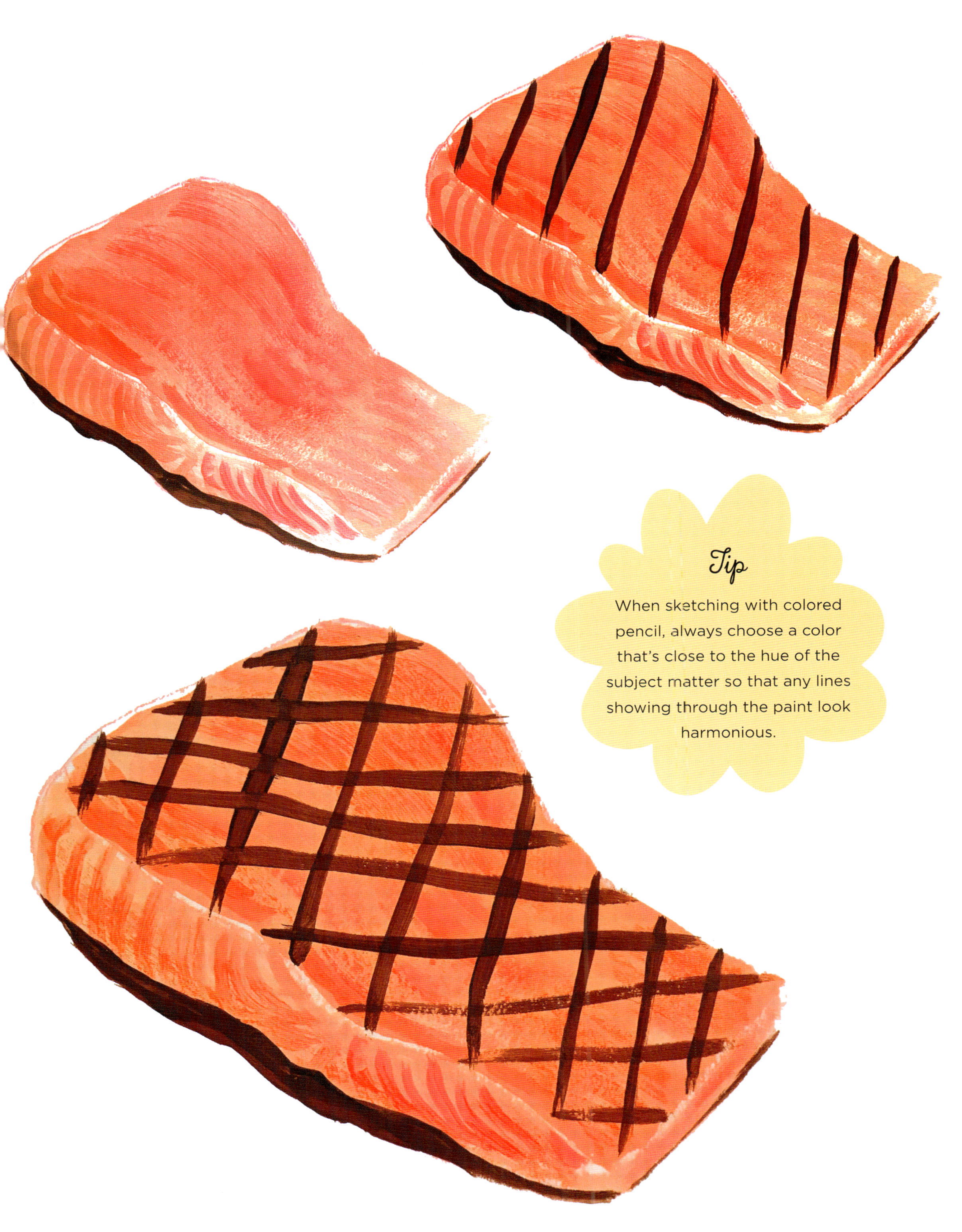

Tip

When sketching with colored pencil, always choose a color that's close to the hue of the subject matter so that any lines showing through the paint look harmonious.

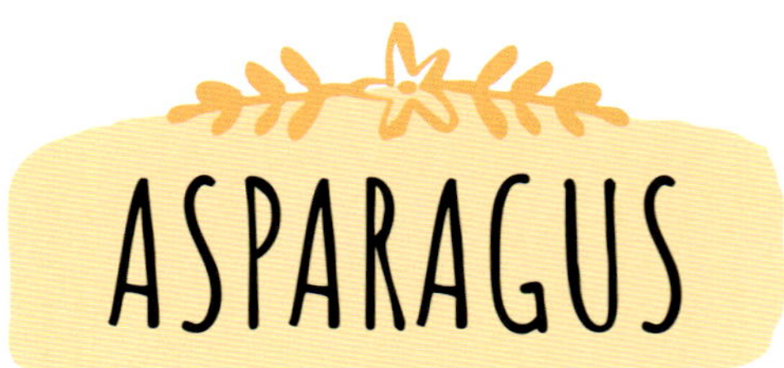

ASPARAGUS

After painting the salmon on the previous pages, consider adding some asparagus to make it a complete meal!

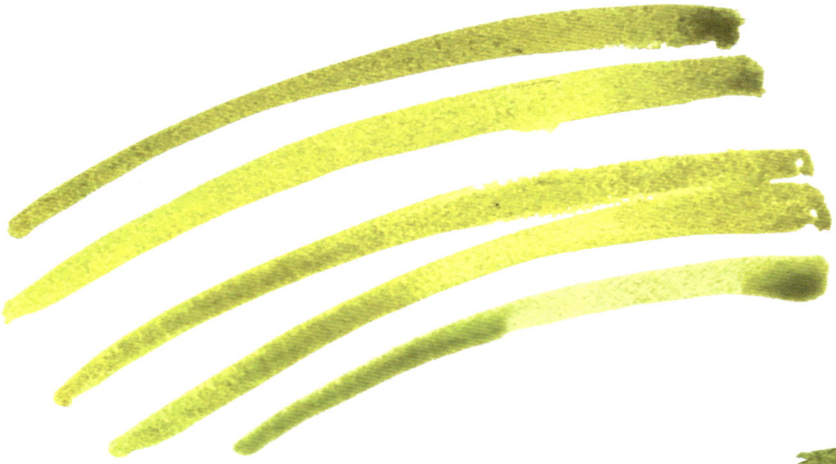

Step 1

Use a light watercolor wash to create the general shape of the asparagus spears.

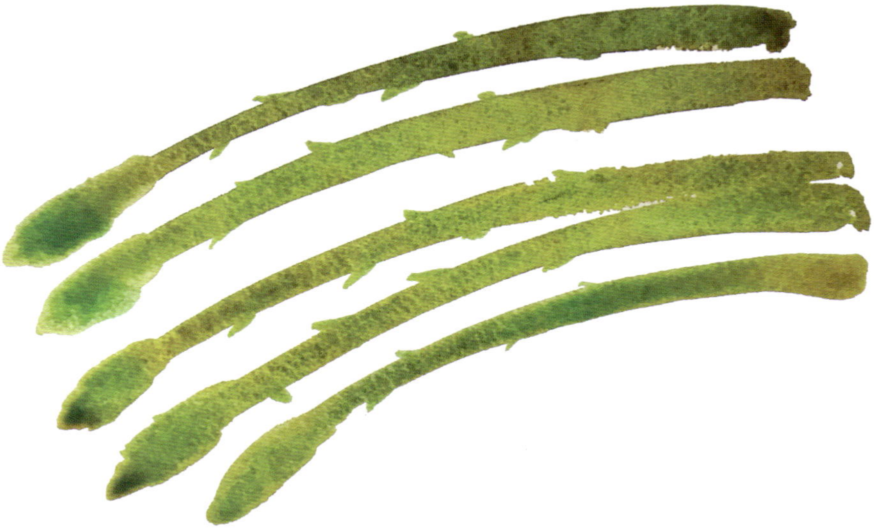

Step 2

While the first wash is wet, tap color into the spears to begin adding more dimension. Also add the heads of the asparagus spears.

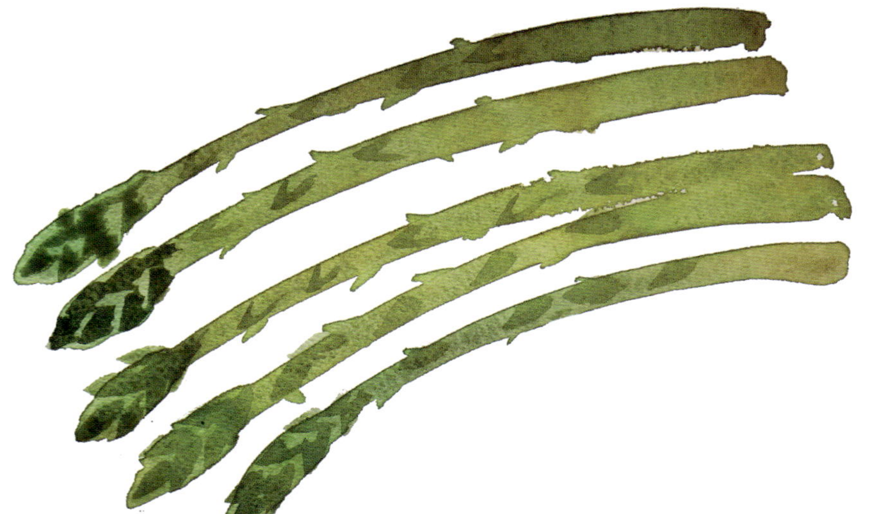

Step 3

Using the tip of a #4 round brush, draw some of the pigment out from the asparagus to enhance tiny triangular scales on each spear.

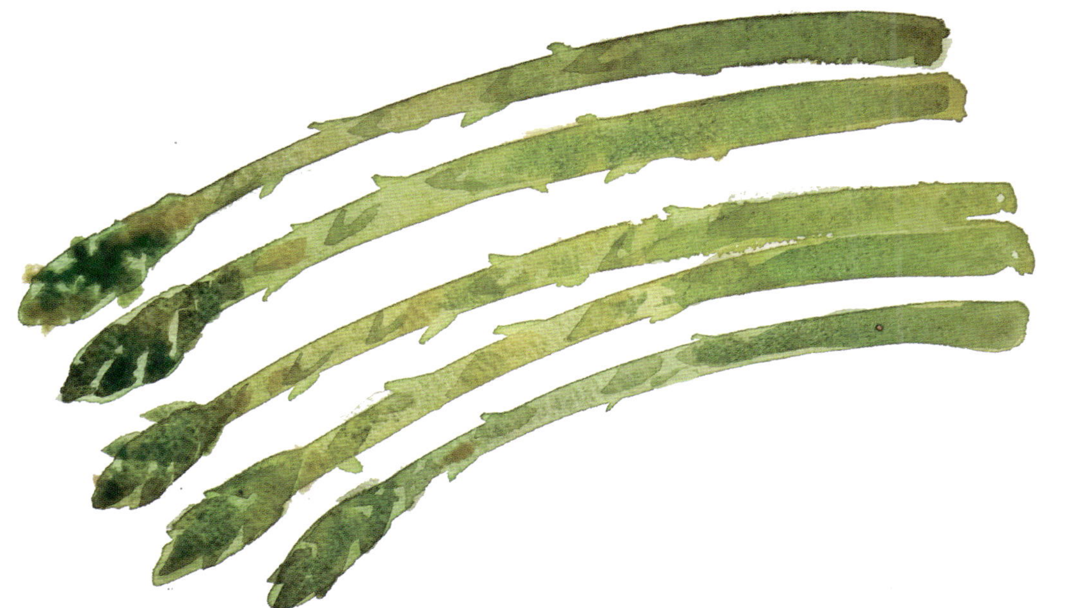

Step 4

Let the first layers dry, and then add a darker hue of green and raw sienna for detail in the scales. This will take some back-and-forth until each spear has the right amount of contrast.

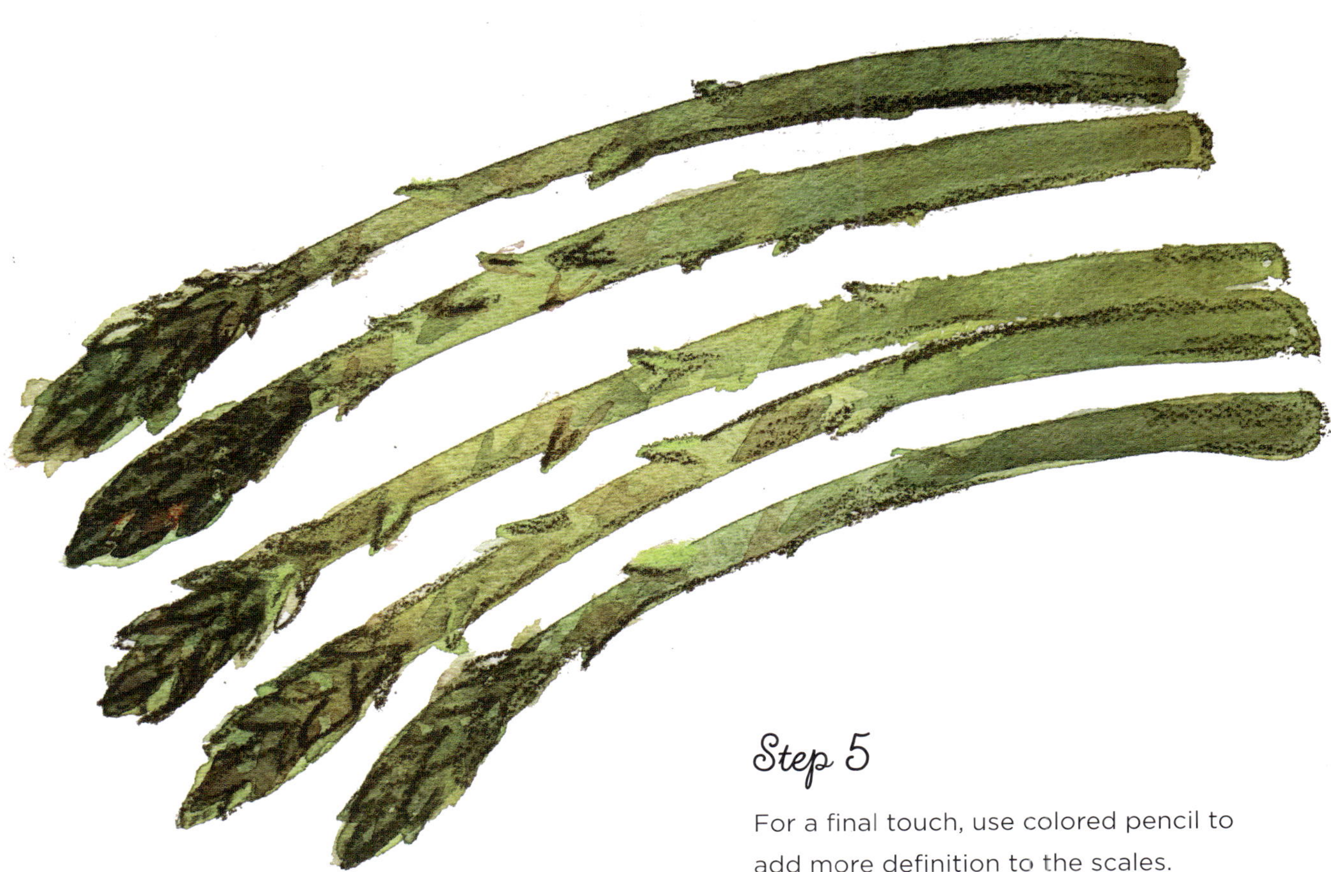

Step 5

For a final touch, use colored pencil to add more definition to the scales.

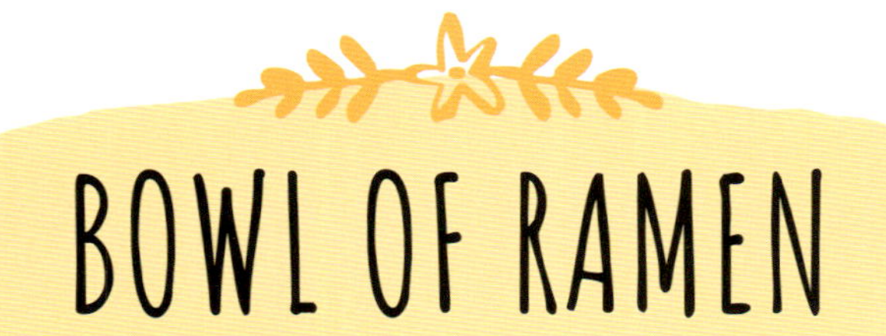

BOWL OF RAMEN

This fun little project emphasizes silhouette and pattern.

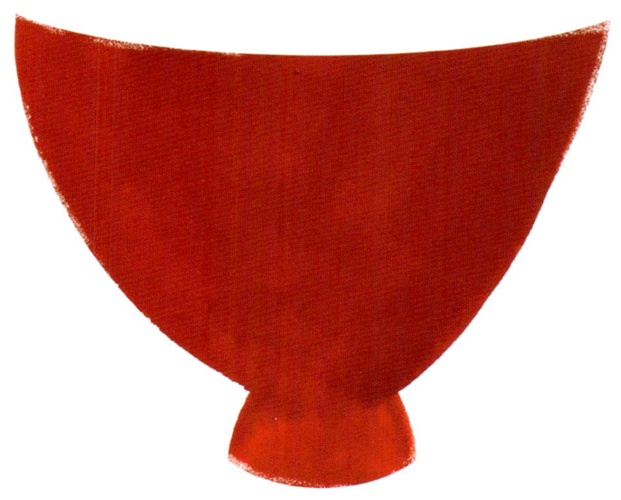

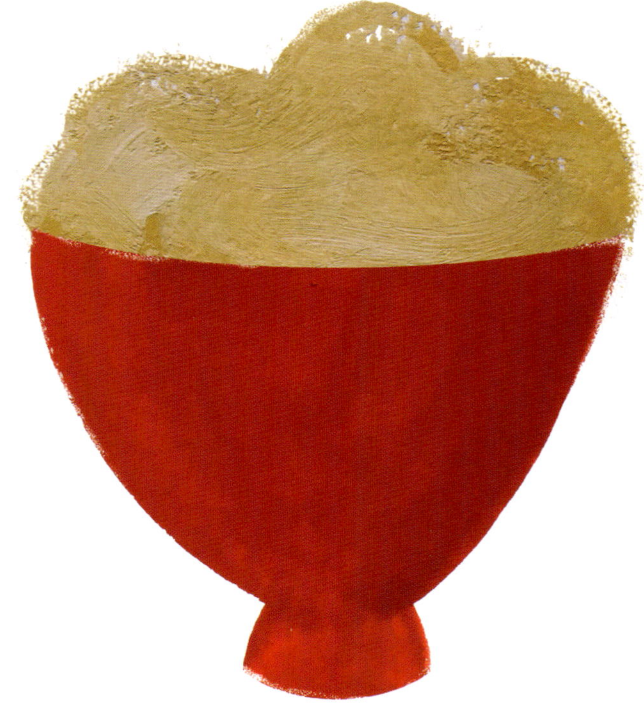

Step 1

Use red gouache to create a simple footed bowl shape. Then mix a tint of raw sienna and white to make the basic mass of what will become the ramen.

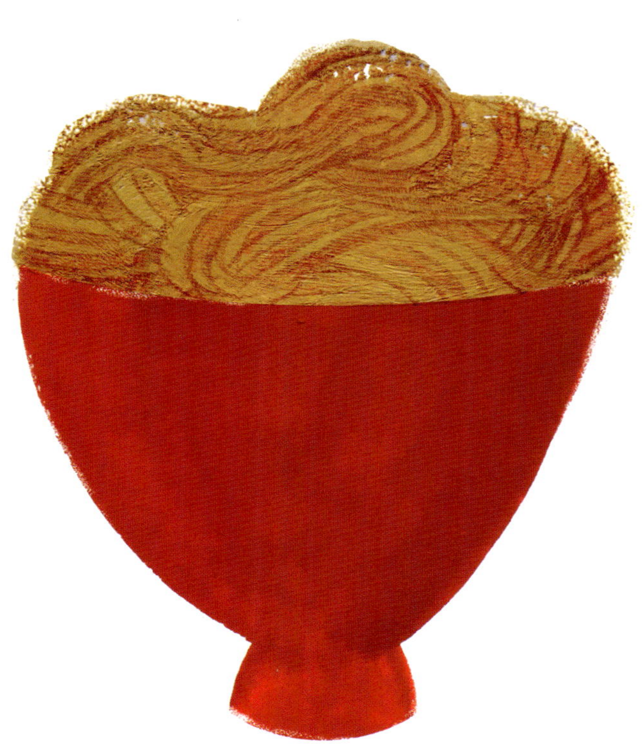

Step 2

Let the paint dry, and then use a dark brown colored pencil to define the strands of the ramen. Look closely at how ramen noodles twist and turn. Drawing over matte gouache is lots of fun, but this look can also be accomplished using a liner brush dipped in brown gouache. If you need additional texture, use the drybrush technique to scrape along the outer edges of the ramen mass. This will give it additional dimension, as well as texture.

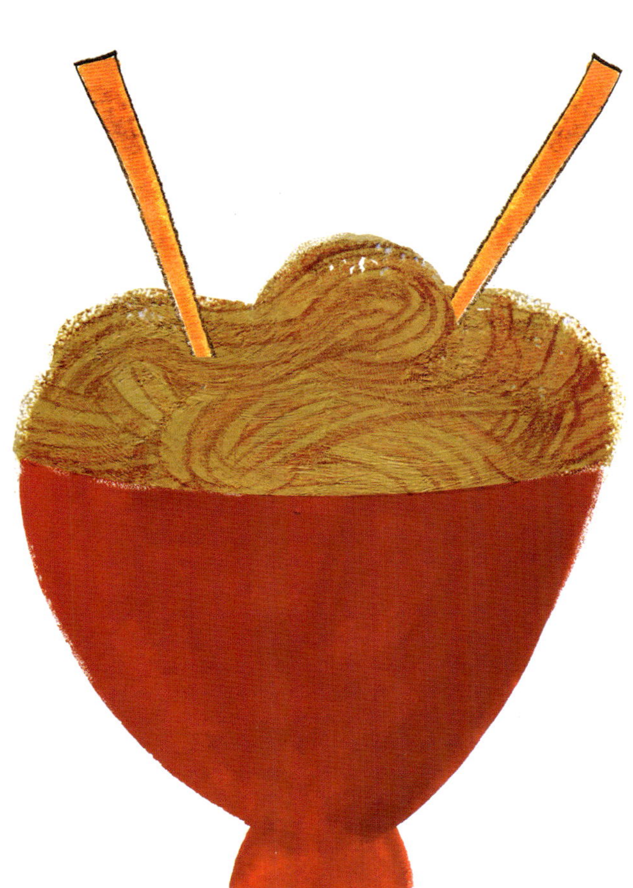

Step 3

Create chopsticks by painting opaque, elongated triangular shapes over the entire dried illustration. Be mindful of how the chopsticks descend into the ramen, making sure that they appear tucked under the noodles in the right places. You can also add spices or additional edibles into the mix if you want to take it a step further.

Step 4

I've added a decorative pattern of flowers to one side of the bowl. That's what's fun about gouache: its opaqueness makes it possible to add details on the painted surface.

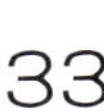

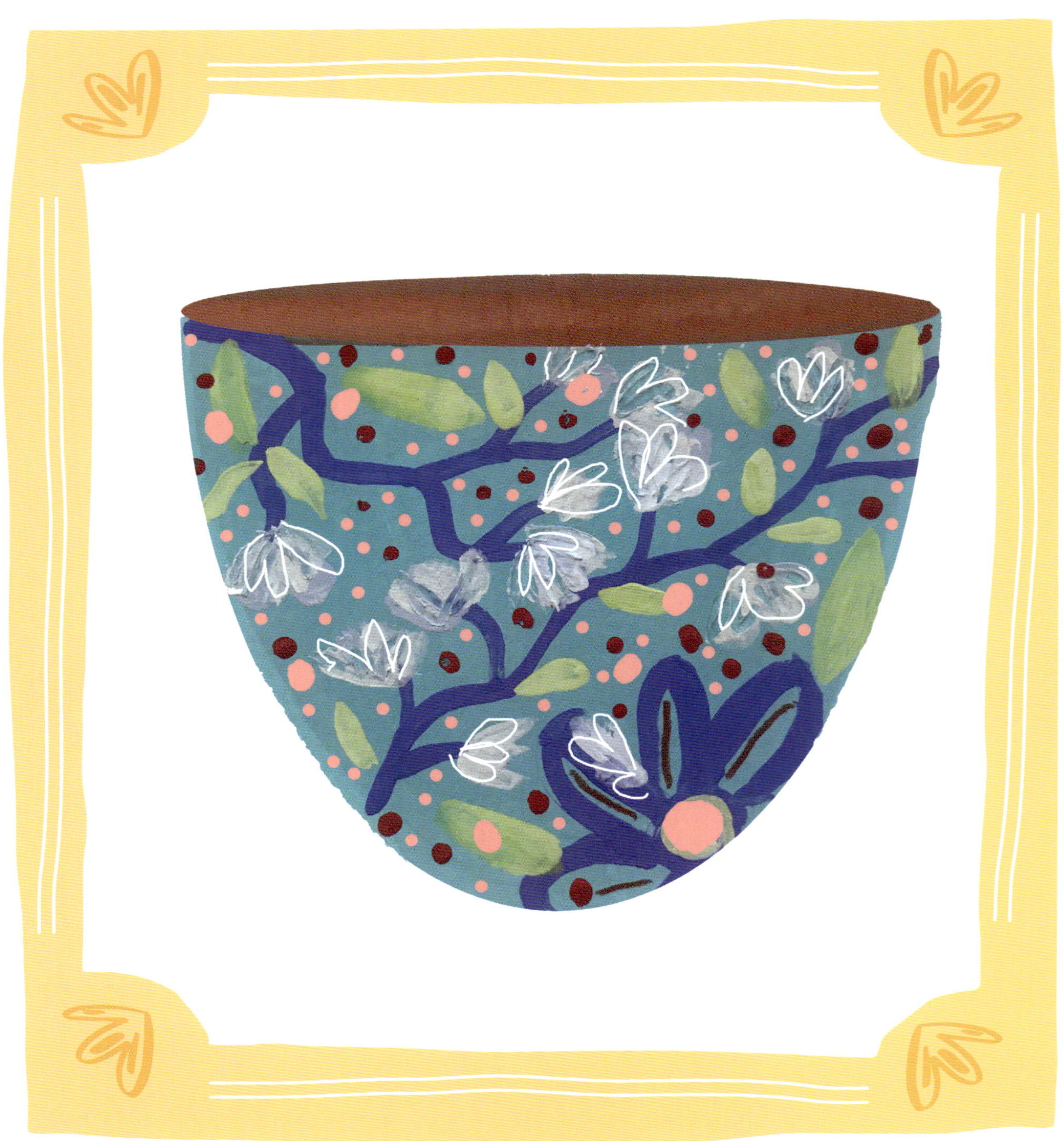

COLOR STORIES

Cool colors would complement the ramen in the bowl as well. What else might you eat with your bowl of ramen? Maybe you'd like to add a soft-boiled egg, mushrooms, or green onions? These are all easy to paint using just a few colors!

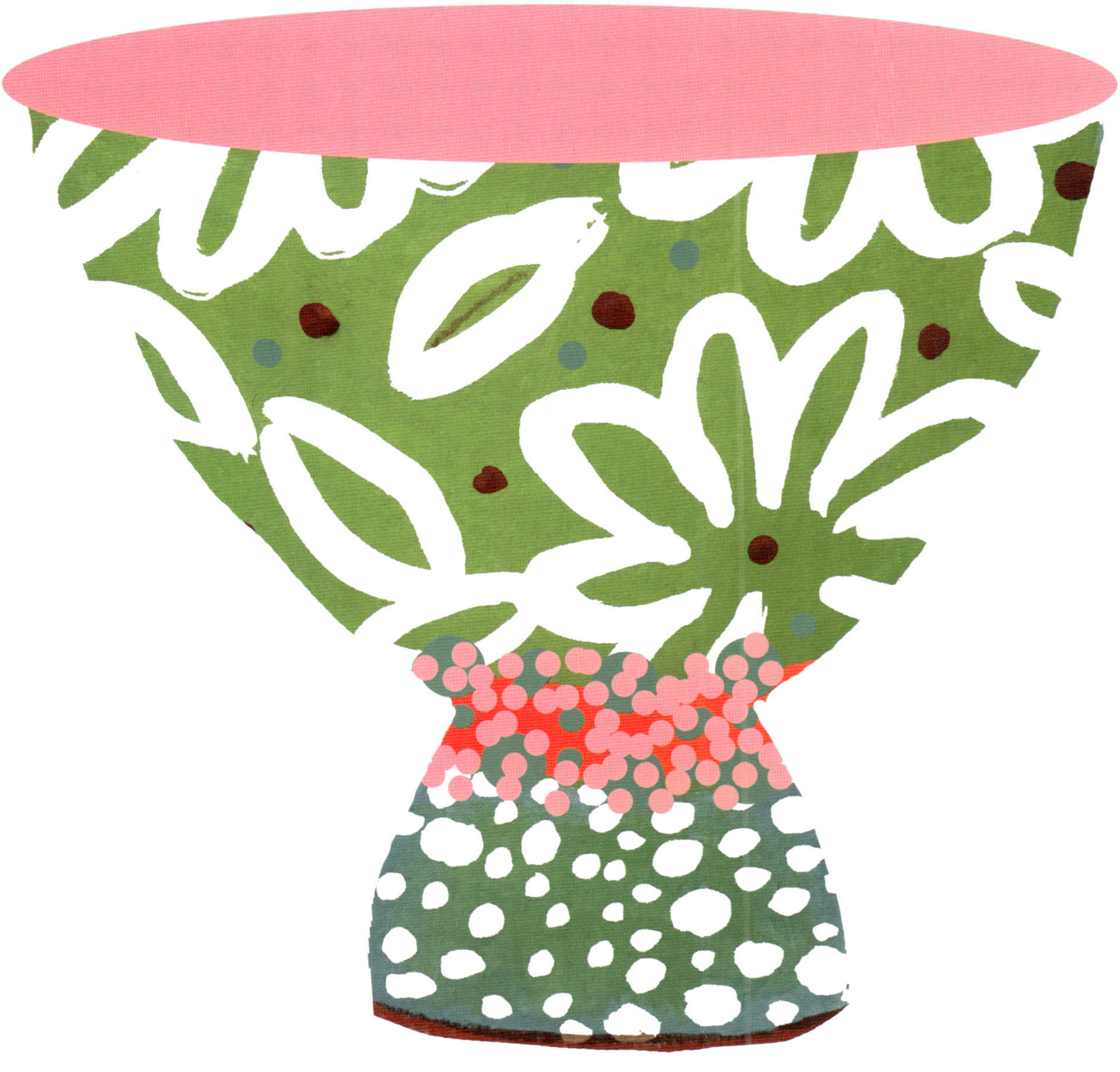

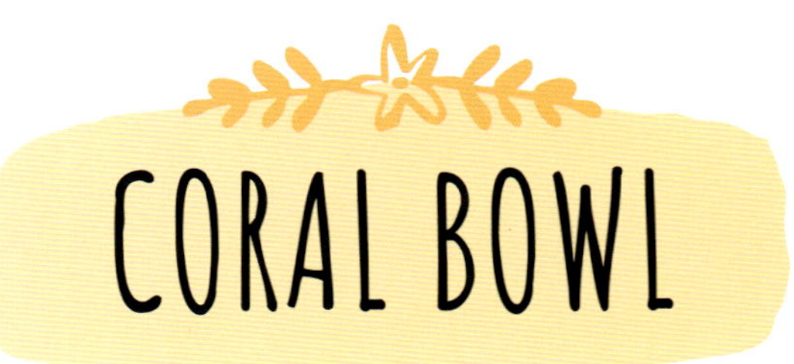

CORAL BOWL

You can use gouache to paint this fun, decorative bowl—both because of this paint medium's vibrant colors as well as its good layering properties.

Step 1

Create the bowl consisting of a simple shape with a small-footed base. Think of this part as a smaller bowl turned upside down.

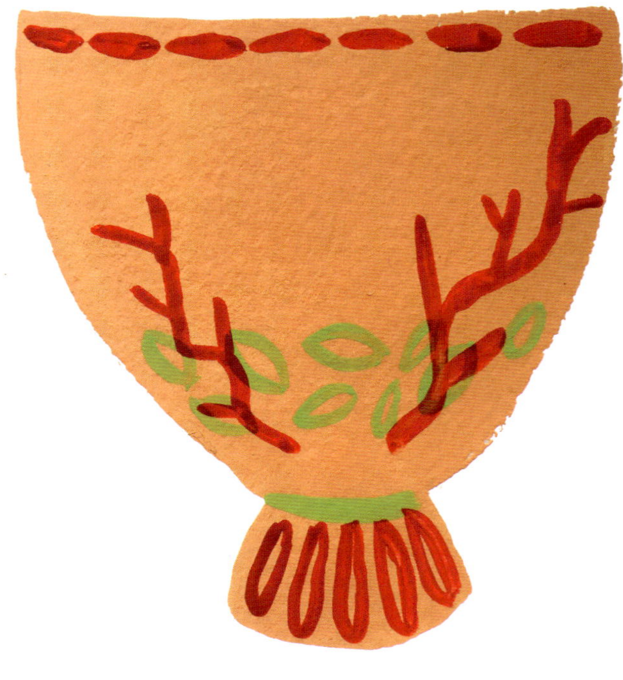

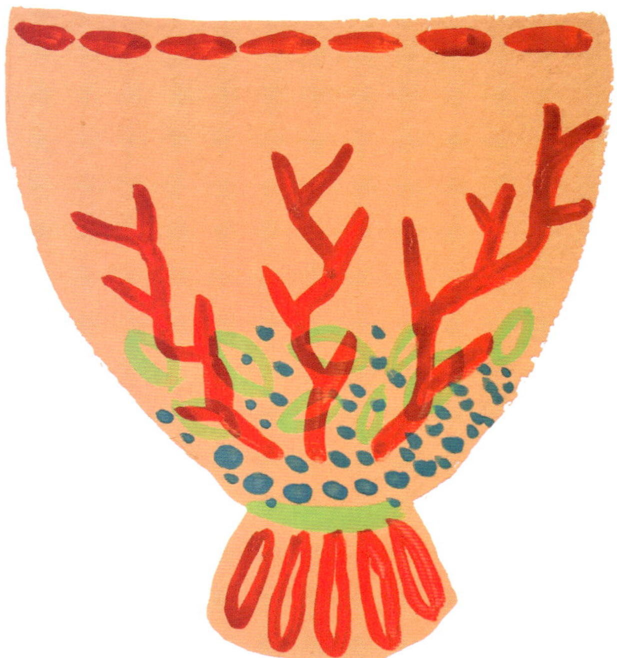

Step 2

Add decorative details in leaf-green and red. This is a great time to use the colors and imagery of your own preference. This example has a coral theme, but any pattern or color scheme will do.

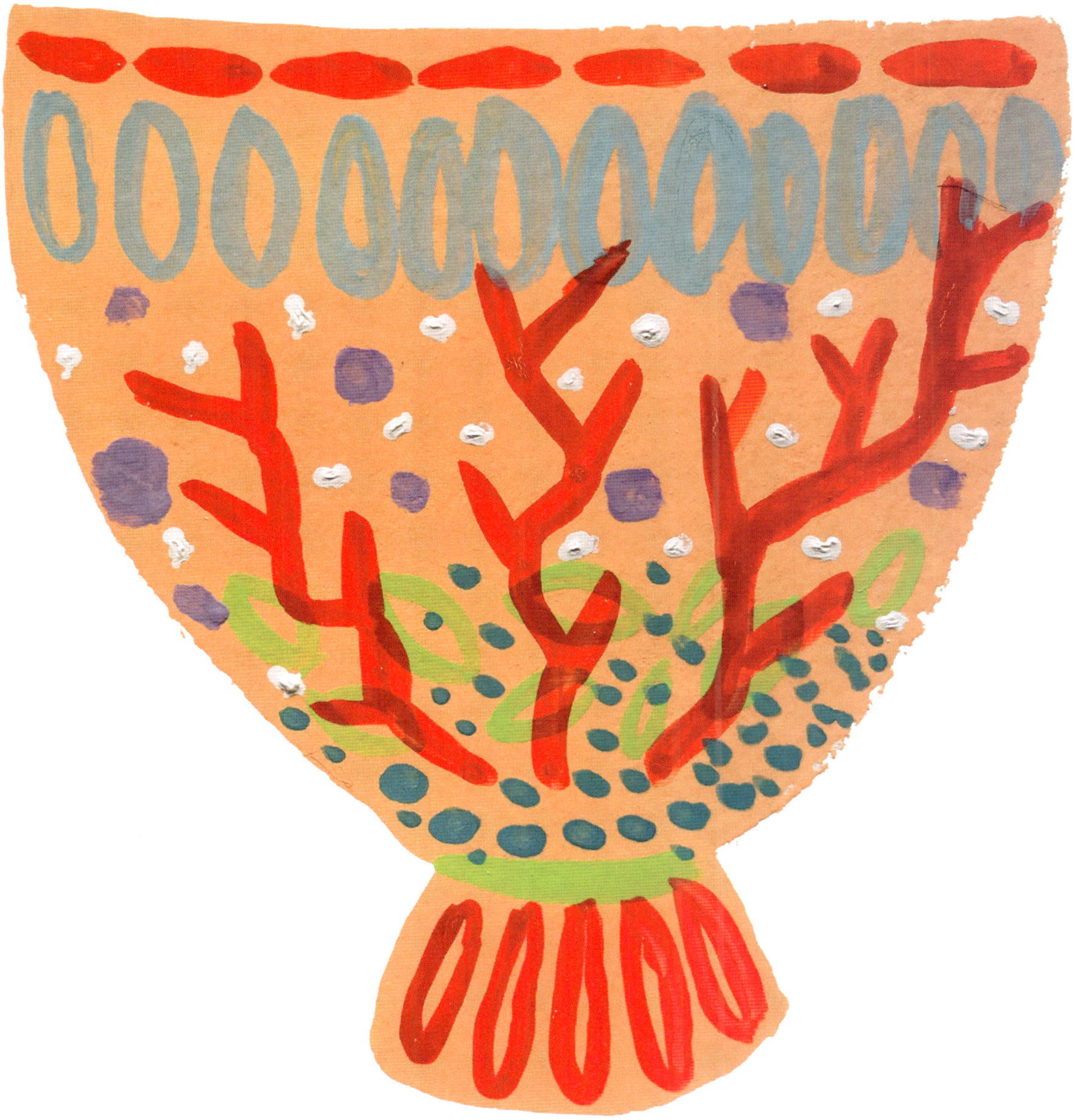

Step 3

I haven't planned my marks, which makes for some fun experimentation. Make the bowl in any hue with any subject; this is merely a starting point.

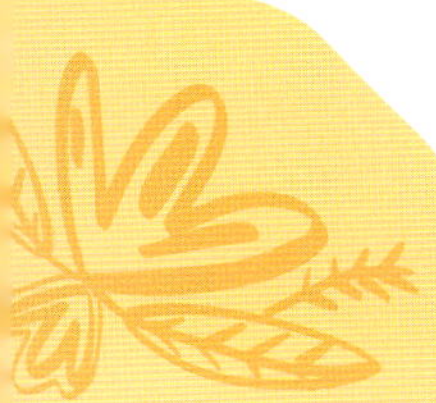

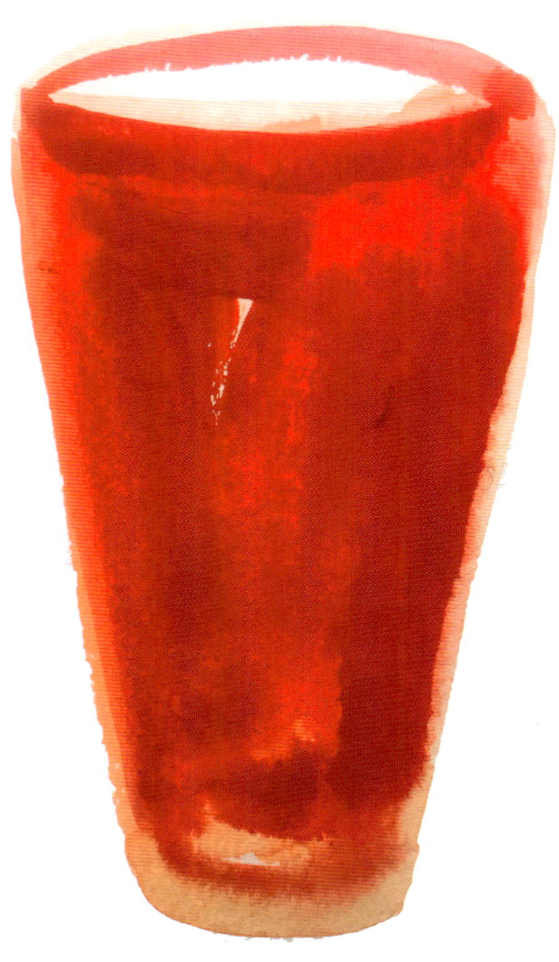

BLOODY MARY

Let's move on to drinks, specifically cocktails!

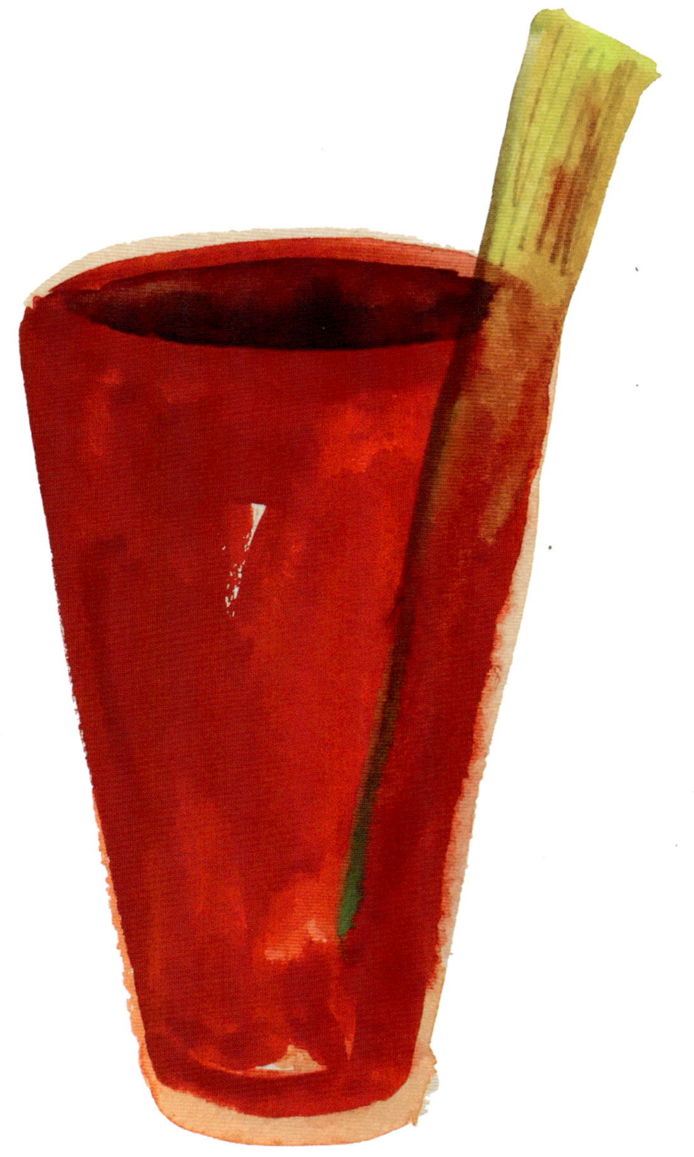

Step 1

Begin by mapping out the dominant red color of the glass. Then add celery, shrimp, and olives, and refine these elements step by step. As you can see, the progress is gradual.

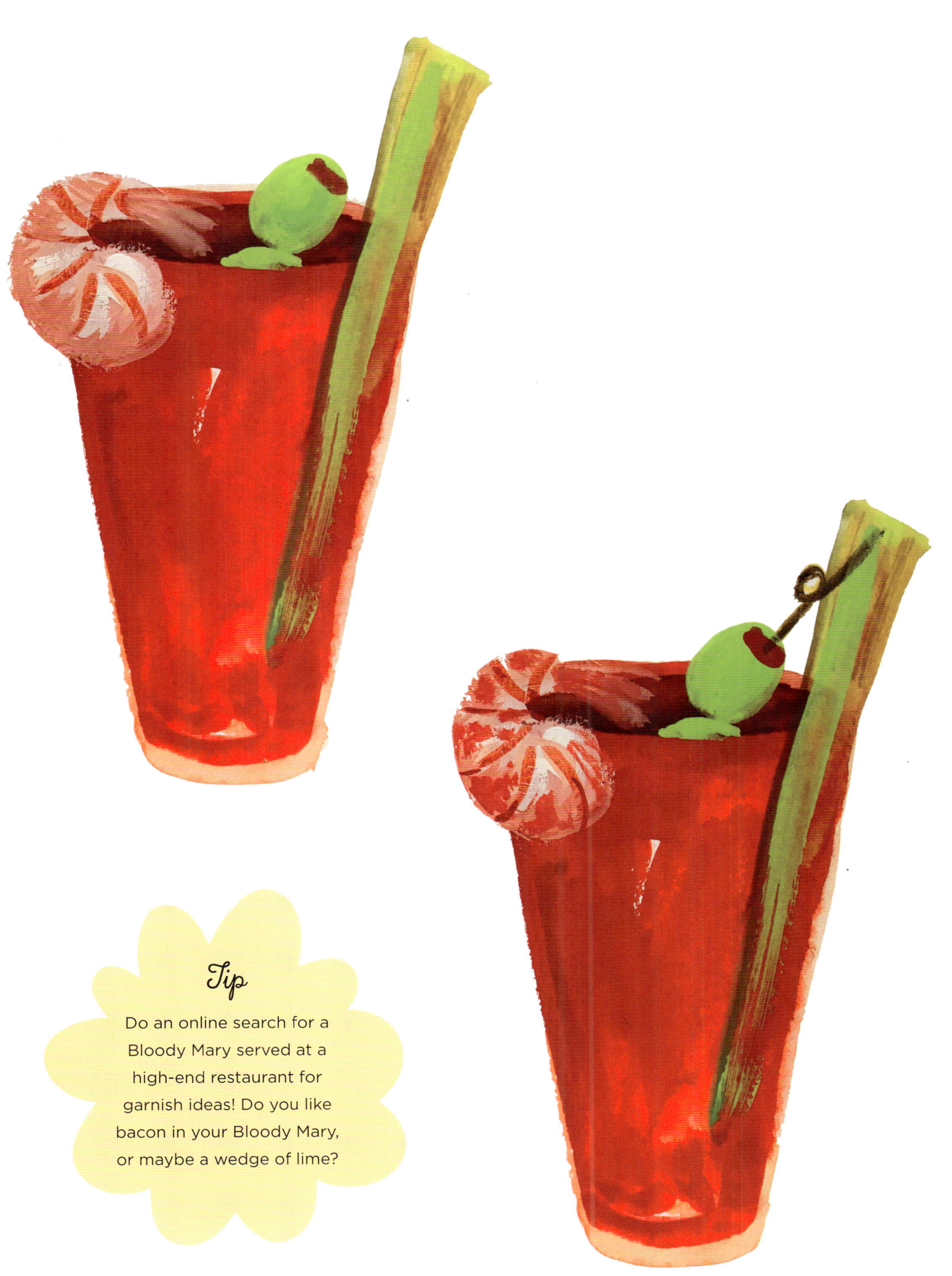

Tip

Do an online search for a Bloody Mary served at a high-end restaurant for garnish ideas! Do you like bacon in your Bloody Mary, or maybe a wedge of lime?

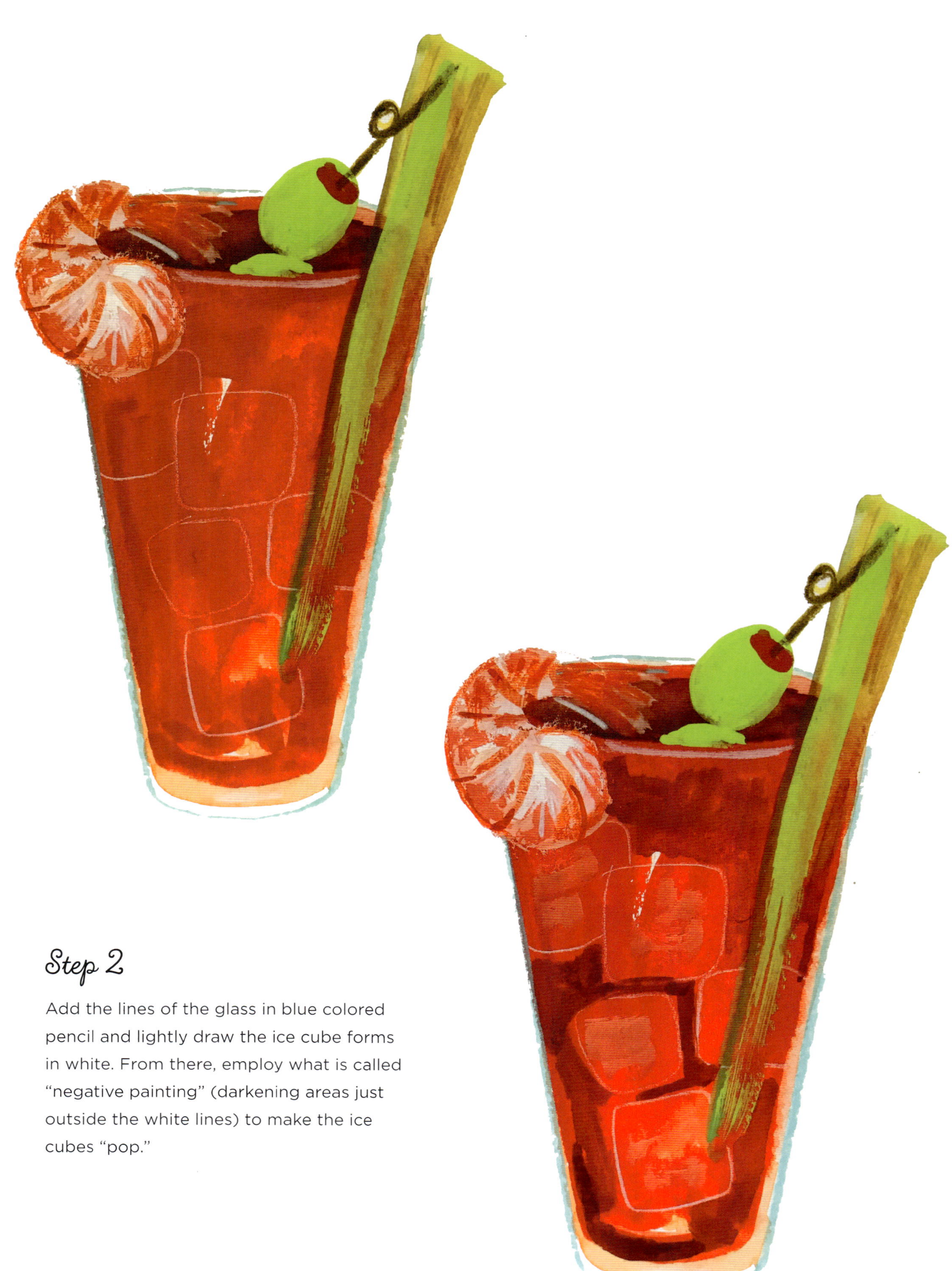

Step 2

Add the lines of the glass in blue colored pencil and lightly draw the ice cube forms in white. From there, employ what is called "negative painting" (darkening areas just outside the white lines) to make the ice cubes "pop."

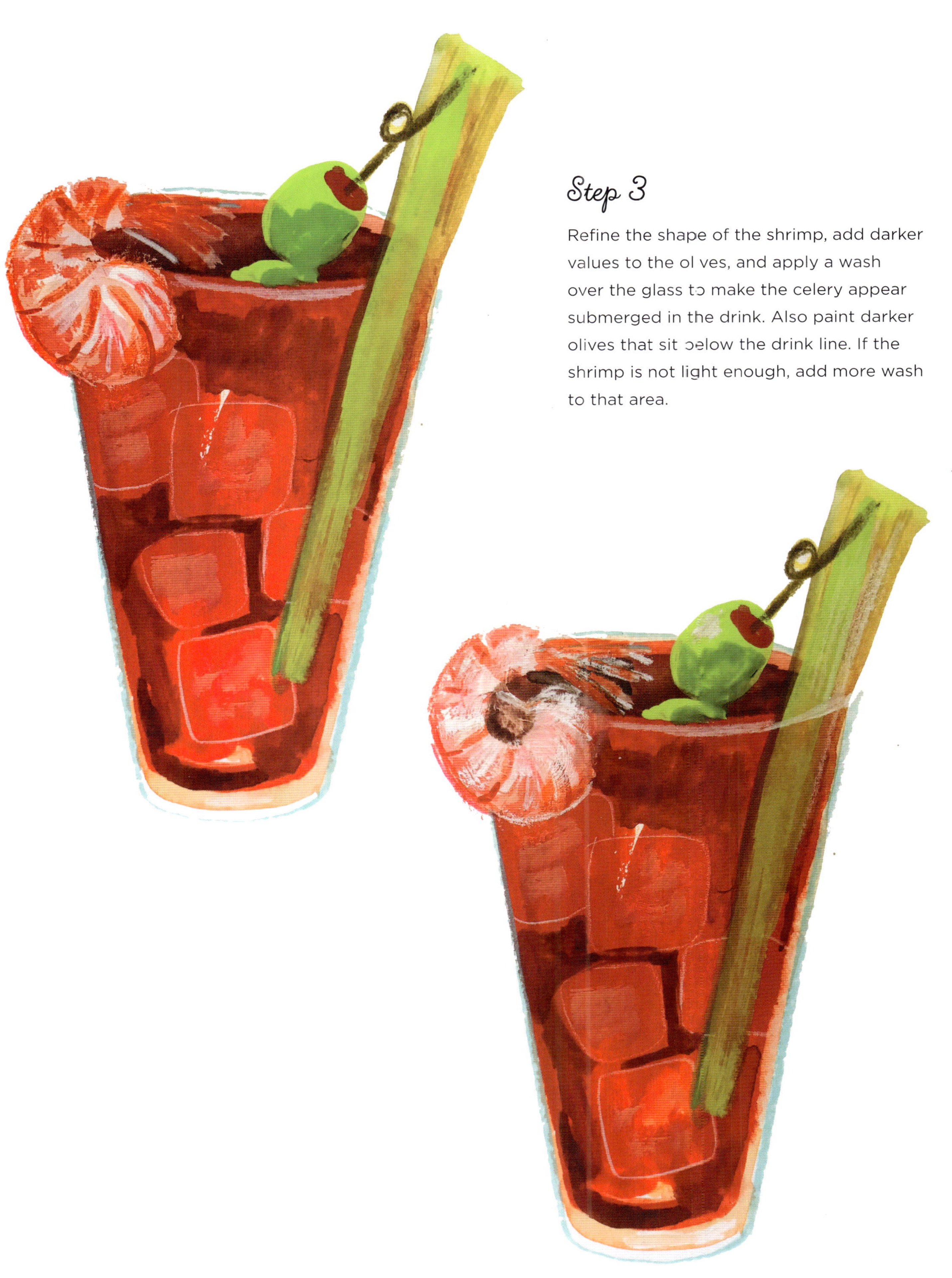

Step 3

Refine the shape of the shrimp, add darker values to the olives, and apply a wash over the glass to make the celery appear submerged in the drink. Also paint darker olives that sit below the drink line. If the shrimp is not light enough, add more wash to that area.

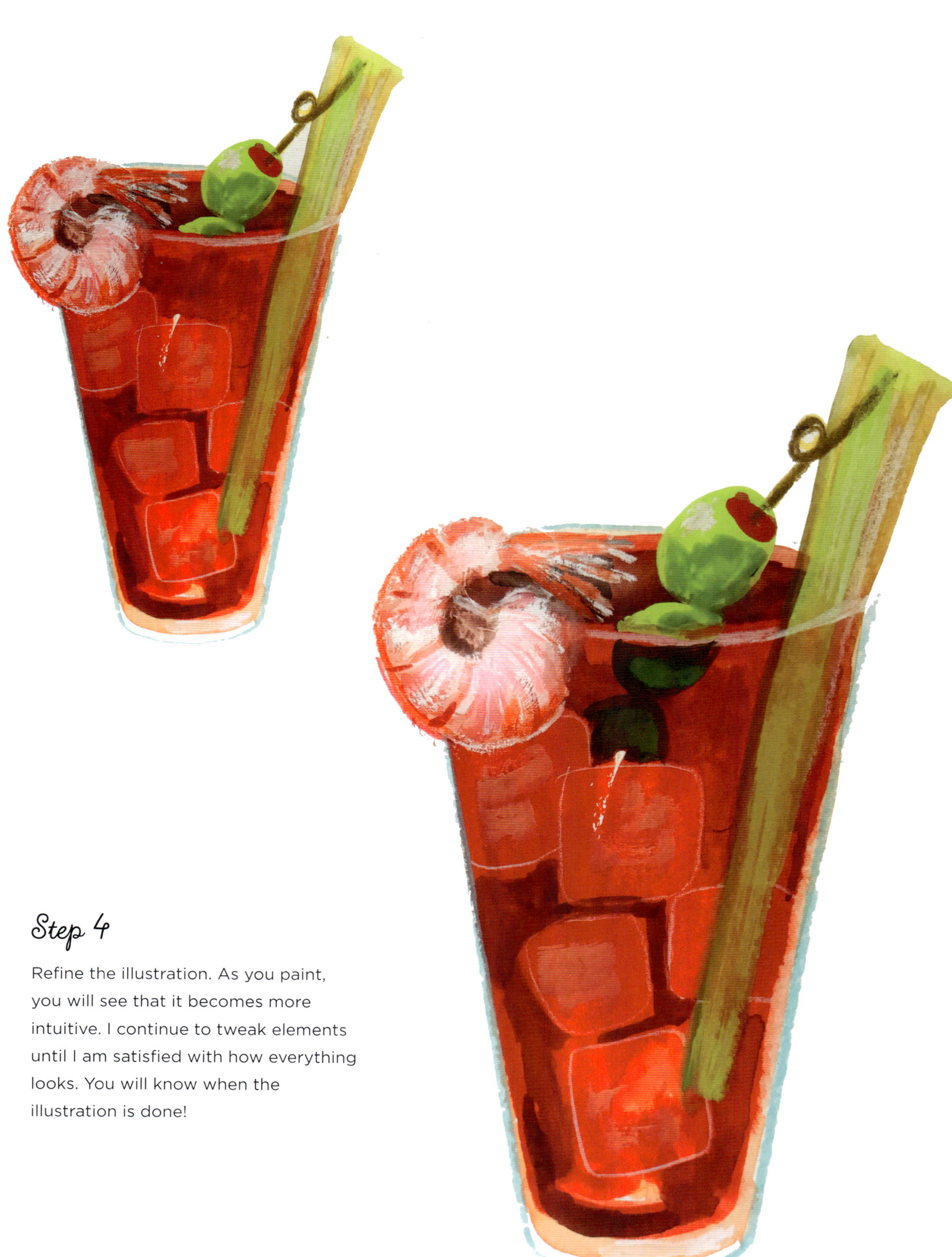

Step 4

Refine the illustration. As you paint, you will see that it becomes more intuitive. I continue to tweak elements until I am satisfied with how everything looks. You will know when the illustration is done!

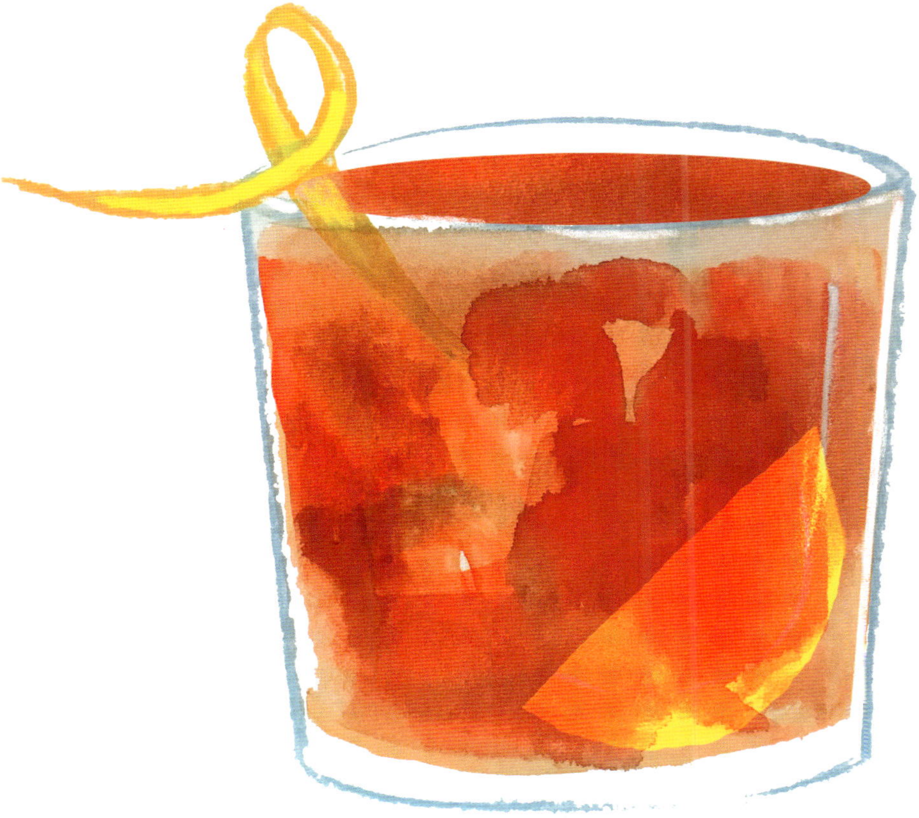

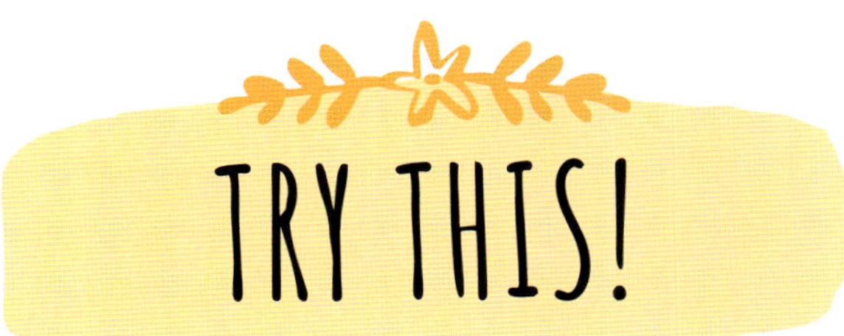

A Negroni is a popular Italian cocktail that looks red, like the Bloody Mary, but it usually comes in a short, squat glass and is garnished with a slice of orange. What other cocktails or mocktails might you like to paint? Maybe you prefer a glass of sparkling water garnished with a lemon slice?

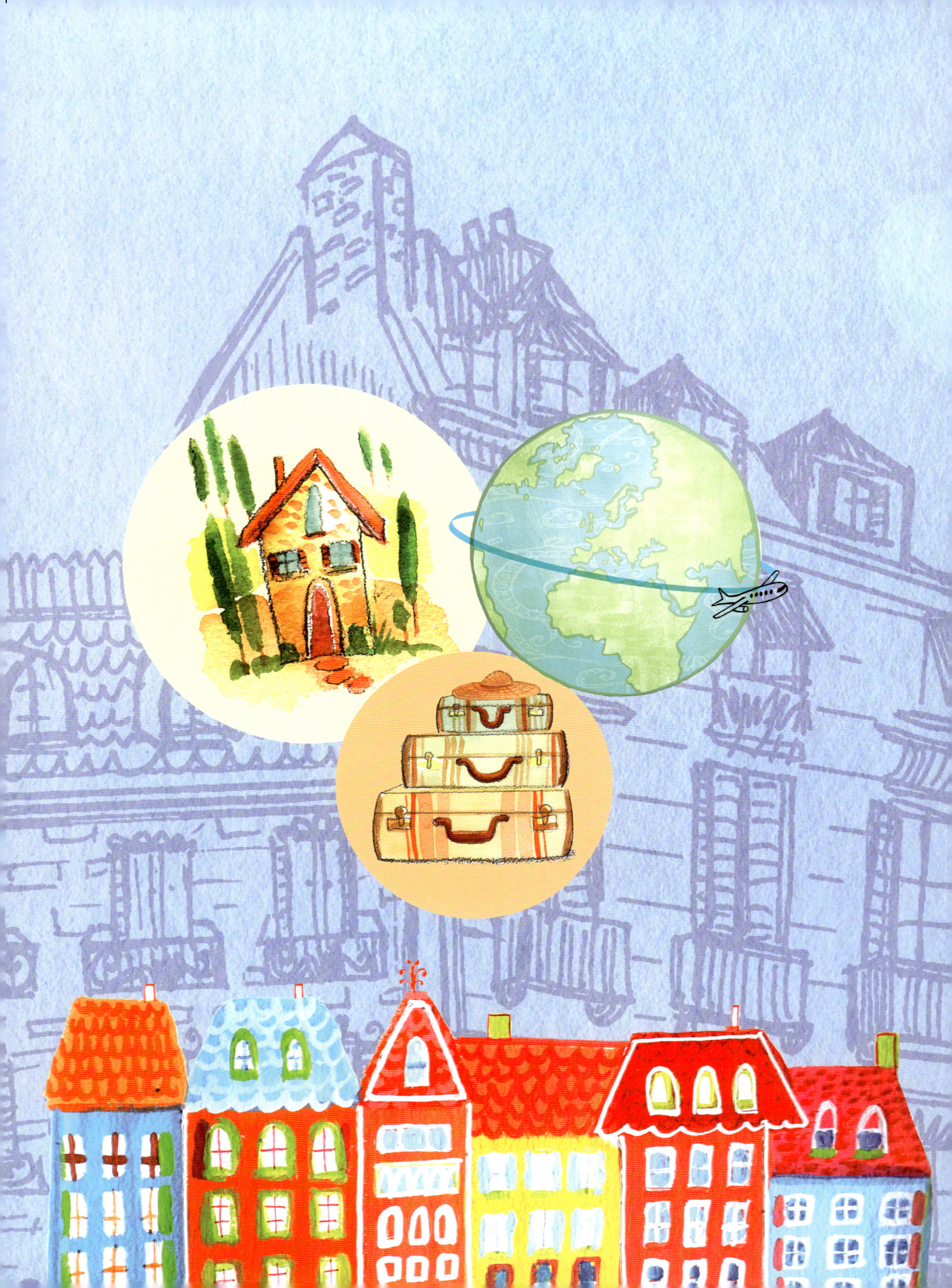

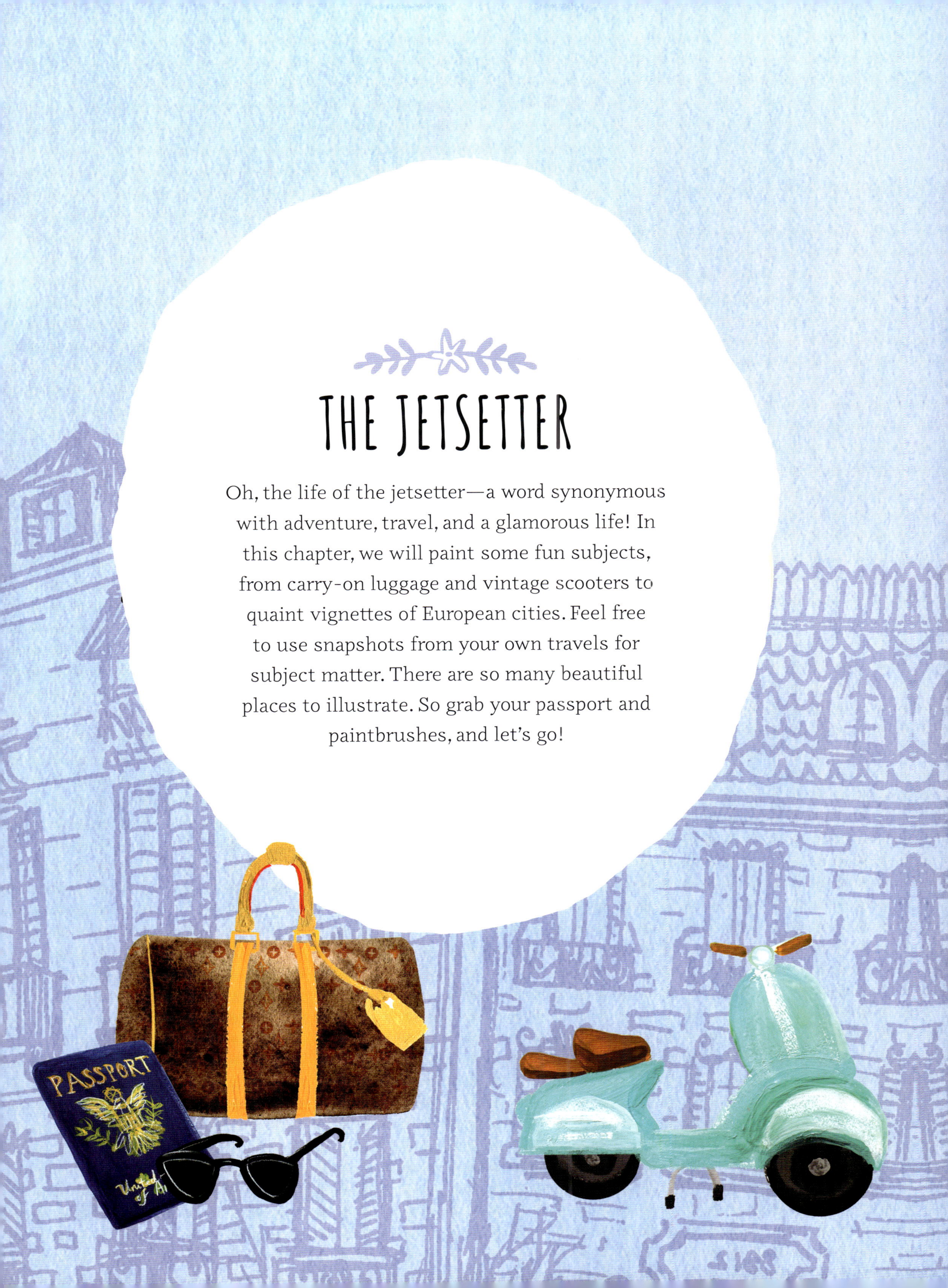

THE JETSETTER

Oh, the life of the jetsetter—a word synonymous with adventure, travel, and a glamorous life! In this chapter, we will paint some fun subjects, from carry-on luggage and vintage scooters to quaint vignettes of European cities. Feel free to use snapshots from your own travels for subject matter. There are so many beautiful places to illustrate. So grab your passport and paintbrushes, and let's go!

DESIGNER CARRY-ON

This project has a luxurious vibe, but any color combination or pattern would be welcome on this handbag!

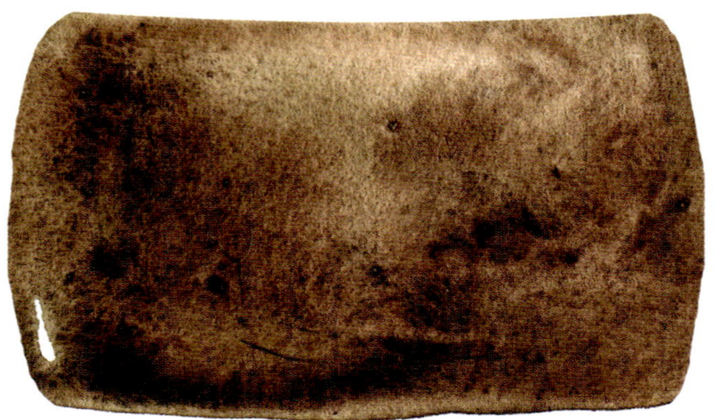

Step 1

Use watercolor here to create a wash for a basic duffel bag shape, allowing the water to pool in some areas to mimic the darker recesses of the canvas material.

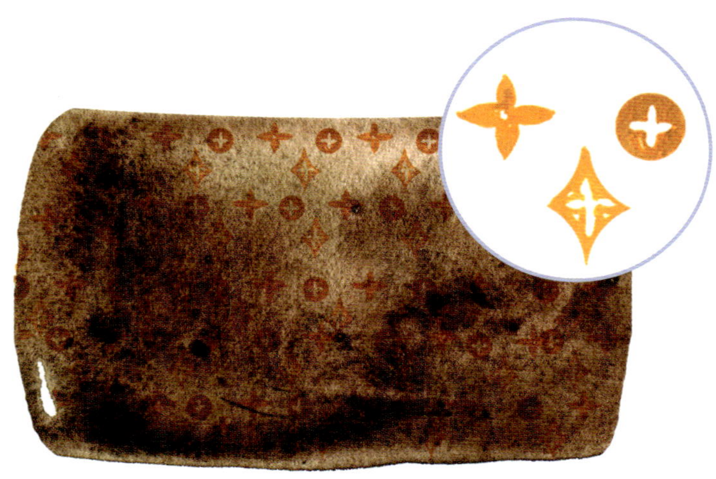

Step 2

Once this layer dries, use a liner brush to paint little icons across the entire surface. Mix a warm caramel hue so that the icons blend into the background canvas. (See inset for a larger view of the icons.)

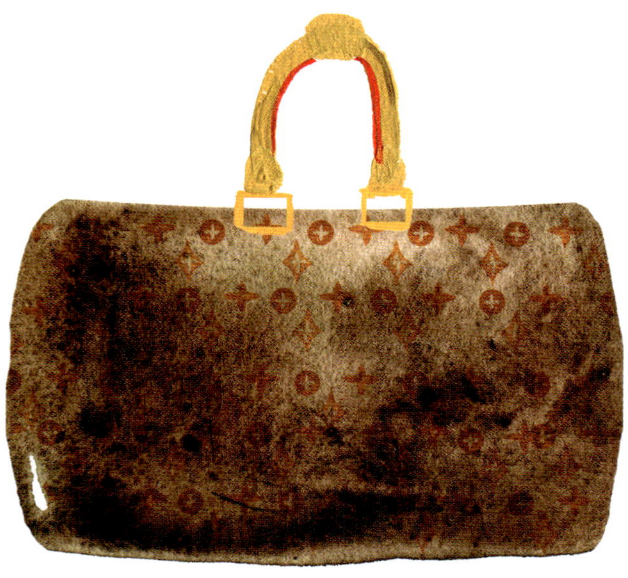

Step 3

Use gouache to create the handle and buckles. Watercolor and gouache are fun to interchange and layer in an illustration, as the combination of transparent and opaque is quite eye-catching.

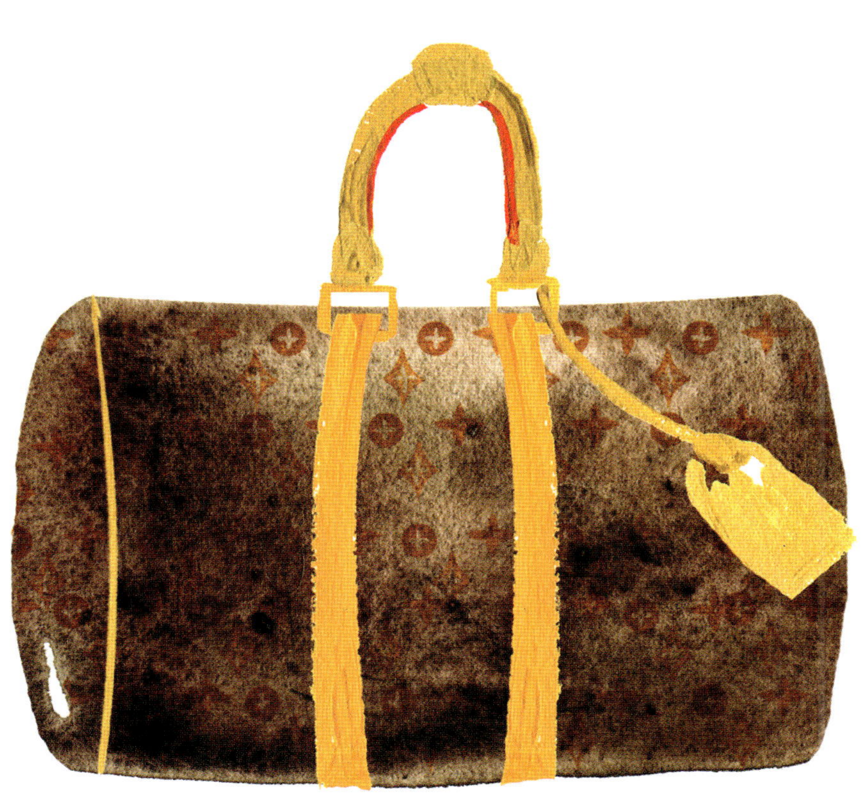

Step 4

Lastly, add the leather cross straps, piping, and luggage tag using gouache.

TRAVEL IN STYLE

After painting a carry-on bag, why not add a passport and some cute shades to your travel-inspired art? A passport case could make for another fun painting project!

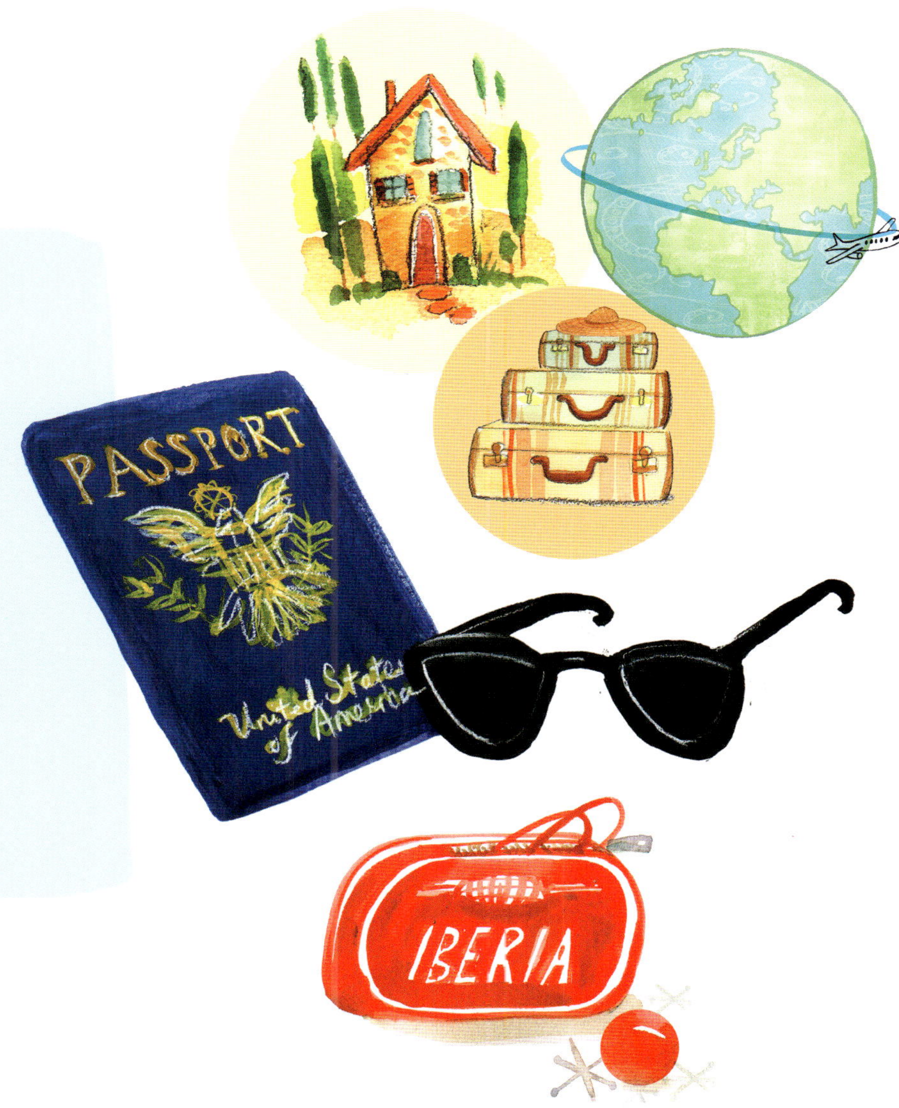

PARISIAN FLOWER MARKET

This project evokes visits to flower markets in European cities. For inspiration at home, try visiting a flower stand in your city or search online for reference photos.

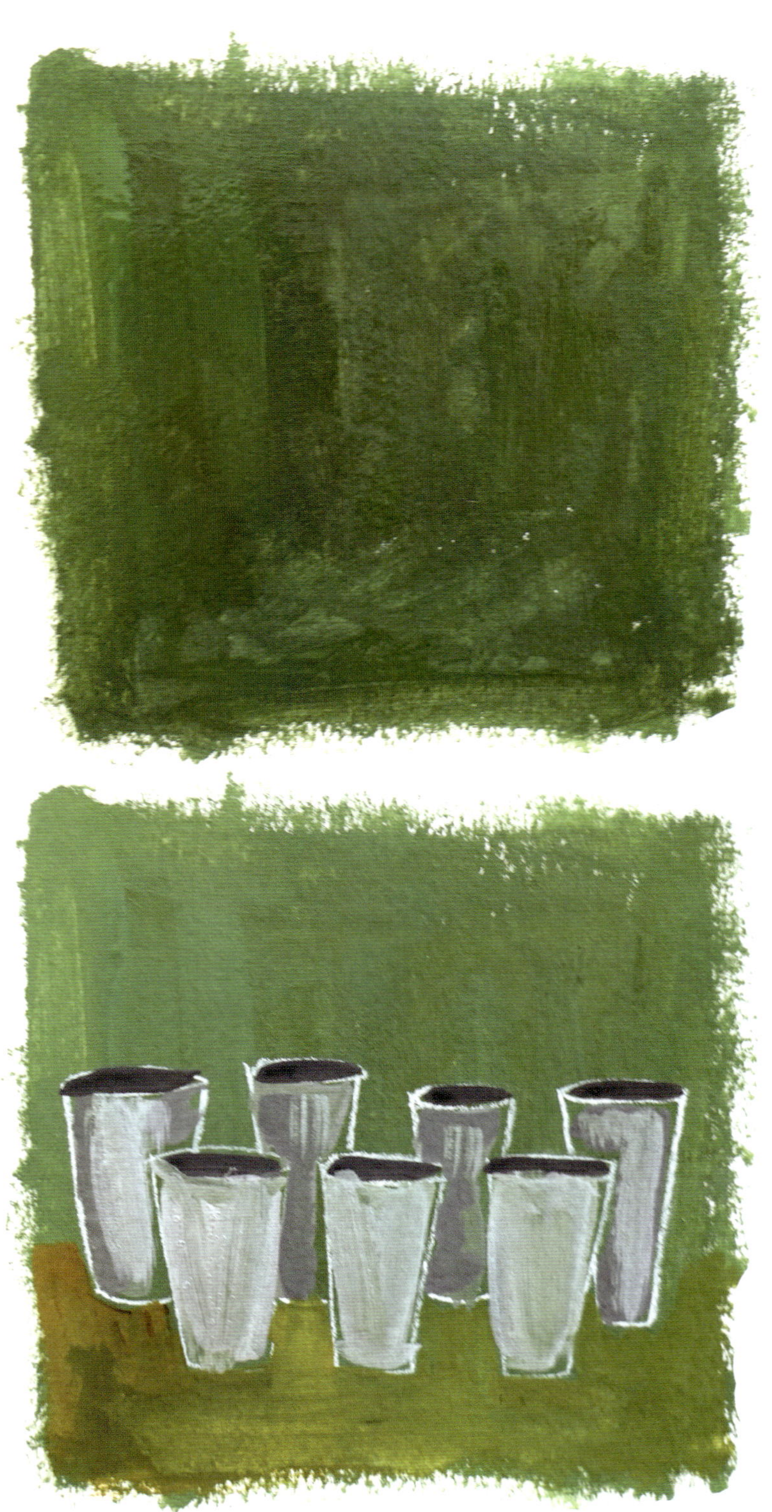

Step 1

Using gouache and the drybrushing technique (page 15), create a simple background of a rough-hewn square. This draws more interest than a solid square, as the flowers will eventually break the border.

Step 2

With a white charcoal pencil, draw the flower buckets. Then use shades of gray gouache to paint layers and form the buckets' colors and darker insides, . Add a touch of raw sienna to give the illusion of a wooden base.

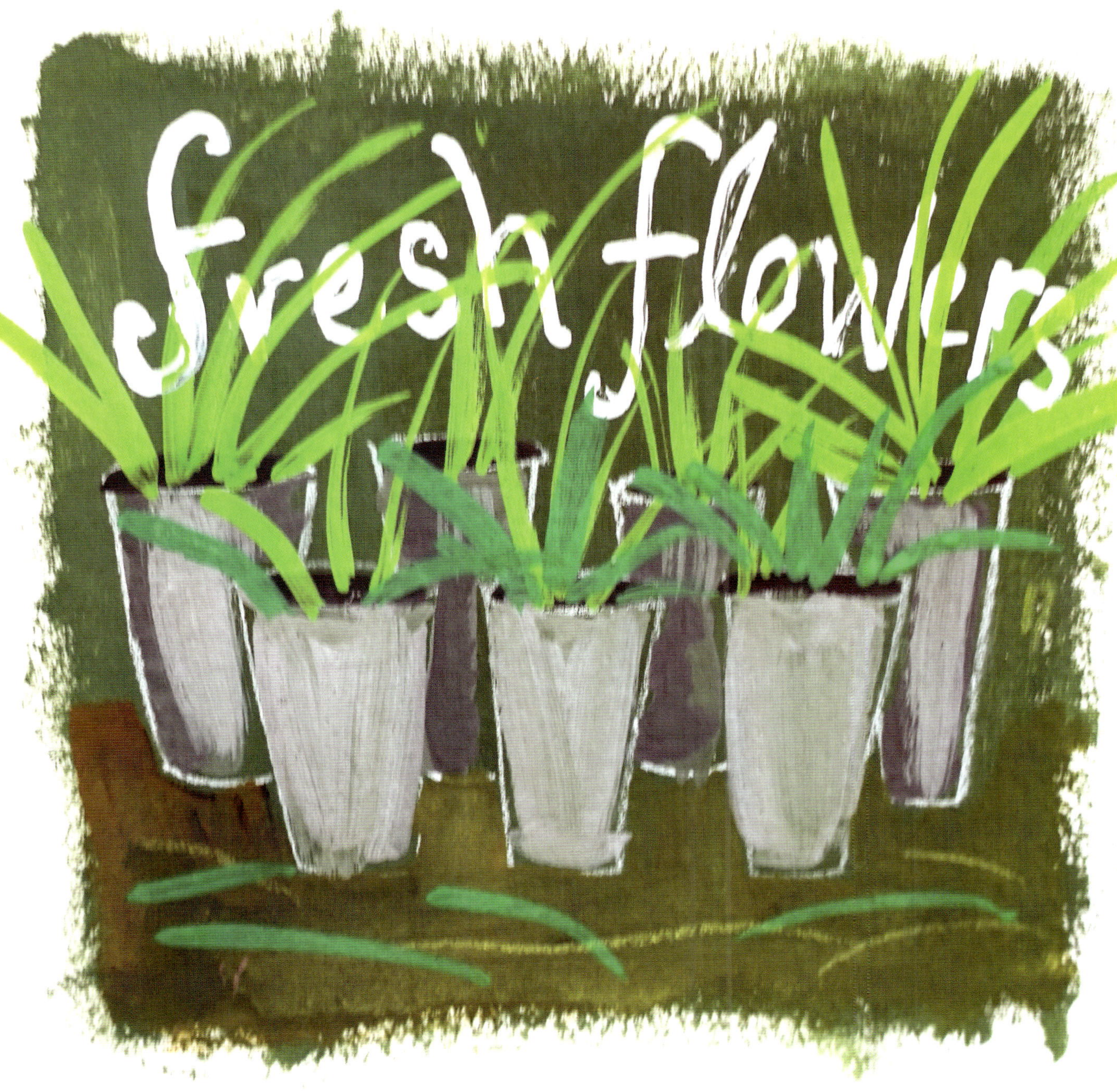

Step 3

Add the "fresh flowers" lettering using white acrylic ink. Let this dry; then add the greenery in various hues of gouache. Be sure to drag your brush up and out here to give the illustration energy and so that the lettering recedes behind the flowers.

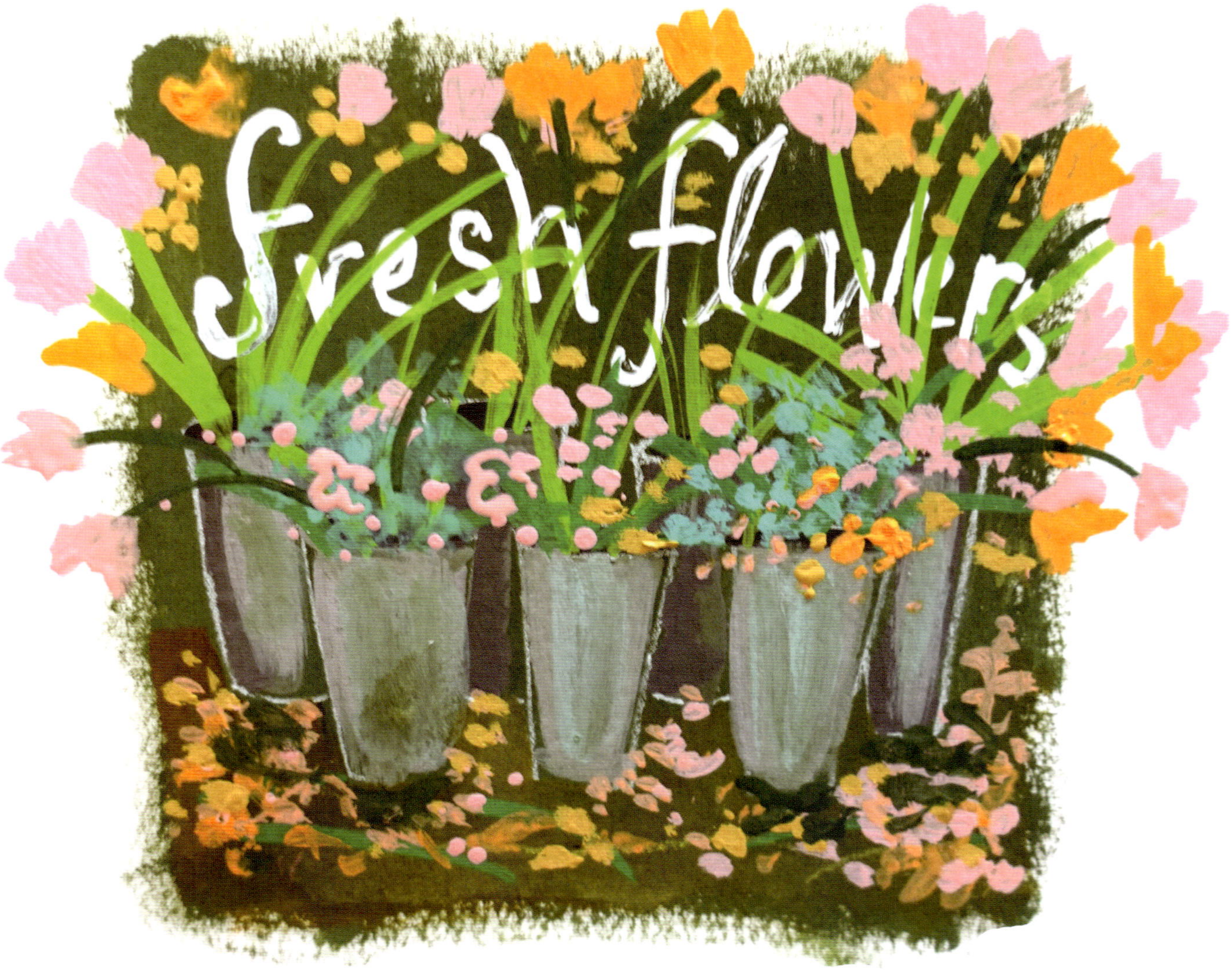

Step 4

Use assorted colors of gouache to create the flowers. Experiment with using the end of your brush to mimic smaller blooms. I've used the tip of a round brush to create fallen petals, as well as darkened the background to add contrast.

Choose any colors and play with different types of flowers.

You may choose to stand back and assess now. Gouache is a wonderful medium for layering, so have fun here and feel free to add your own touches!

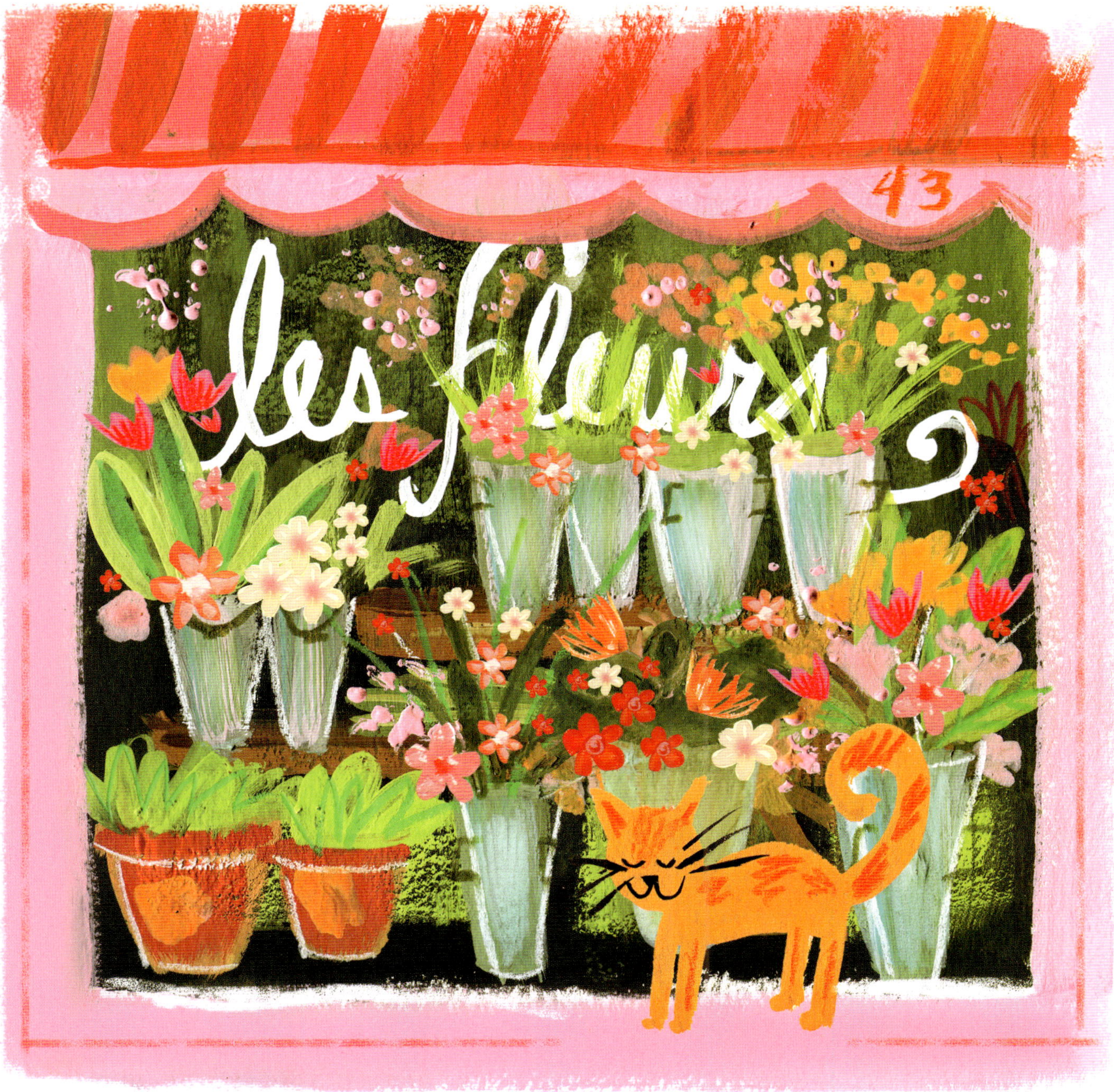

FRENCH FLAIR

Here is another option for a flower market illustration that uses an alternative color story and features a shop pet added into the mix.

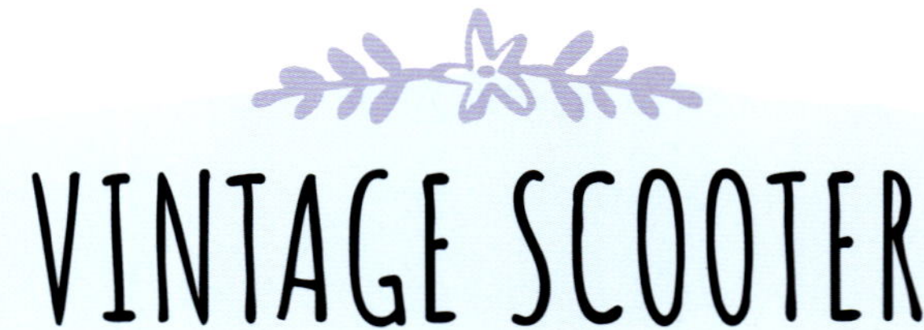

VINTAGE SCOOTER

I've chosen to use gouache here because of its amazing vibrancy and opacity—reminiscent of the Mediterranean sea or the potted plants on an Italian balcony.

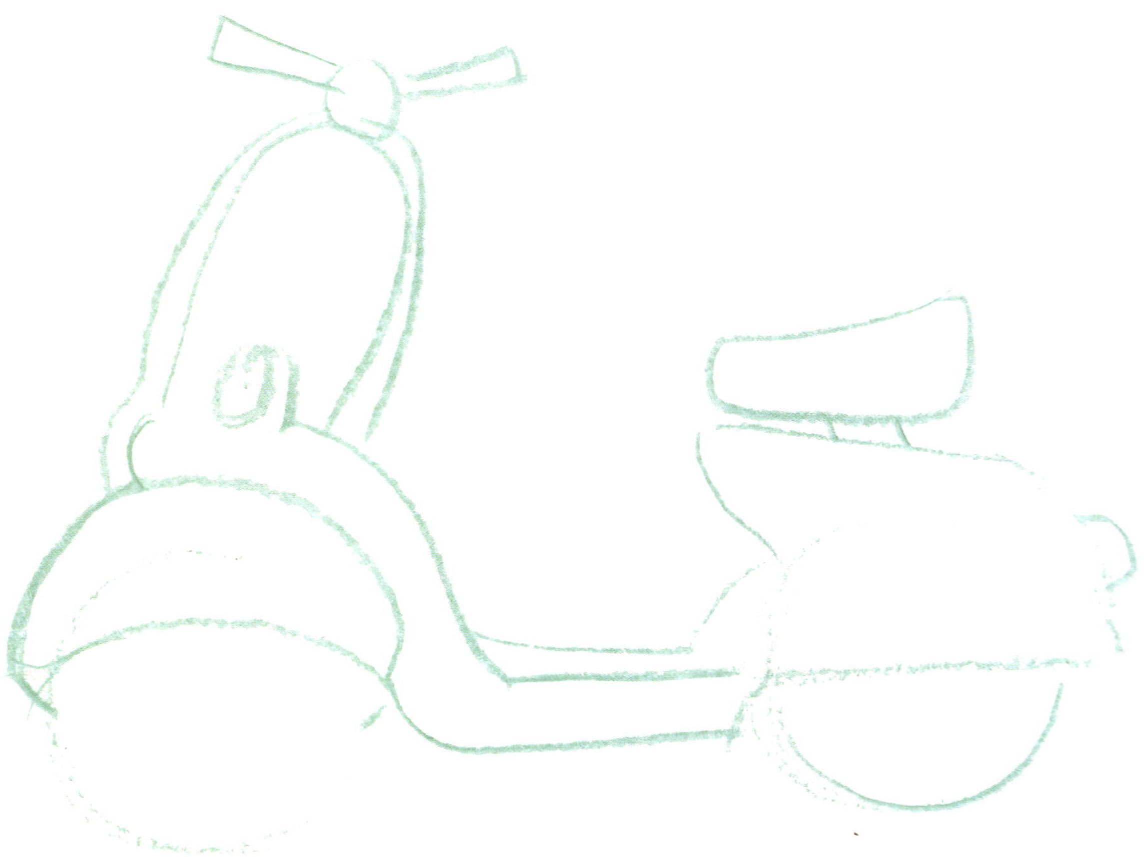

Tip

These tires will eventually tuck beneath the frame and wheel wells and can be refined in later steps.

Step 1

Start by making a light drawing using a turquoise colored pencil.

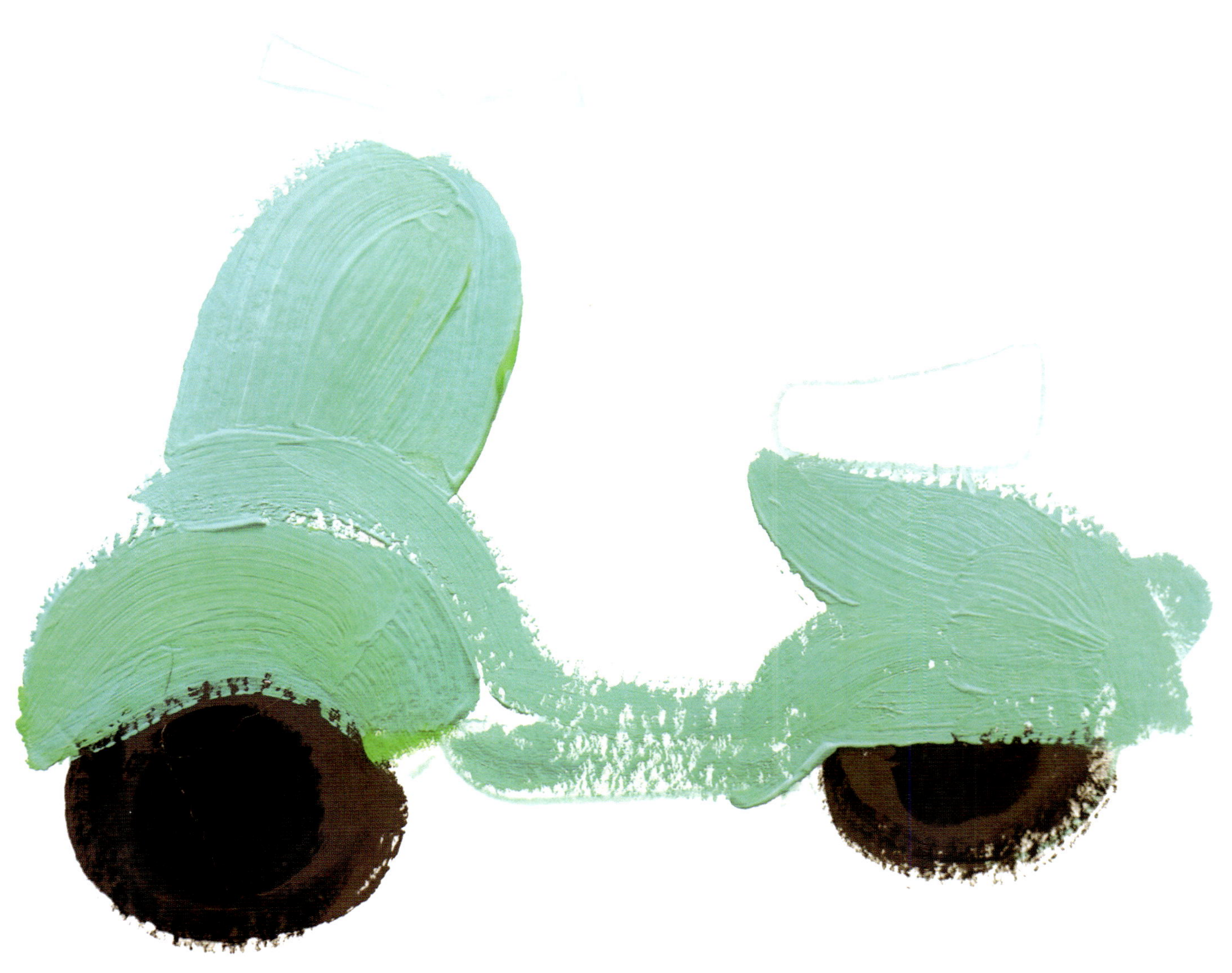

Step 2

Apply bright turquoise gouache to form the basic shape of the scooter; then use black for the tires.

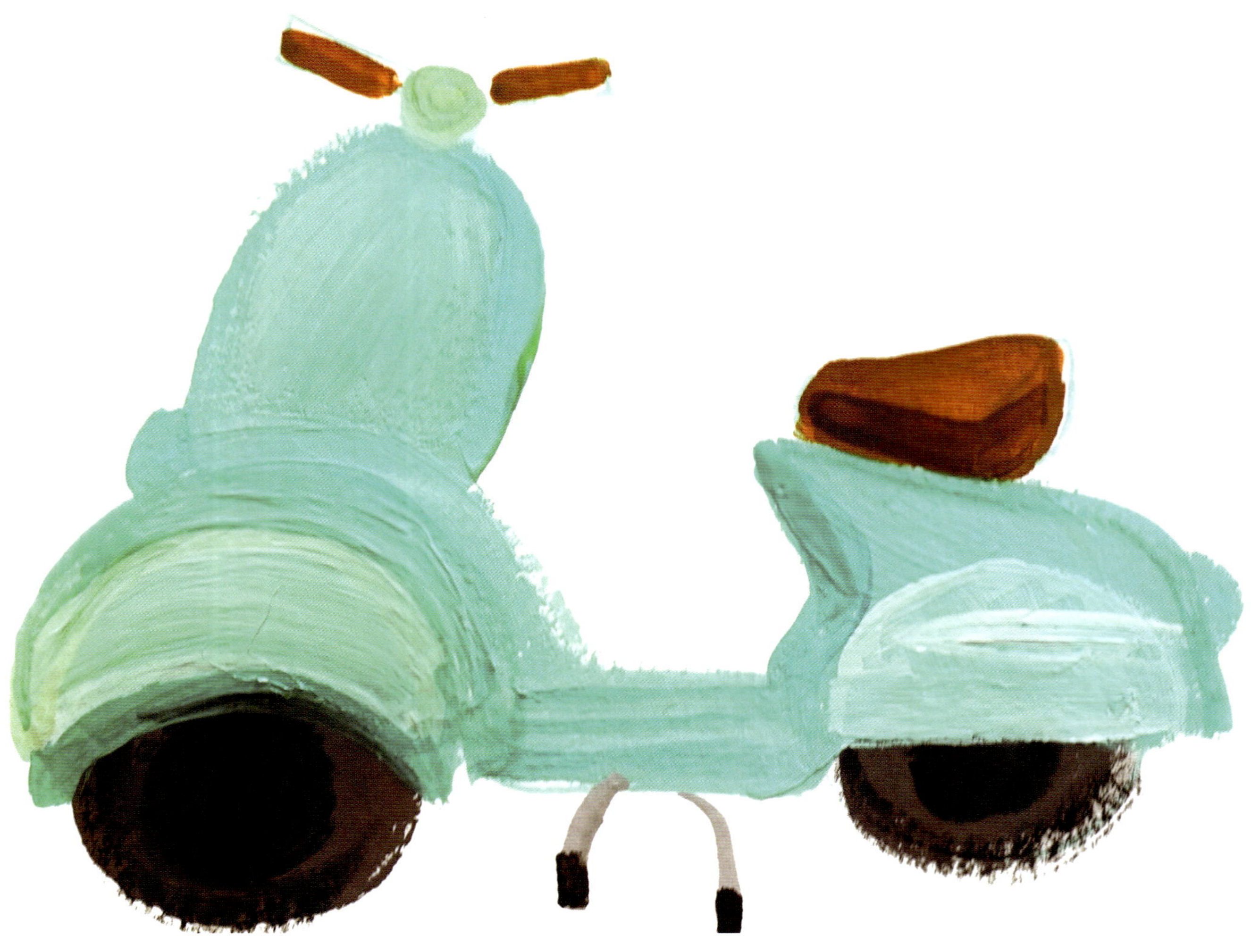

Step 3

Make a tint using turquoise and some white. Use this mixture to add reflective areas to the wheel well, as well as the raised areas of the scooter shield. You will see the scooter begin to take more shape now as this step gives the object depth.

Mix raw sienna and white to form the handlebars and seat. To add depth to the leather seat, use raw sienna straight from the tube to make the side a shade darker than the tint that was made with white. Mix gray paint to form a simple kickstand and black to form its caps.

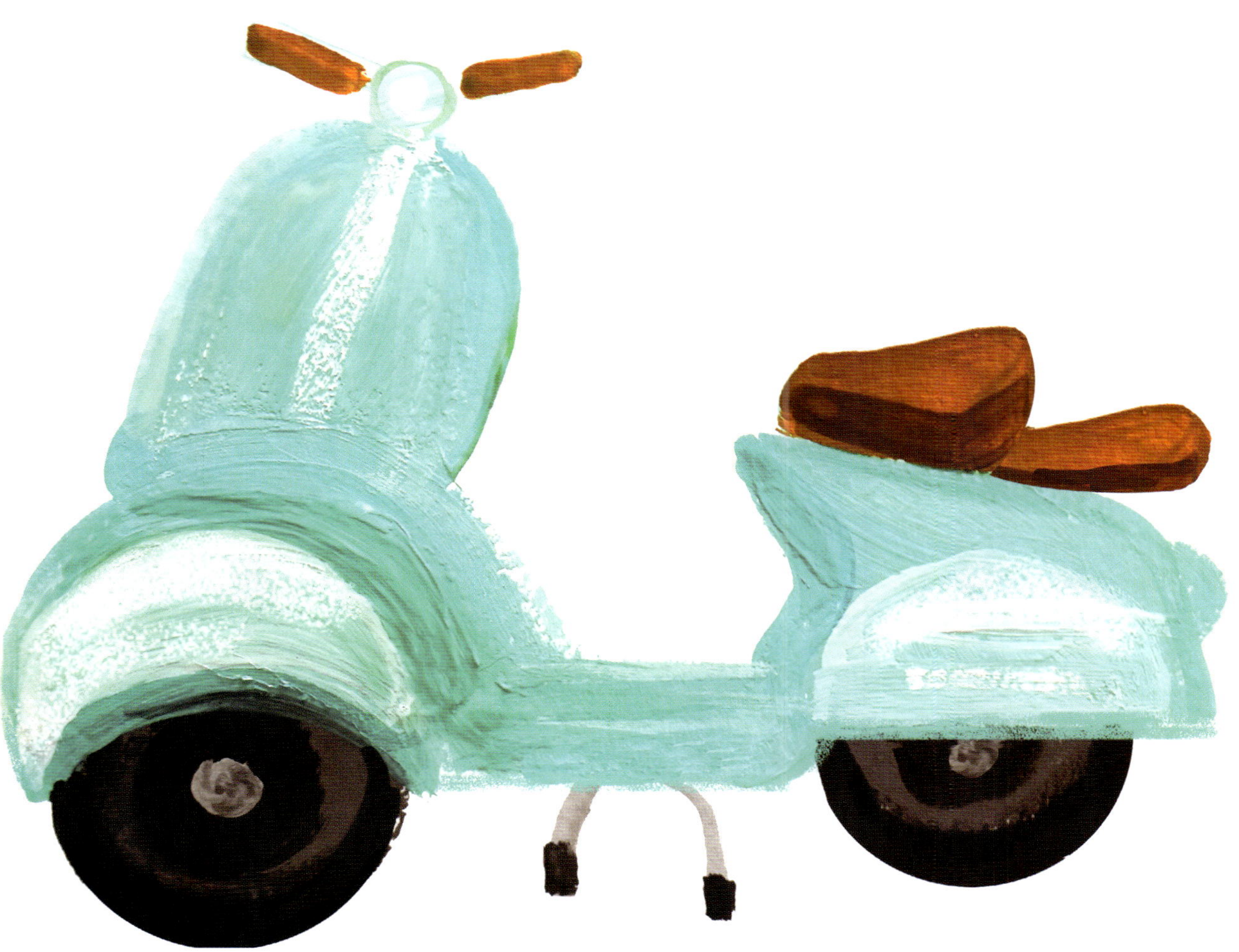

Step 4

Finally, add additional highlights to make the raised areas of the body "pop." Add a second seat on the back of the scooter using some of the leftover raw sienna mix. Then add details to the wheels to give them more dimension.

You can use white paint to clean up any areas that need refining. This is the perfect time to round out those wheels a bit or add any highlights. Then it's time to whisk through the streets of Roma. *Andiamo!*

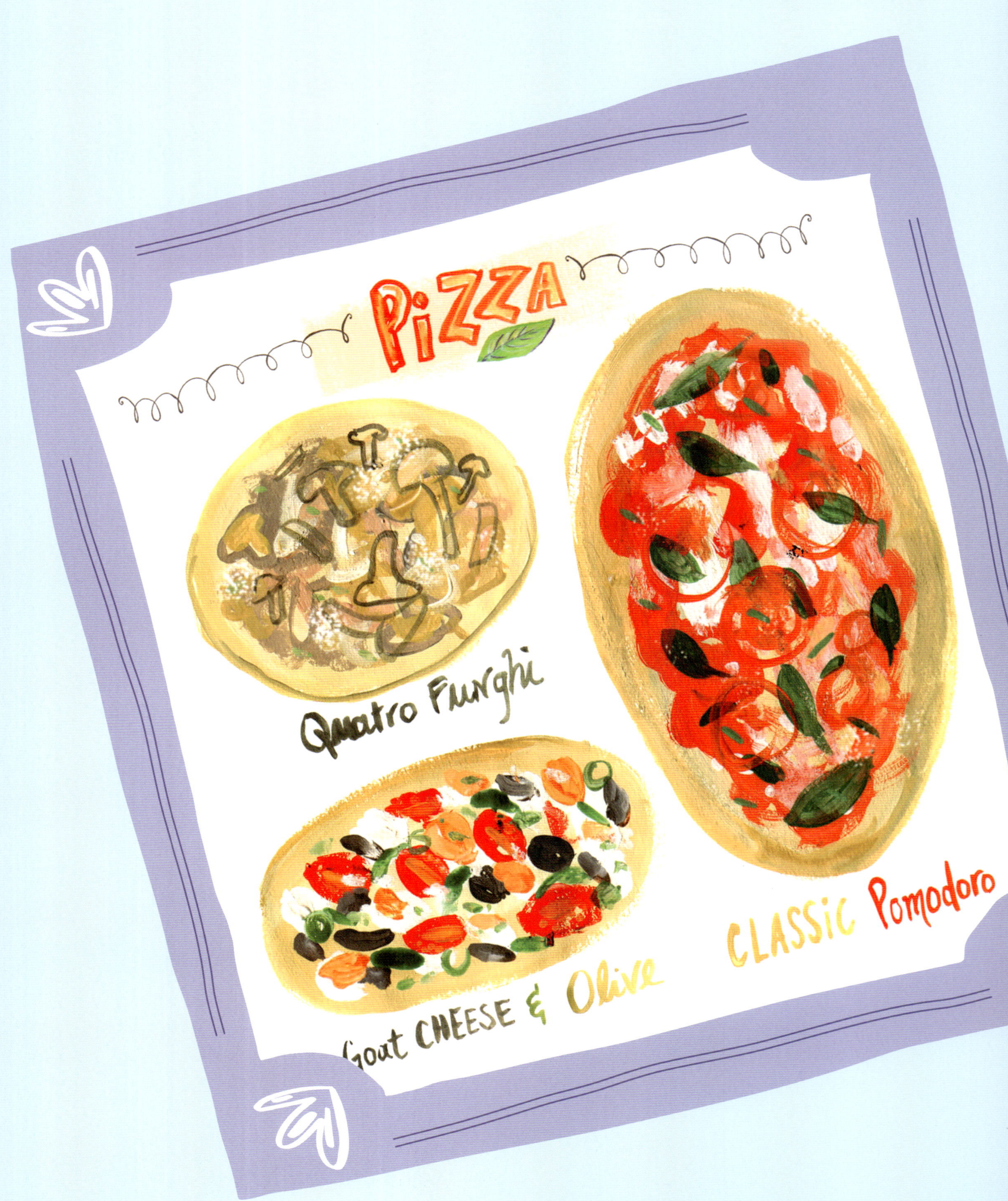
PiZZA
Quatro Funghi
Goat CHEESE & Olive
CLASSIC Pomodoro

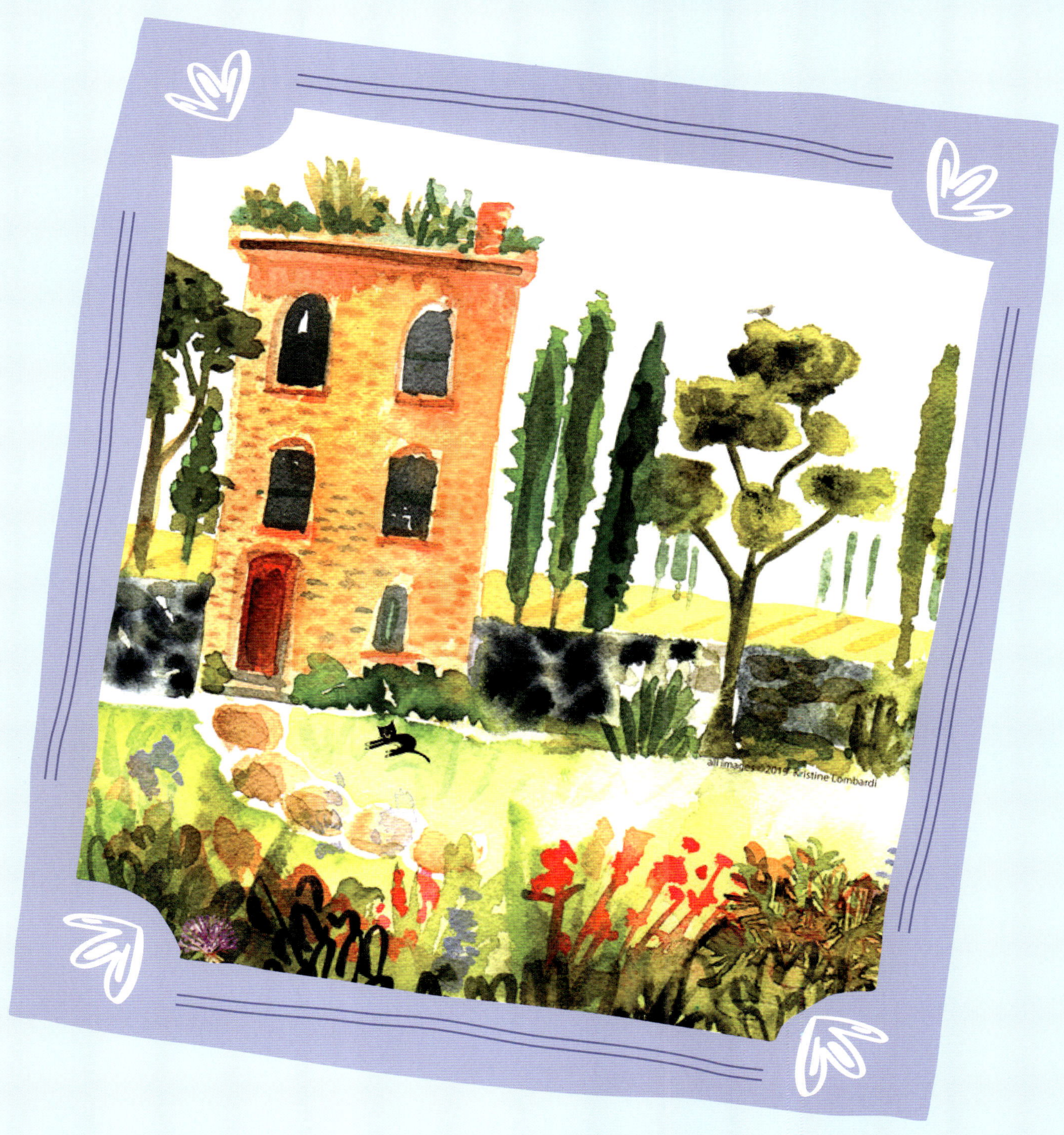

ITALIAN INSPIRATION

If you ever run out of painting ideas, think about your favorite place (mine's Italy!) and what you might see there, and try painting that. Look online for reference photos of Tuscan villas, cypress trees, pasta dishes, and more.

COPENHAGEN STREET SCENE

This scene was inspired by the colors and architecture in the ancient city of Copenhagen, Denmark. Modern buildings mix with colorful townhouses to create a beautiful, unique skyline in this Scandinavian capital.

This fun project uses gouache as the primary medium.

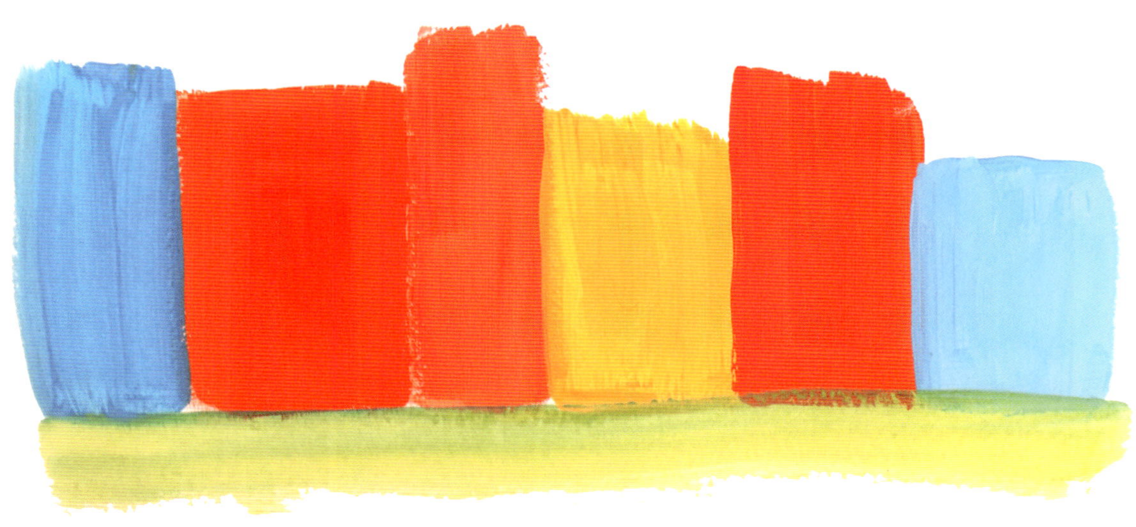

Step 1

Paint simple, vertical shapes in warm, sunny colors with a flat brush.

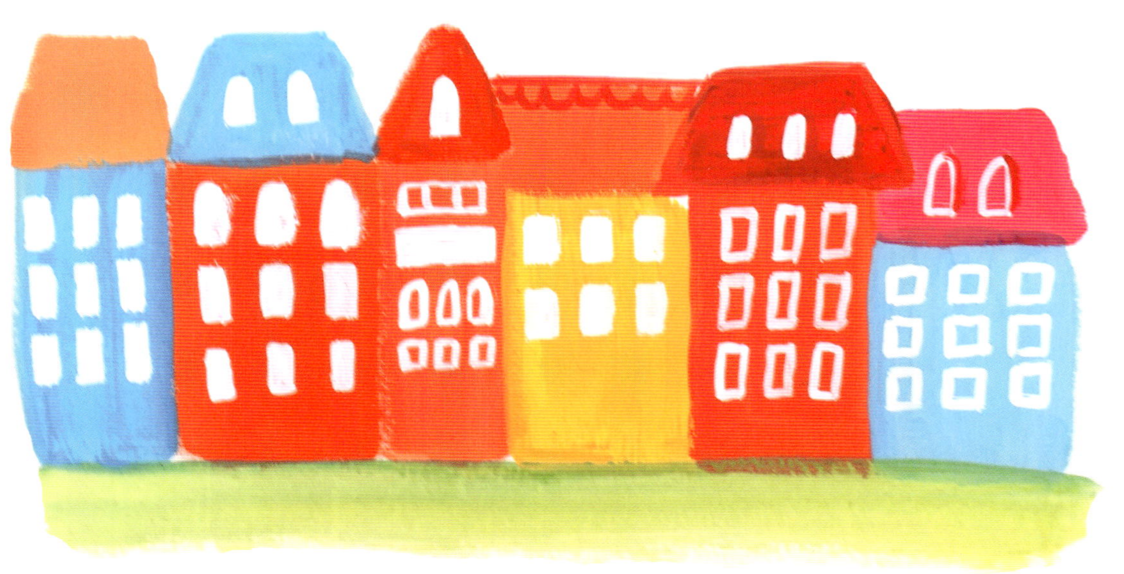

Step 2

Add triangular and trapezoidal roof shapes. These will form the facades of the buildings.

Because of its incredible opacity, white acrylic ink can be used to create the window shapes. Add scalloped details to the roofs using a liner brush.

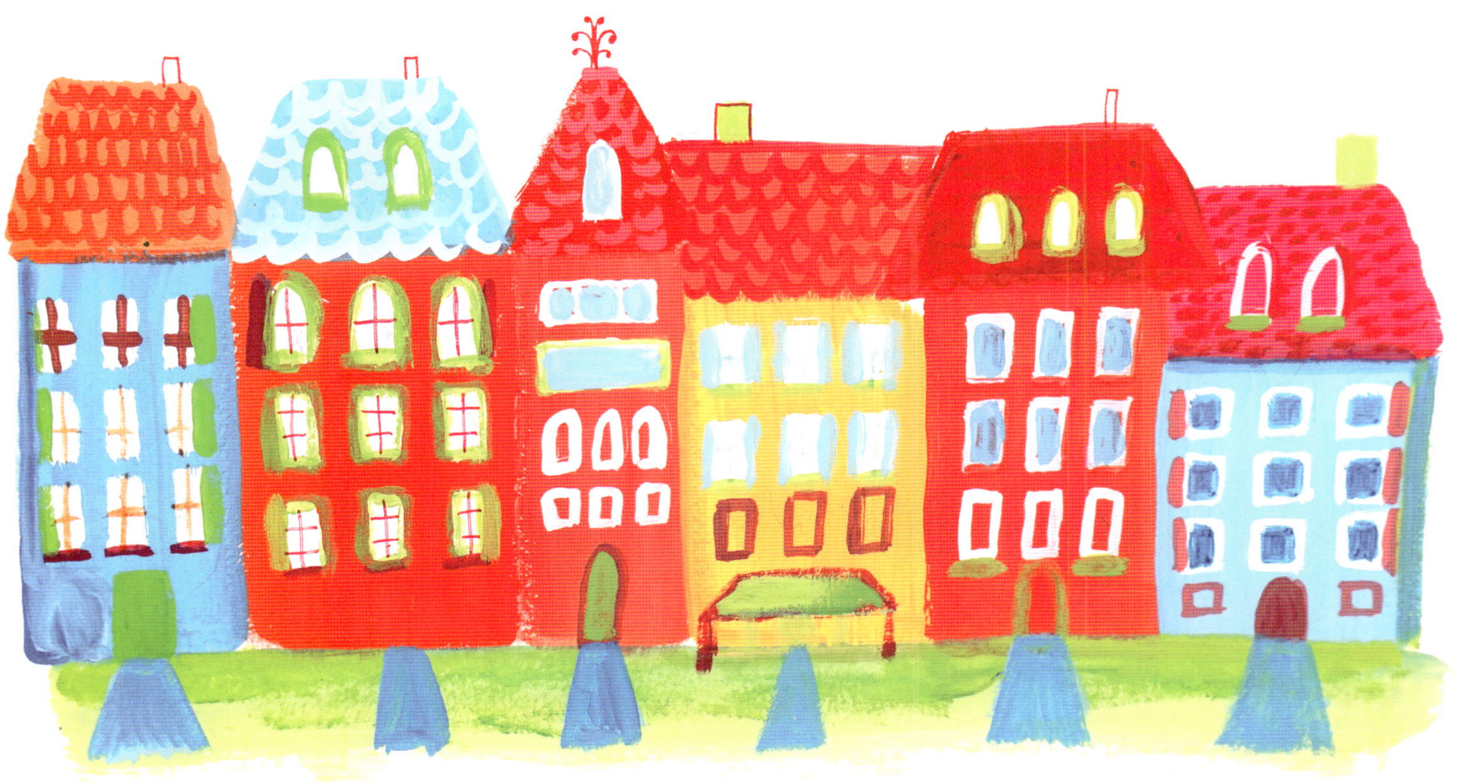

Step 3

This is a fun step and all sorts of details can be added here, from bricks to ornamental decorations, pediments, and so on. Fill some of the windows with color.

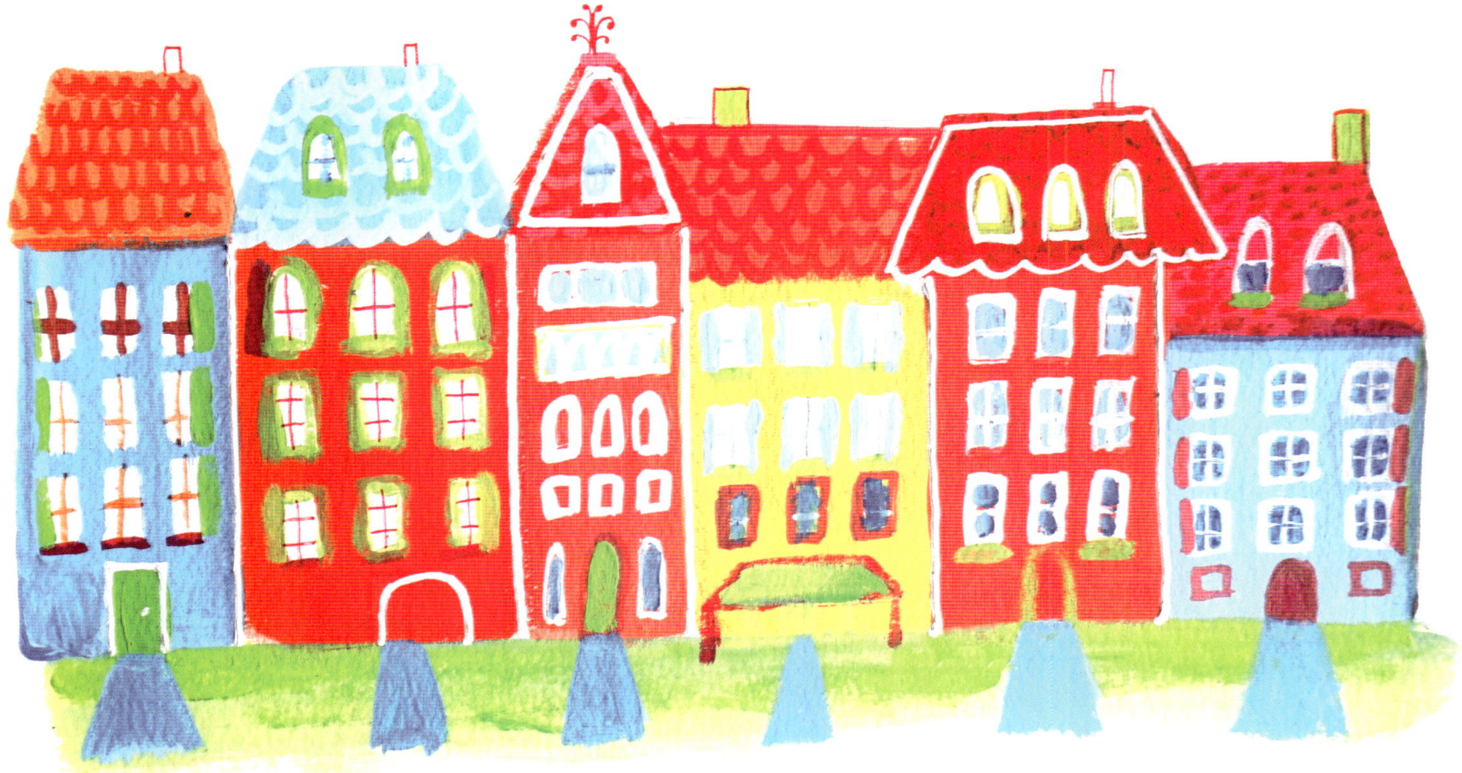

Step 4

Draw windowpanes using a simple gel pen. Feel free to experiment with colored pencils for any details!

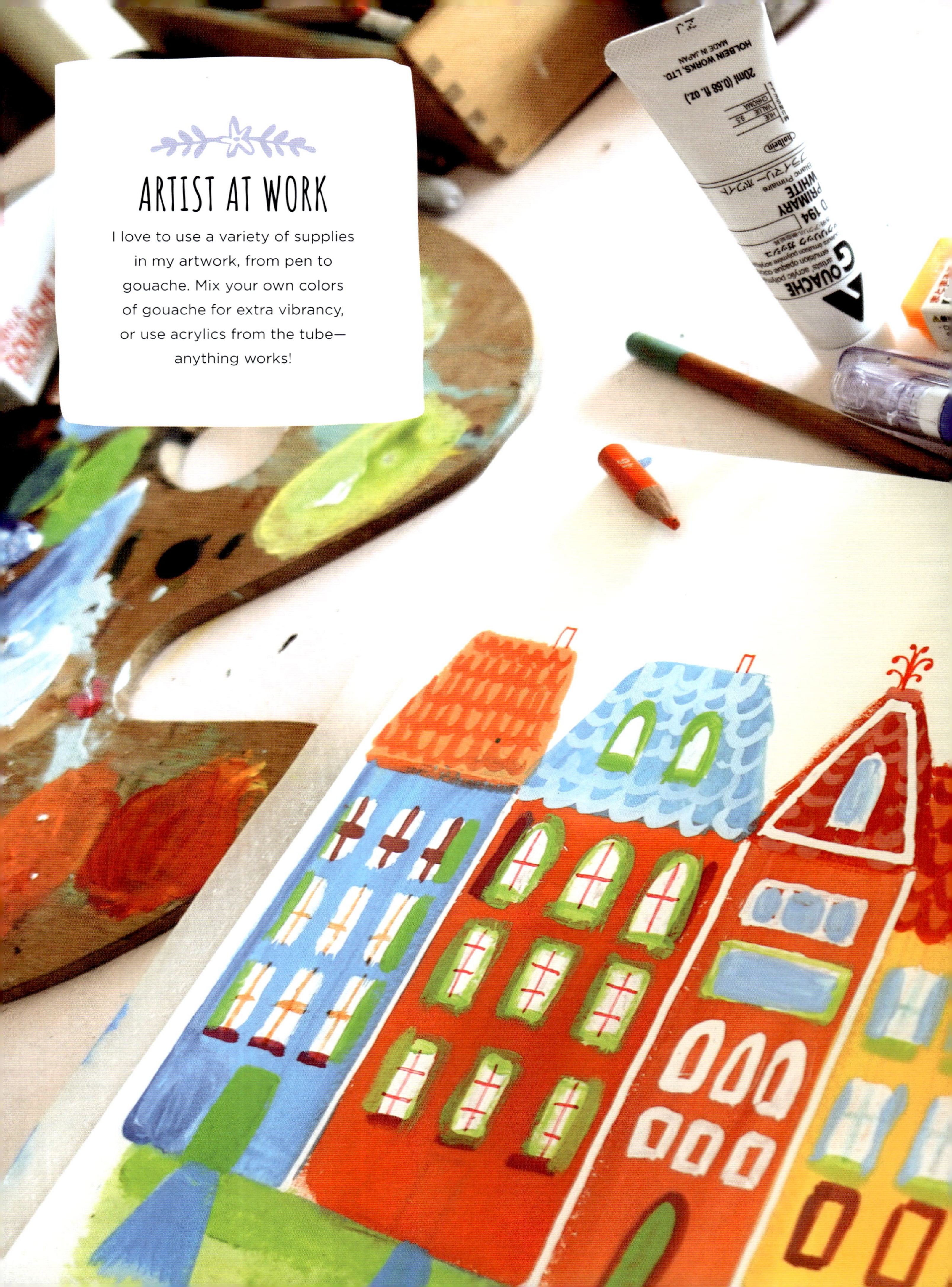

ARTIST AT WORK

I love to use a variety of supplies in my artwork, from pen to gouache. Mix your own colors of gouache for extra vibrancy, or use acrylics from the tube—anything works!

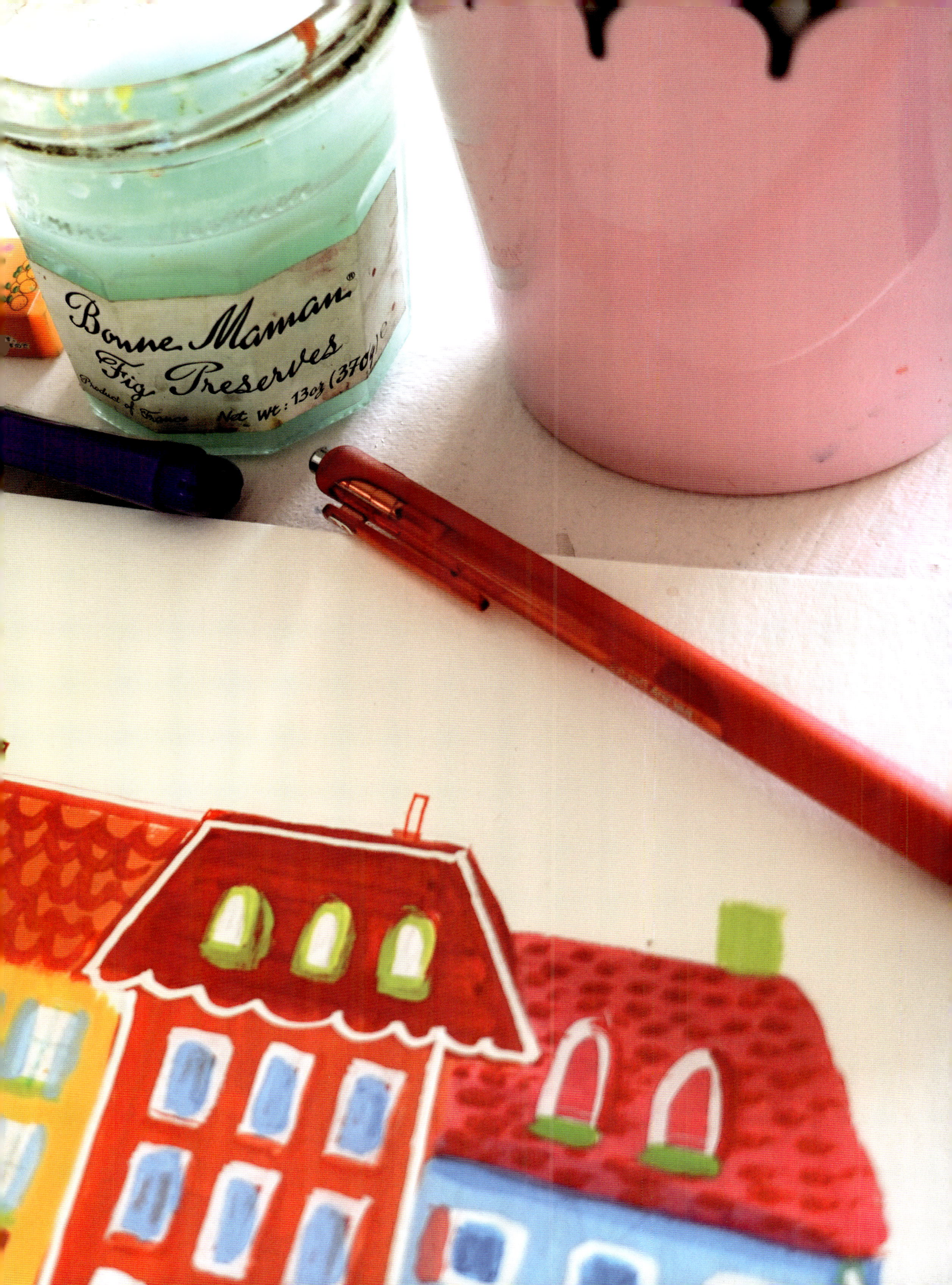
Bonne Maman
Fig Preserves
Net Wt: 13oz (370g)

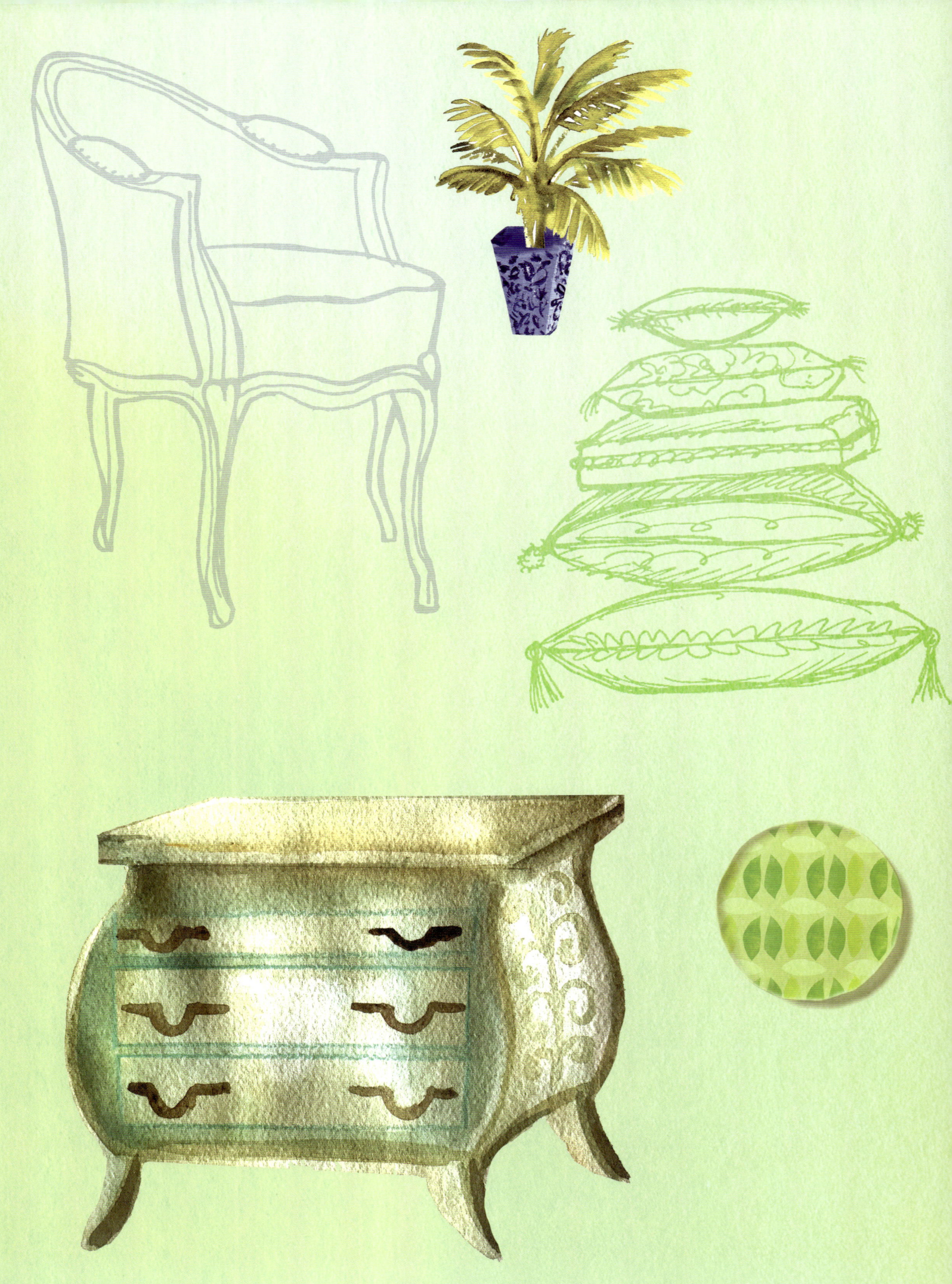

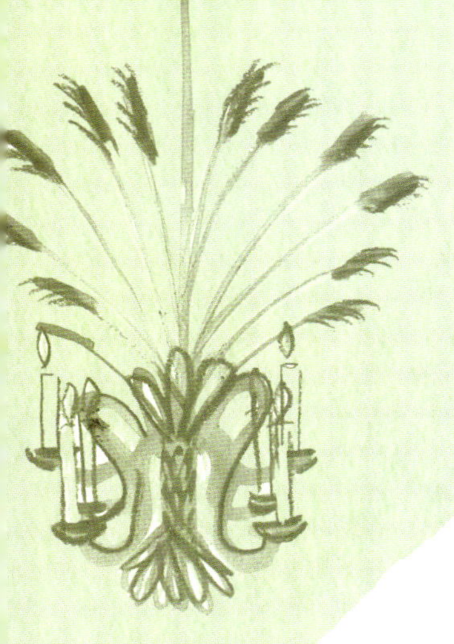

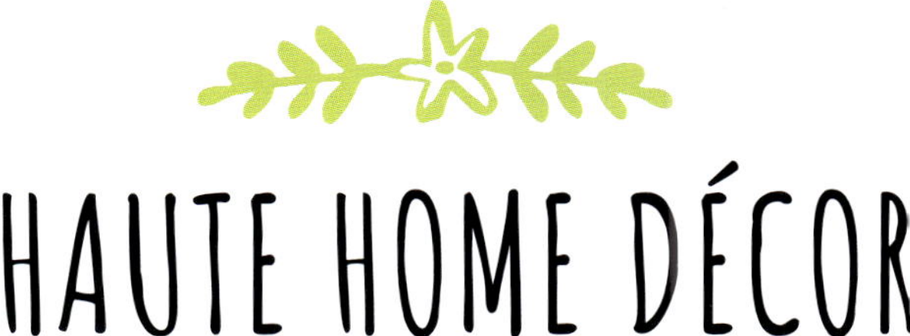

HAUTE HOME DÉCOR

In this section, we will focus on home décor! There are so many different decorating styles and infinite possibilities for subject matter. If you glance around the room you are in now, you will likely see plenty of interesting things that you could paint!

Let's look at three major design styles: midcentury modern, Hollywood regency, and French country. In midcentury modern design, clean lines and organic forms are the focus, with accessories often coming in bold colors, as well as quirky patterns and materials. Hollywood regency is all glam! Think colorful and opulent with plenty of metallic finishes, flashy accessories, and lacquered furniture. Imagine a room where a movie star like Joan Crawford would feel at home. French country style is all about elegant simplicity with warm, subtle colors; natural materials; and weathered finishes on wood. The accessories are often distressed or come with toile or gingham accents. Regardless of your personal decorating style, you will enjoy illustrating home décor. It's so much fun to put your own unique spin on an interior scene by mixing elements of wood, fabric, and metals.

Enjoy!

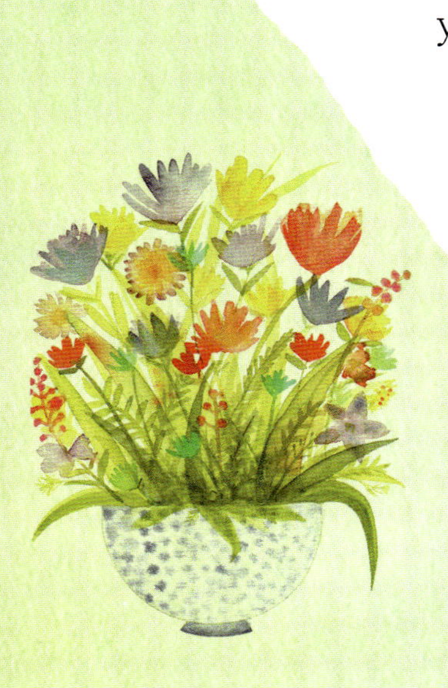

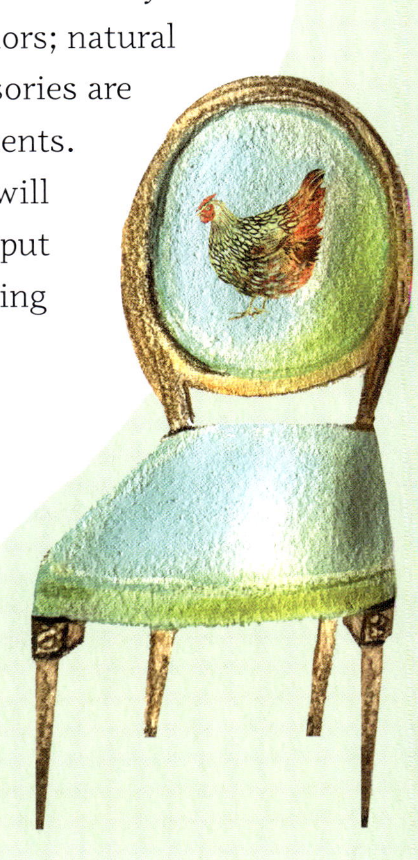

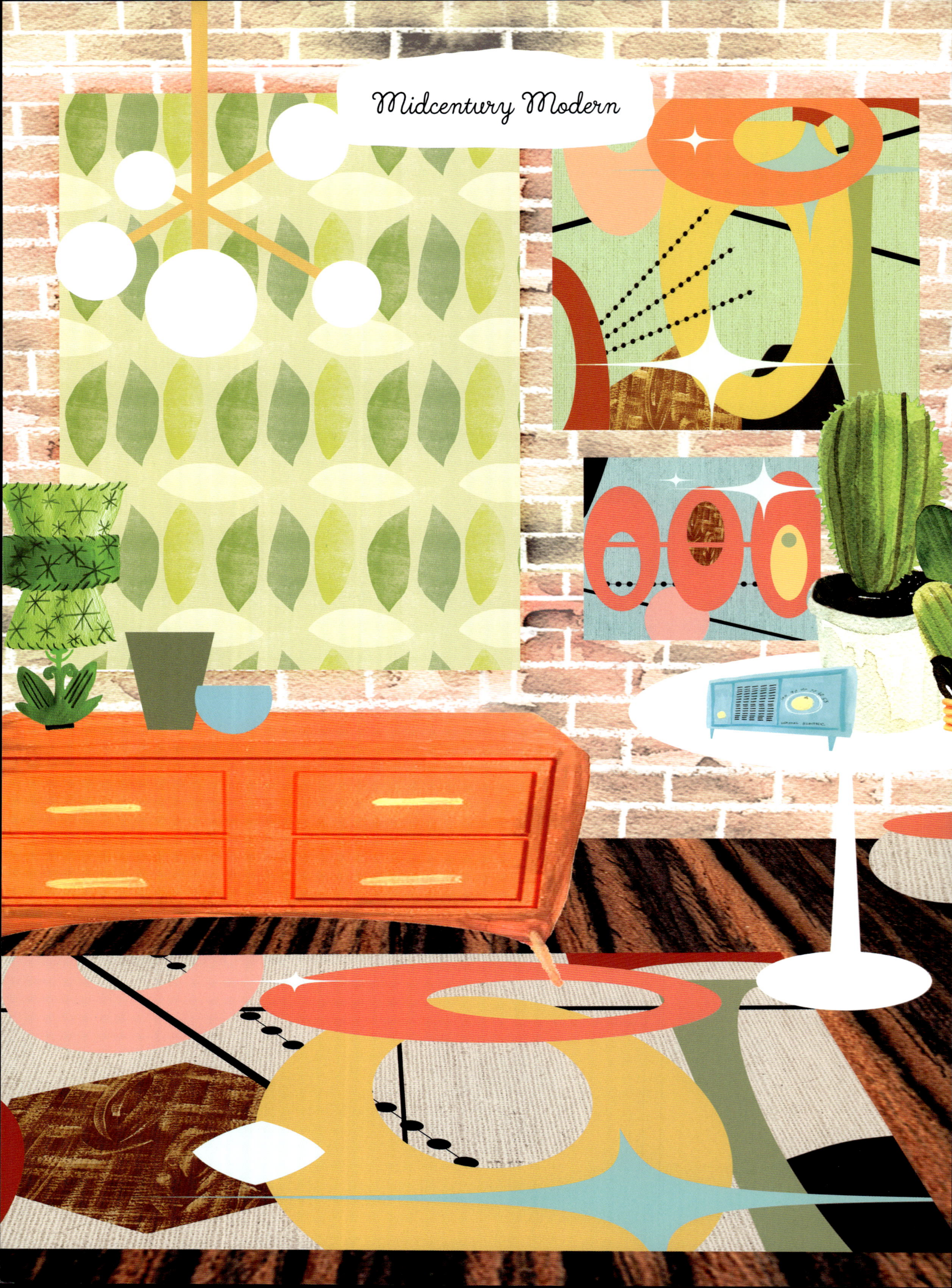
Midcentury Modern

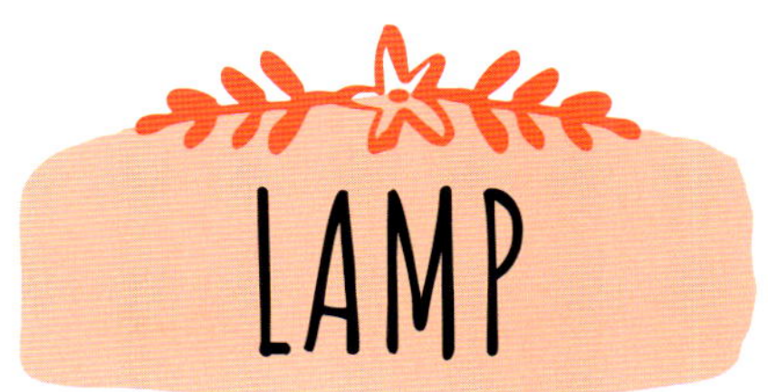

LAMP

Gouache makes the perfect medium for illustrating this quirky midcentury lamp. To use the same colors as I've done, mix salmon pink from magenta, a tiny touch of yellow, and lots of white. To make a batch of the lighter color, just add more white.

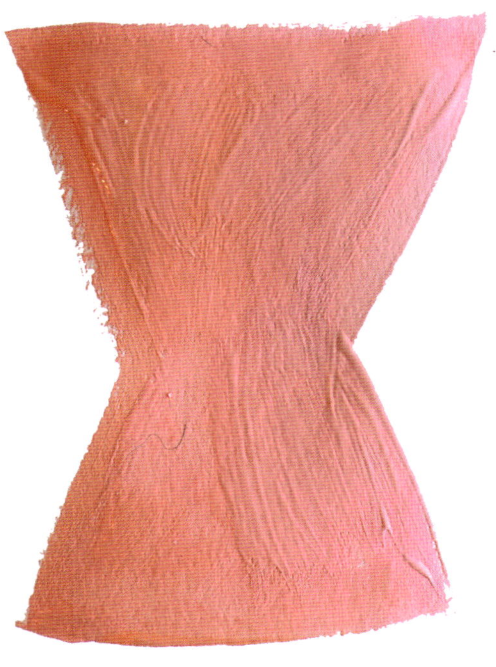

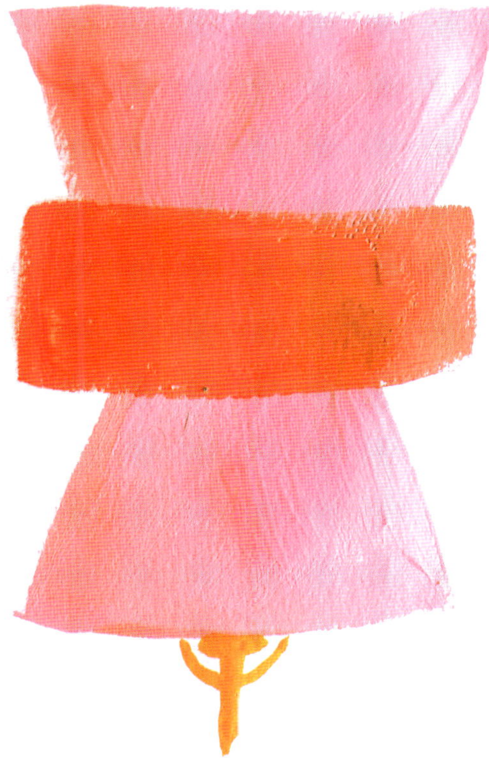

Step 1

Create the lampshade by making an hourglass shape with curves at the top and bottom.

Step 2

Use orange paint to create the broad strip in the middle. You can do this with one bold sweep of your Filbert brush. Then, using your liner brush, apply yellow paint to create the bulb hardware and stem of the lamp neck.

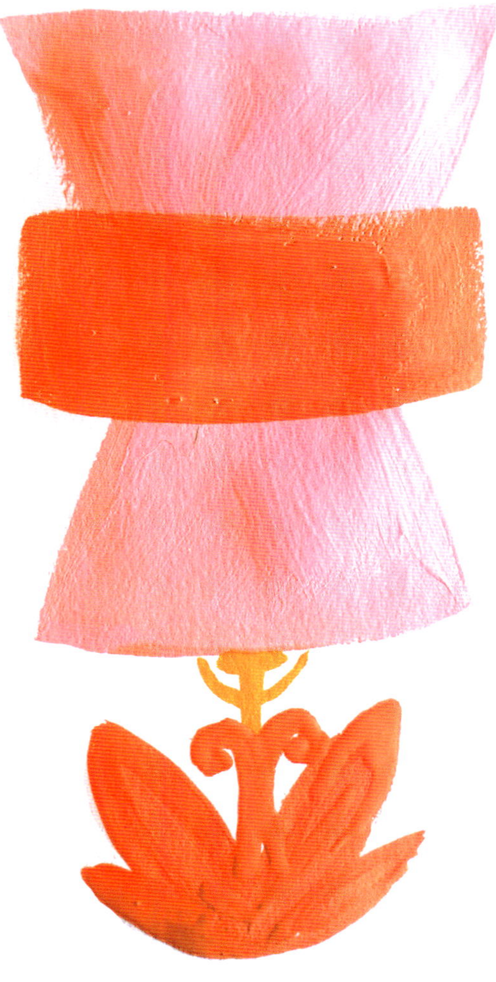

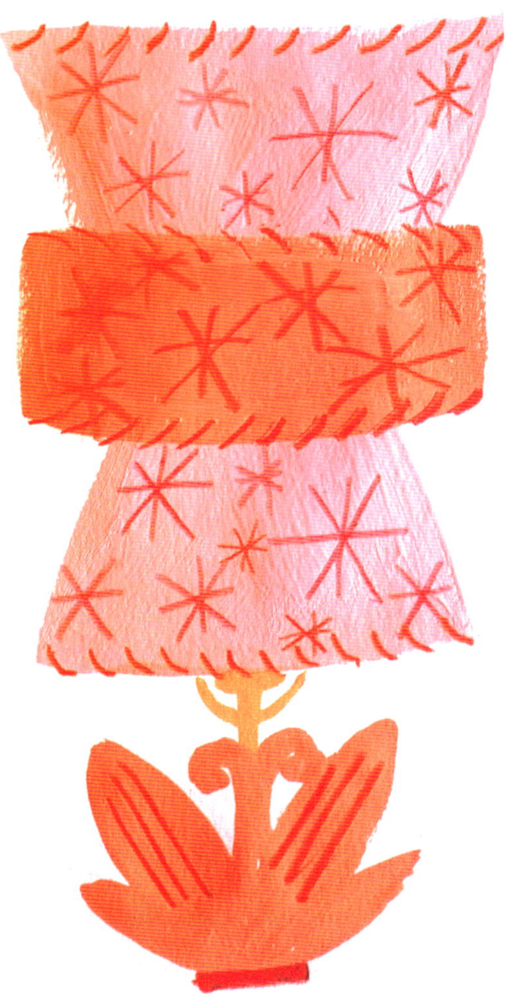

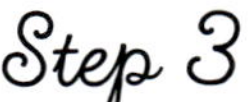

Step 3

To create the base, use the same orange and a #6 round brush to make a V shape by pressing down the point of the brush, and then moving down. Do this on the opposite side as well; then add two smaller leaf shapes on the outer edges. You can use your liner brush to create a curlicue addition in the lamp's base, or something completely different if you'd like.

Step 4

The final step is lots of fun. Use a colored pencil (I've used red and hot pink) to make little starbursts all over the two lampshades. You can then add groove marks to the lamp's base with simple lines, and you're all done!

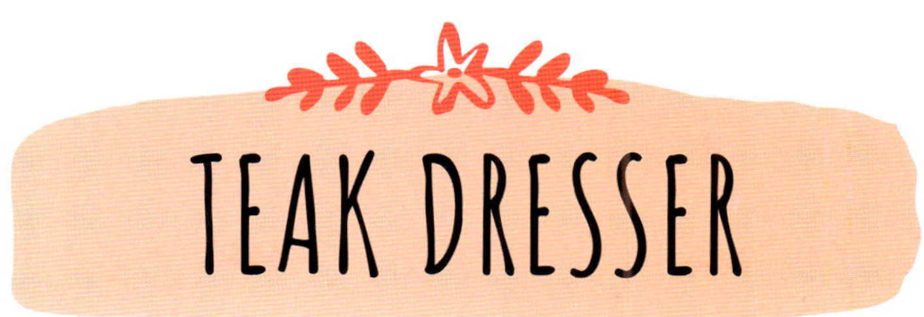

TEAK DRESSER

Teak is a popular material used in midcentury modern furniture for its durability, strength, and luster. Try creating your dresser with different drawer pulls if you like!

Step 1

Start with a simple rectangular shape using raw sienna gouache mixed with yellow to give the teak a warm look.

Tip

Add ample storage to your dresser by making the drawers large and its body long!

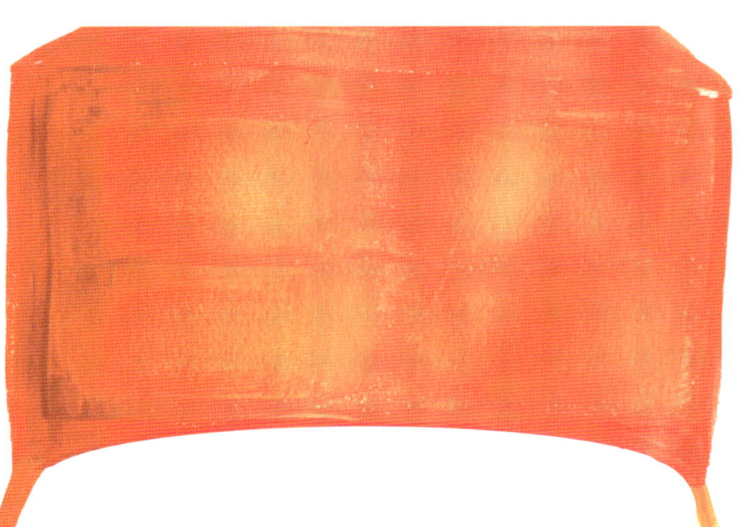

Step 2

Add a curve at the bottom, along with two small, angled legs.

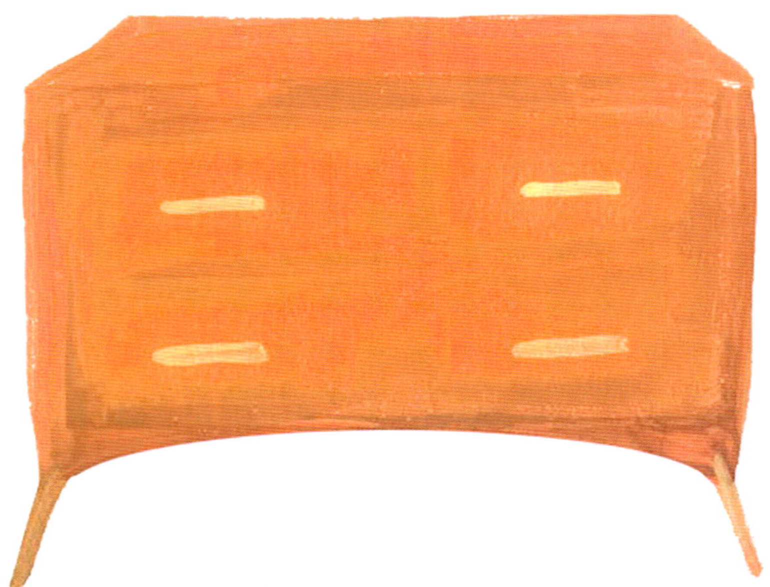

Step 3

Add a top to the dresser, and then some simple handles using a liner brush.

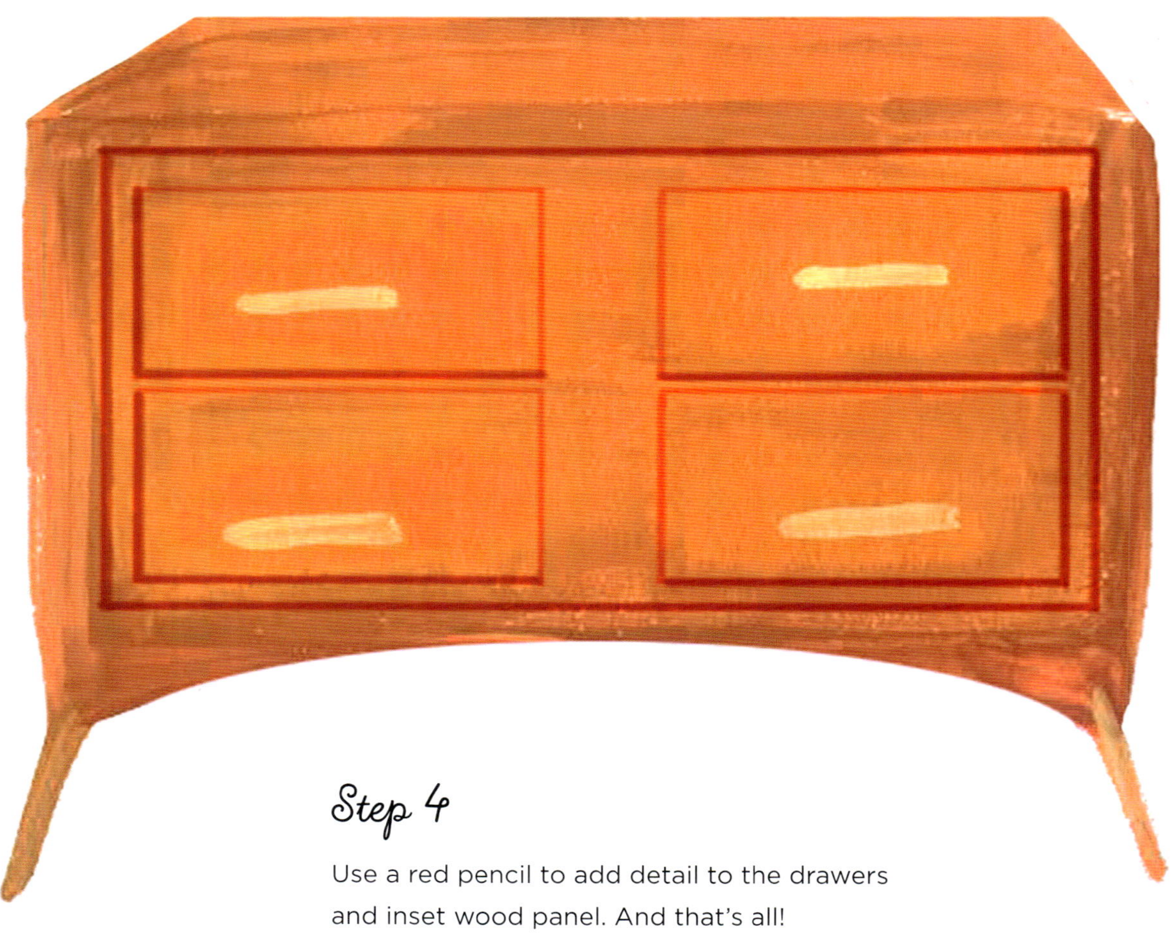

Step 4

Use a red pencil to add detail to the drawers and inset wood panel. And that's all!

RADIO

This fun little midcentury accessory is easy to create and can be painted in any color you like.

Step 1

Start by mixing up some turquoise gouache mixed with white to create a nice bright hue. Then make a simple rectangular shape using an angled brush.

Step 2

Add tapered legs to the base, and then paint a rectangular line within the first rectangle using a darker hue.

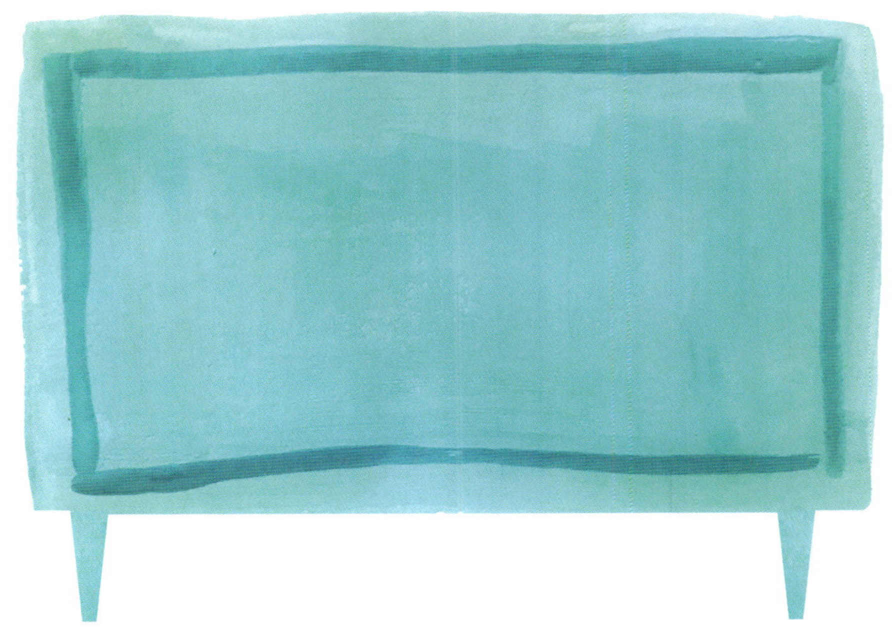

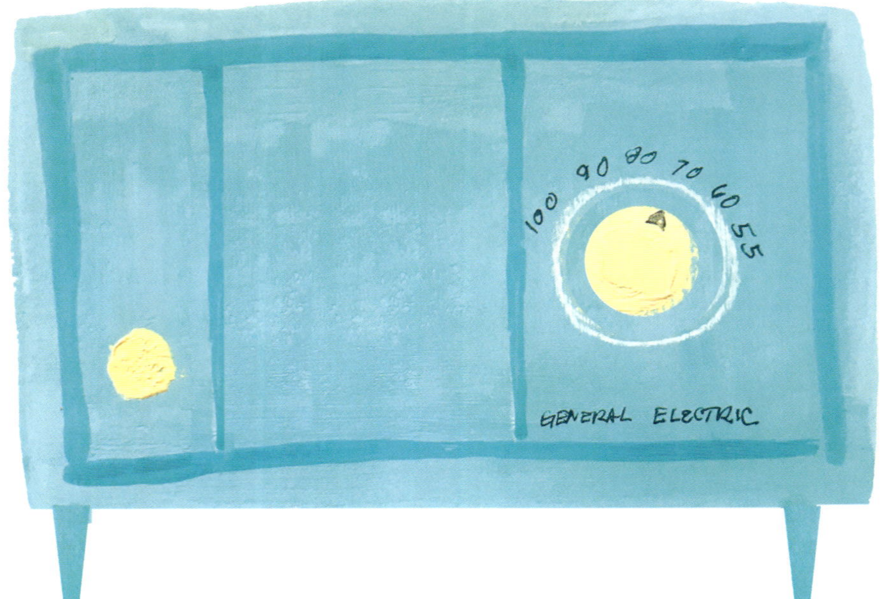

Step 3

Add two vertical lines within the last rectangle, and then create small circles, using a tint of yellow and white, to form the dials. Use a fine-tipped ink pen to write radio frequencies along the large dial, as well as a brand name.

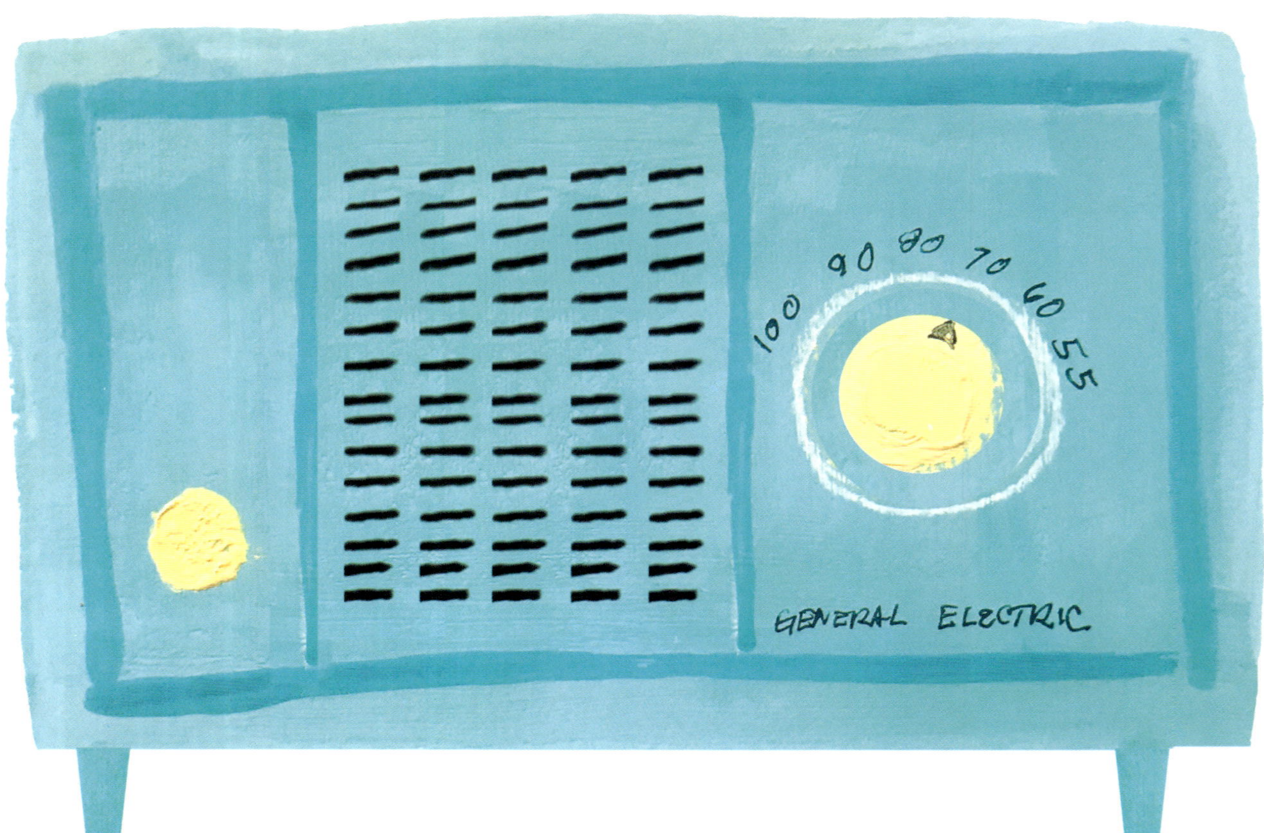

Step 4

Lastly, use a fine-tip black marker to make simple hatch marks that work as the sound slats on the body of the radio. Now it's time for some tunes from the 1950s!

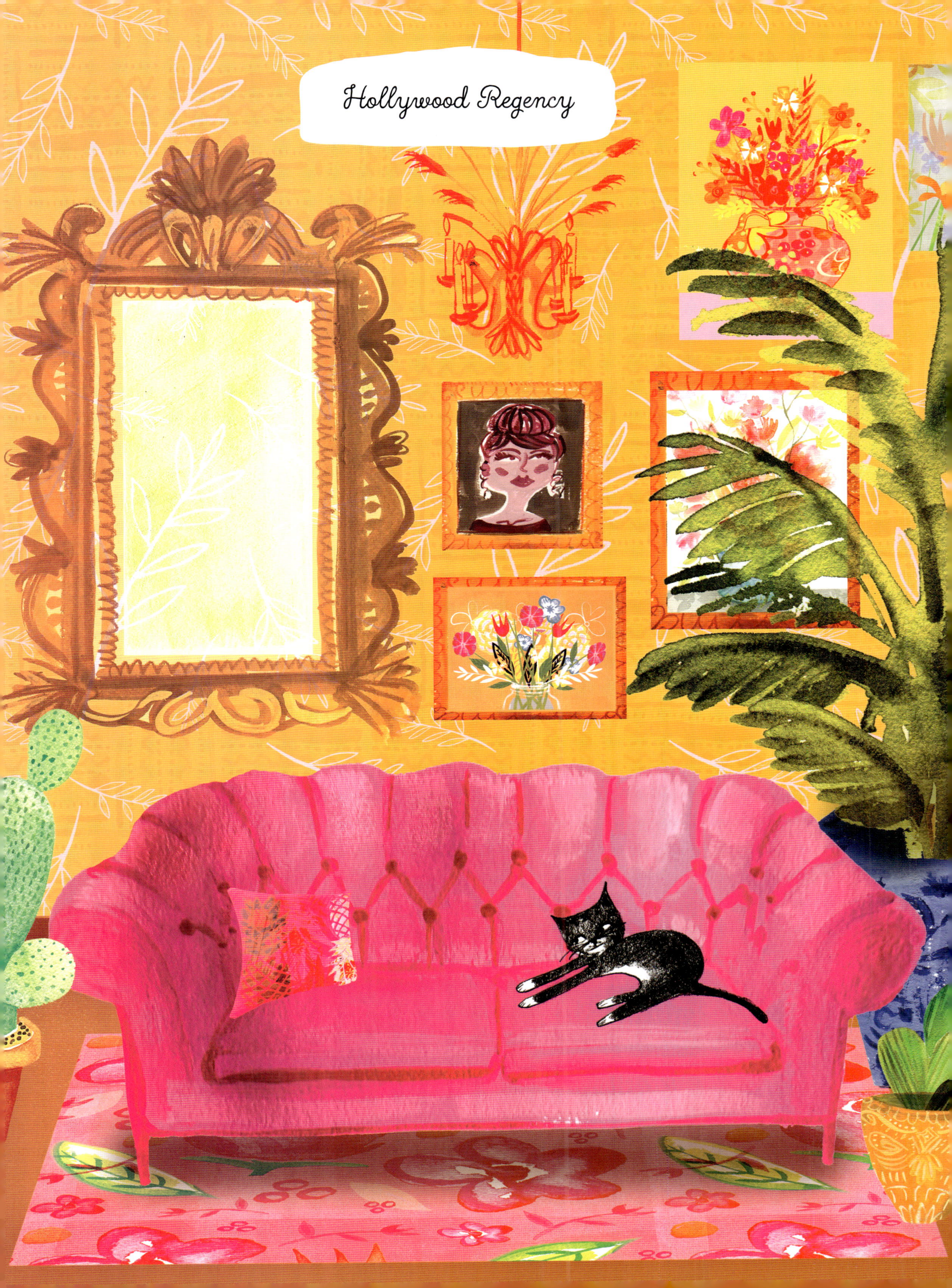
Hollywood Regency

HOLLYWOOD REGENCY MIRROR

You can go really glam with this mirror and the next couple of painting subjects!

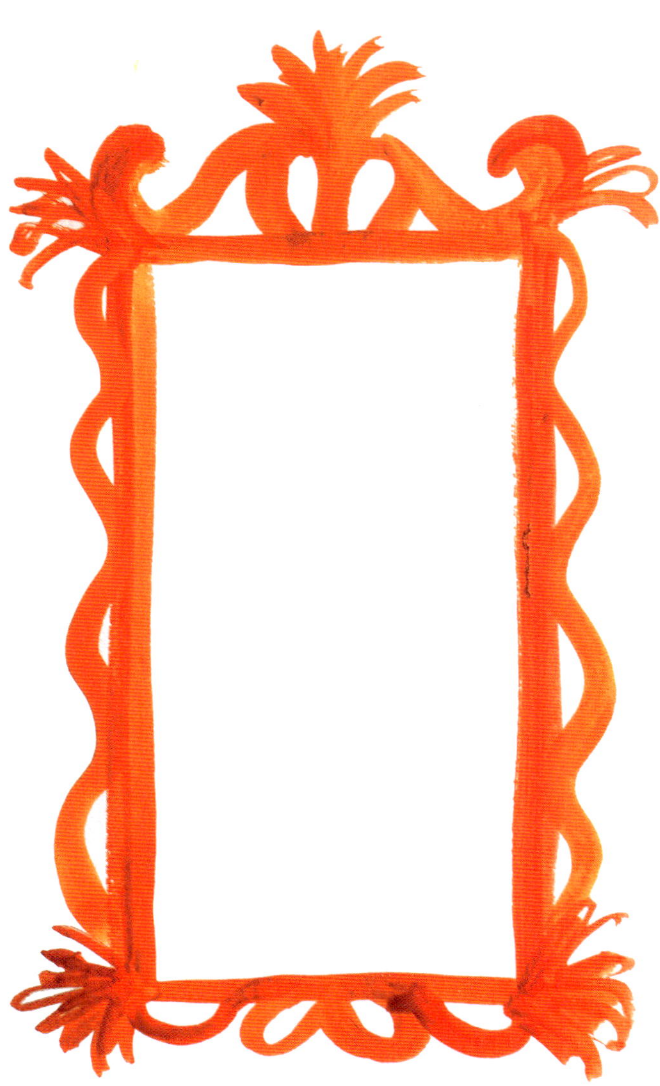

Step 1

Start by having red, yellow, and white gouache on hand, as well as a tiny bit of blue. Mix some orange with the red and yellow. Then paint a simple rectangle in the orange and add touches of red to the corners to create depth. Add loops to the top and bottom of the rectangle.

Step 2

Use a round brush, such as a #4, to make squiggly shapes along the sides, as well as some scrollwork at the top and bottom. Feel free to experiment here and make your mirror as ornamental as you wish. I've used a liner brush to make feathery additions at the corners.

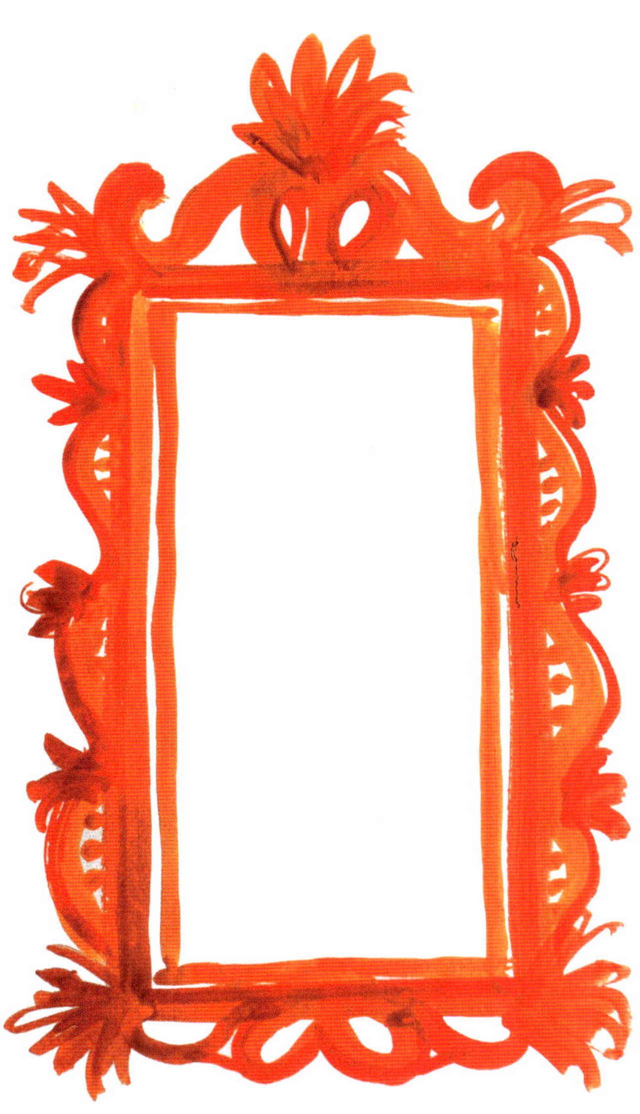

Step 3

Now give the mirror some depth by painting an inset rectangle in red. You can also draw another rectangle in orange to add pronounced and recessed areas. Create horizontal hatch marks in some of the outer squiggly areas, where the white shows.

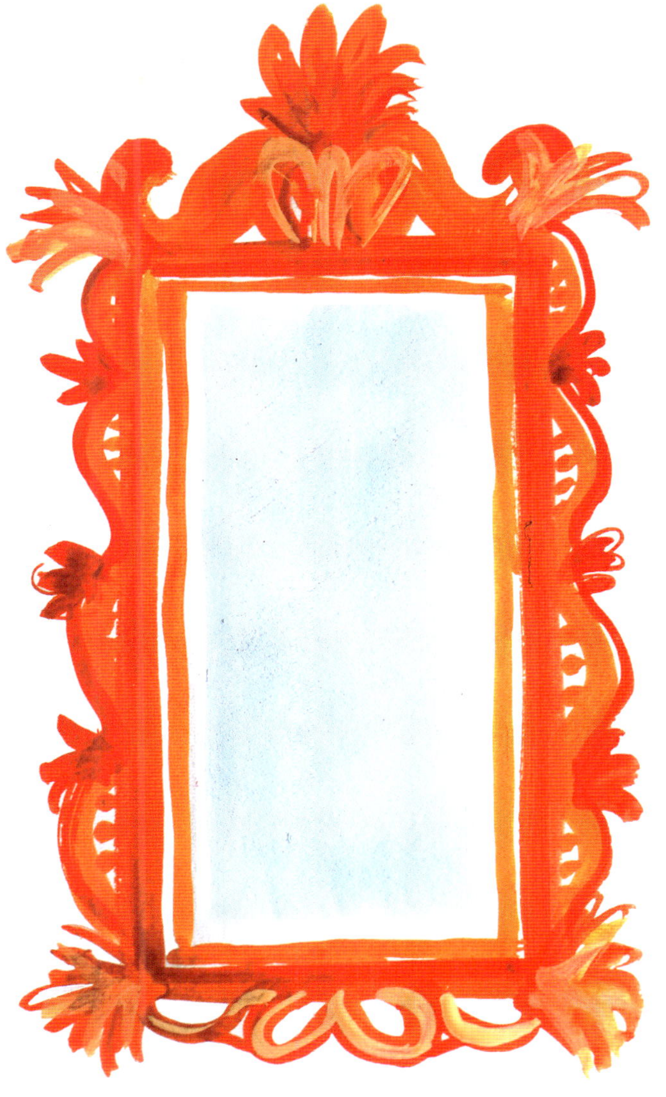

Step 4

To give the mirror highlights, apply a tint of the orange and white over some of the scrollwork in the illustration. Mix a pale gray from lots of white and a tiny bit of blue, adding water to create a wash for the reflective part of the mirror. Using a broad brush, make some light-handed downward strokes for the glass.

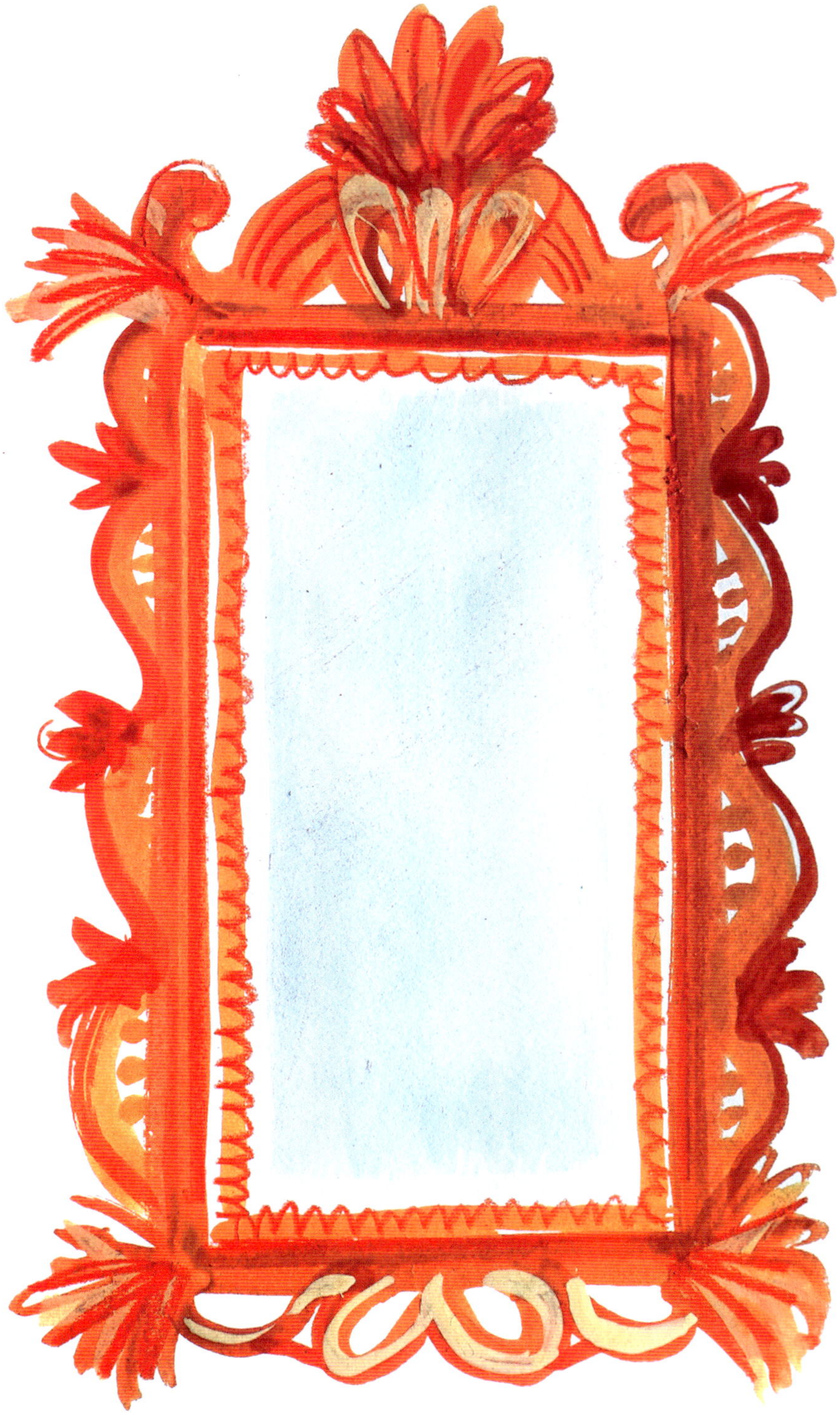

Step 5

Finally, experiment with using a red colored pencil to add embellishments. You can continue to build on the basic design and go as detailed as you wish!

FANCY CHANDELIER

This chandelier may look complex to paint, but it's really quite simple!

Step 1

Using the same palette as you did in the mirror project (pages 72-74), add water to the colors to keep the paint fluid. Draw simple lines to form the chandelier tubing and loops at the bottom, intermittently dipping your liner brush into the yellows, oranges, and reds so that you get a fun, varied color line. Continue adding shapes. Feel free to play around and add scrolls or loops, depending on how ornate you want the lighting fixture to be.

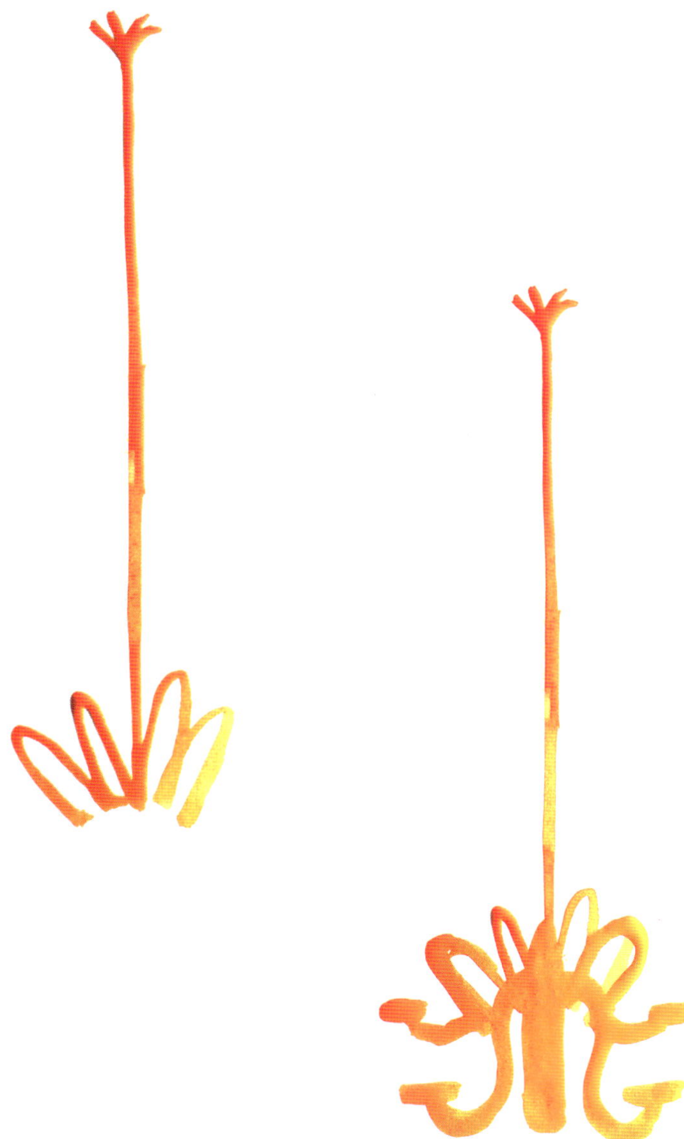

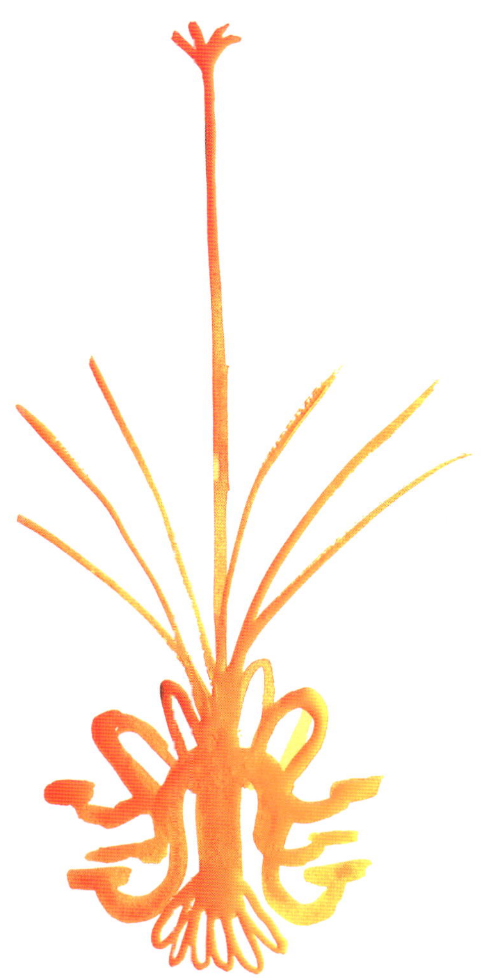

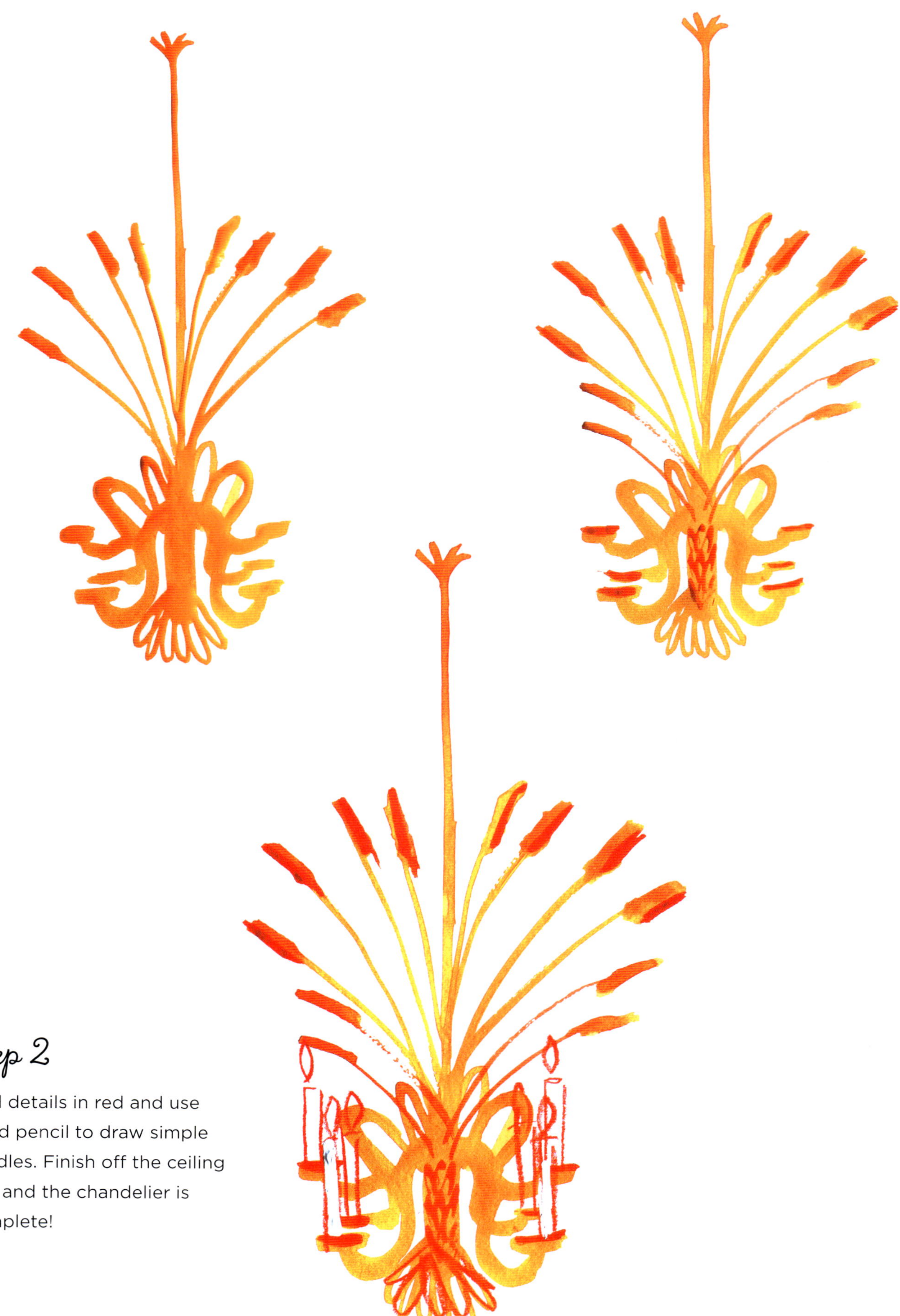

Step 2

Add details in red and use a red pencil to draw simple candles. Finish off the ceiling cap and the chandelier is complete!

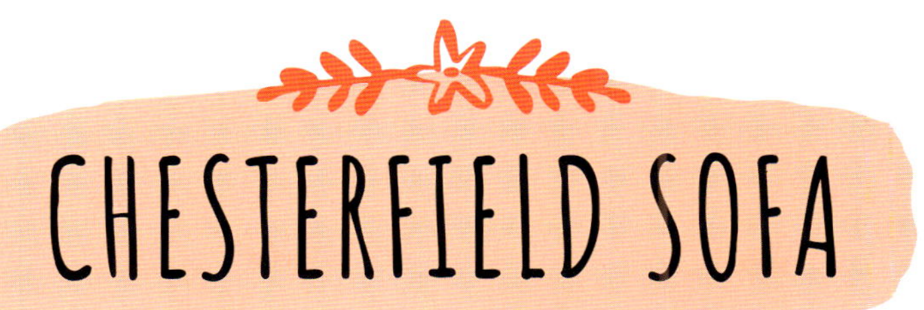

CHESTERFIELD SOFA

It doesn't get much more glam than a hot pink Chesterfield sofa! For this project, we will again use gouache, as it is the best medium to show off this vibrant hue.

Step 1

Use a mixture of magenta and white and an angled brush to form the basic shape of the sofa. Add the arms and create a scalloped top; then create cushions and the tufted back with line work in magenta.

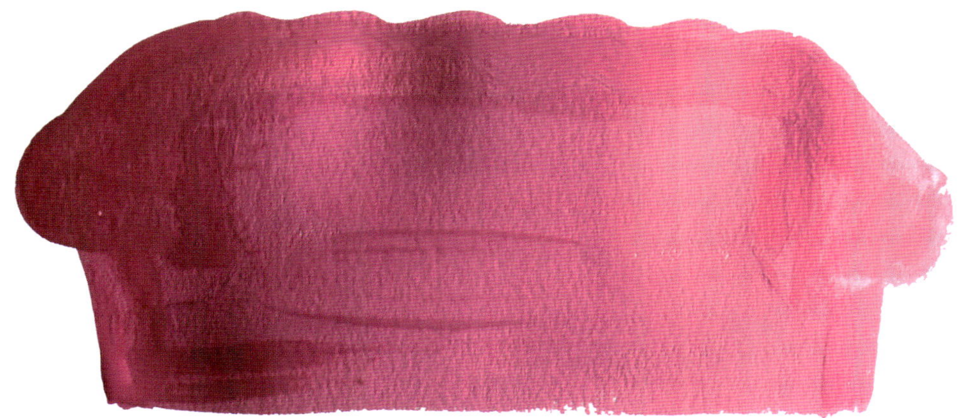

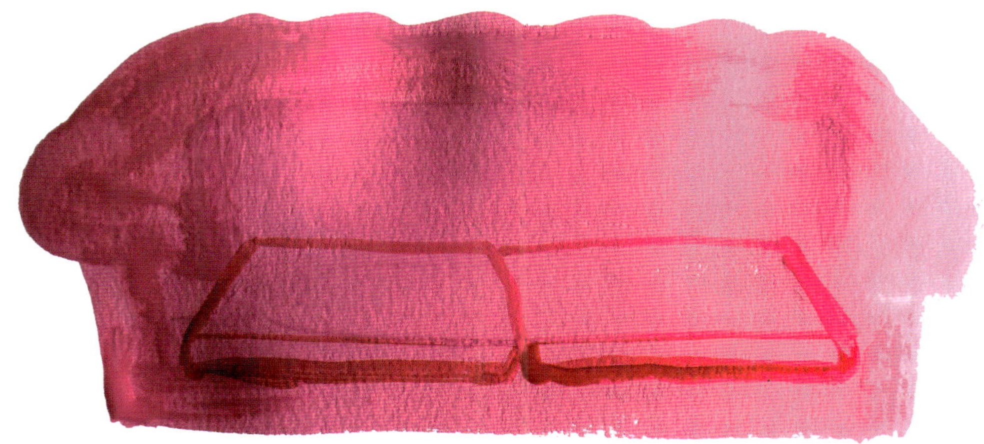

Step 2

Add legs and other details, using a wash of hot pink to give more contrast to the cushions, as well as shadows beneath them. Mix white into the original mixture and grab an angled brush. Add highlights to the top of the upholstery where the light would hit. Now it's time to put on a gown and invite your friends over for cocktails!

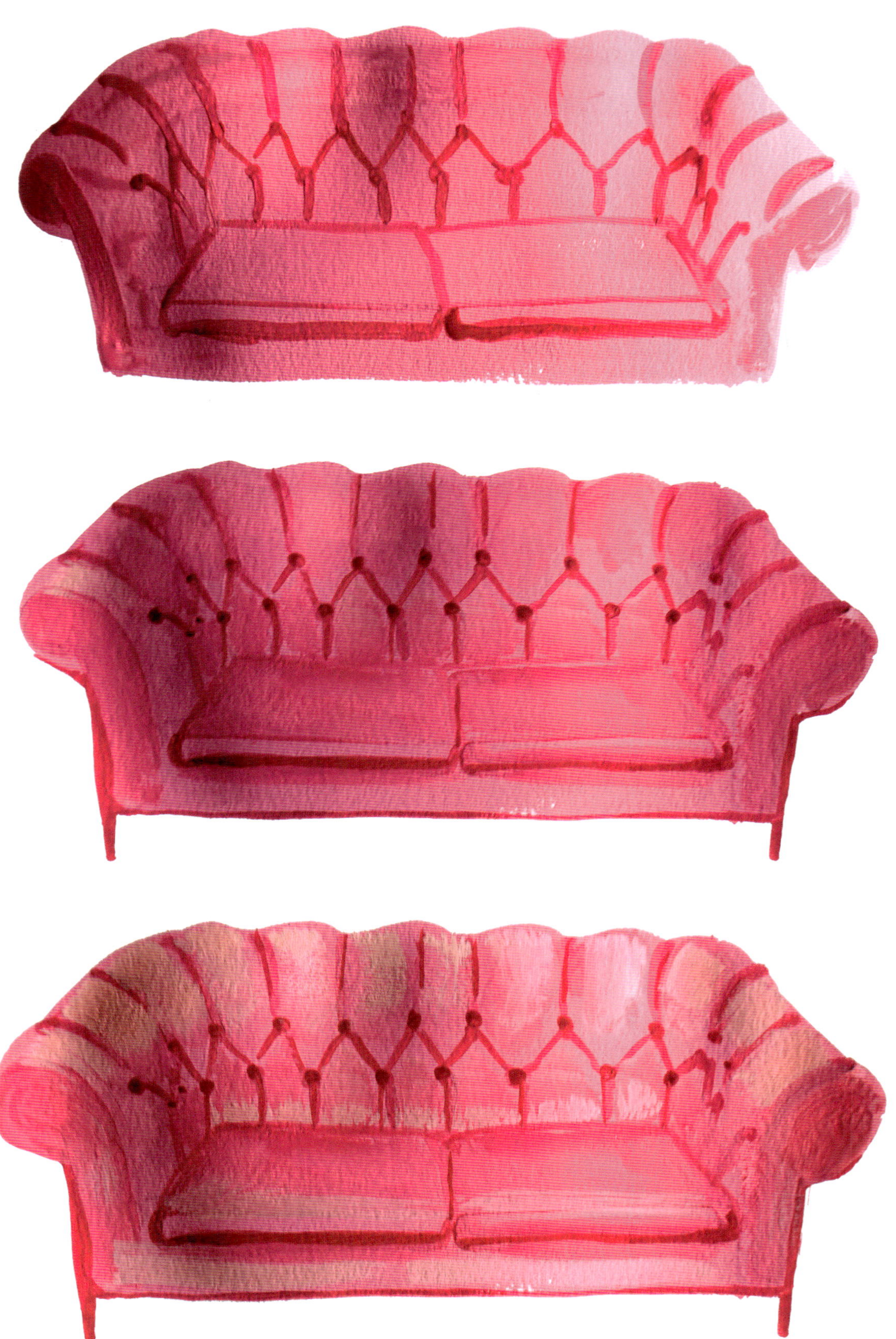

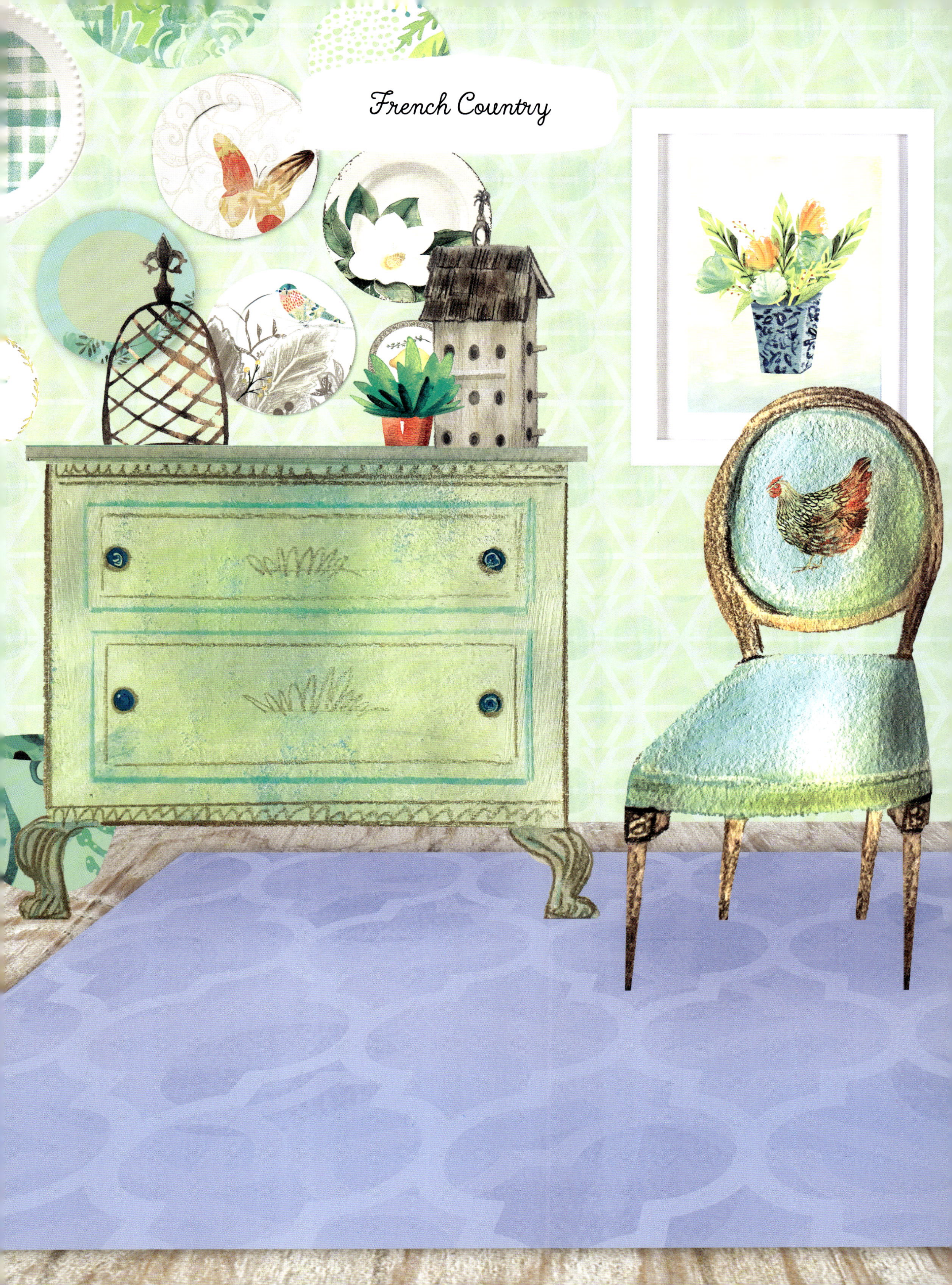
French Country

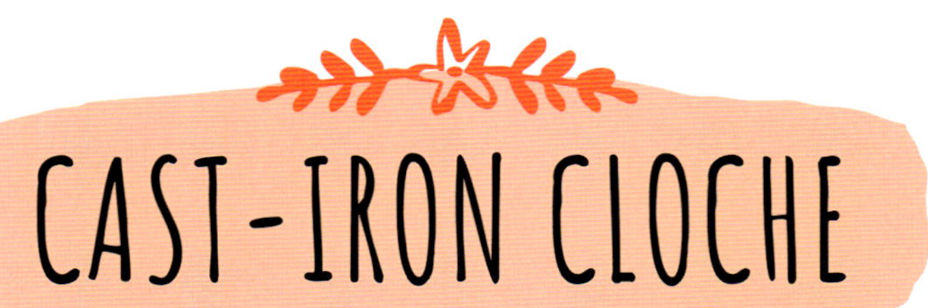

CAST-IRON CLOCHE

This fun little watercolor project uses only raw sienna and black.

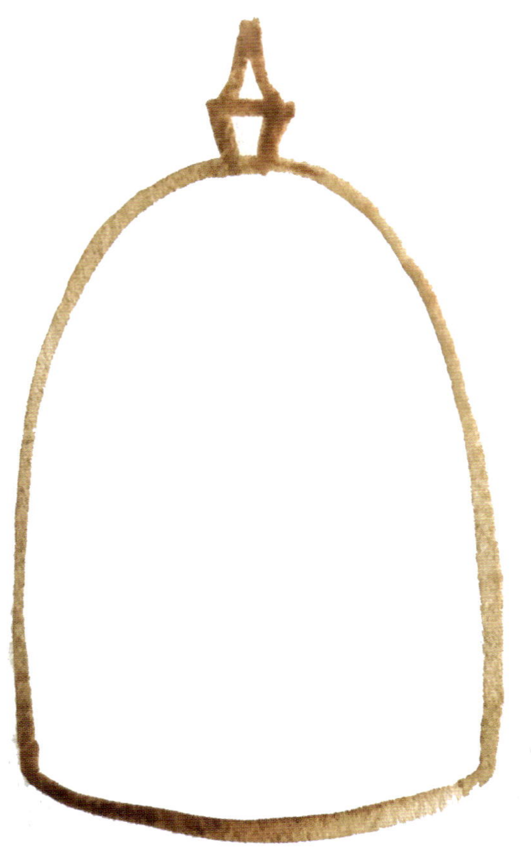

Step 1

Create a simple dome shape with a liner brush. Use plenty of water here; you will use the wet-into-wet technique (page 15) for much of this project. Add the topper and curved lines, using lots of water.

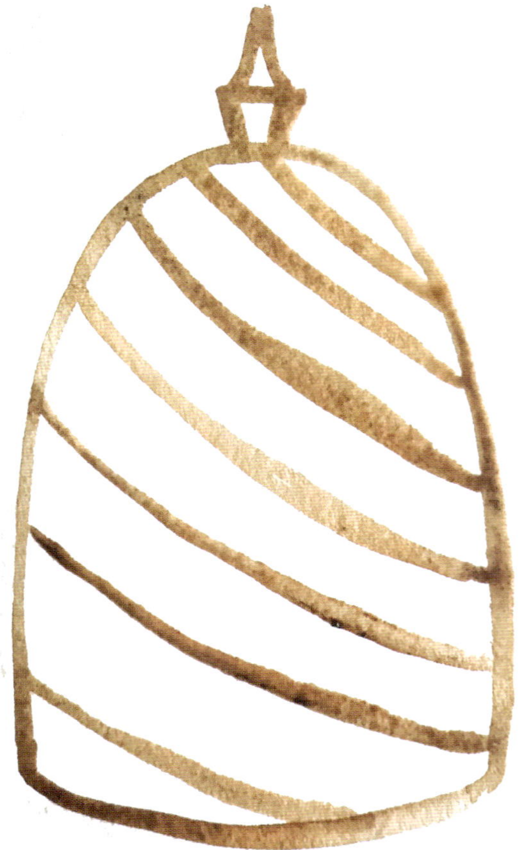

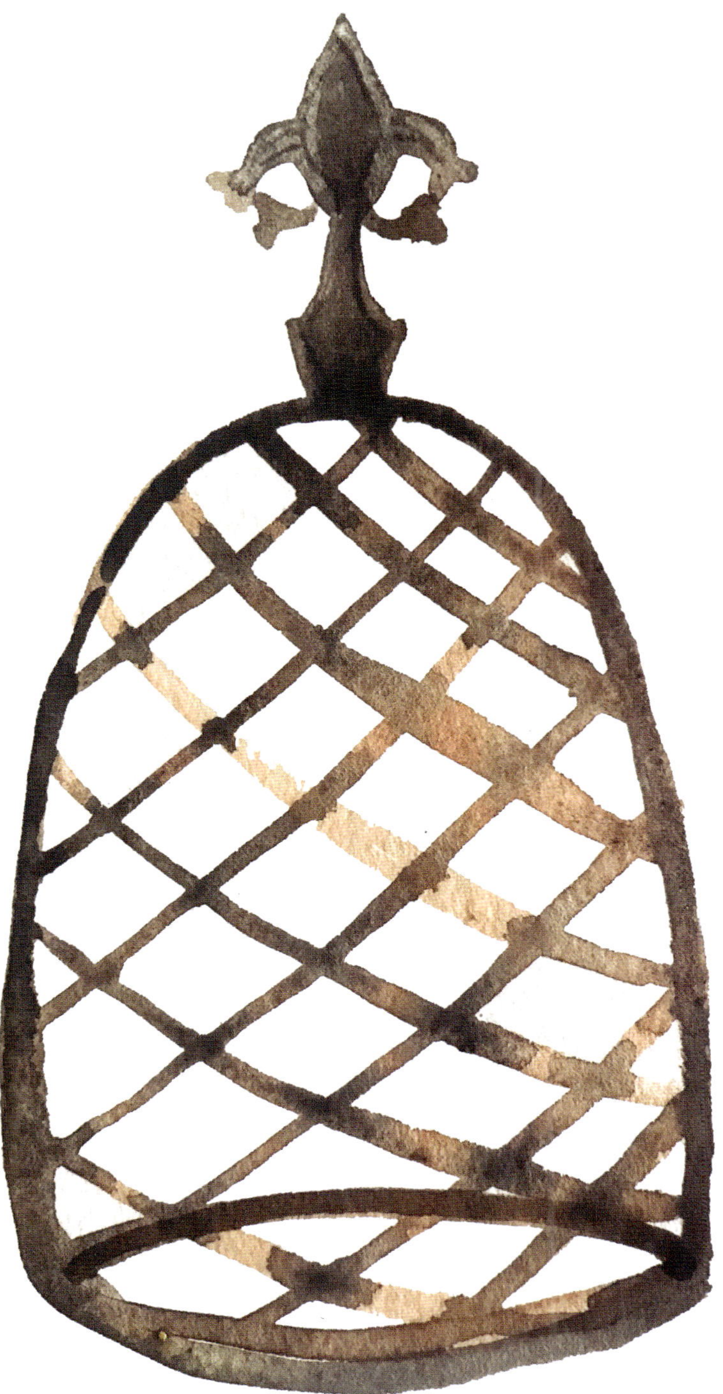

Step 2

Then add lines in the opposite direction, as well as an oval at the bottom to create dimension. Finally, add detail to the fleur-de-lis and continue tapping pigment into the wet areas until the cloche has a nice, variegated finish like cast-iron.

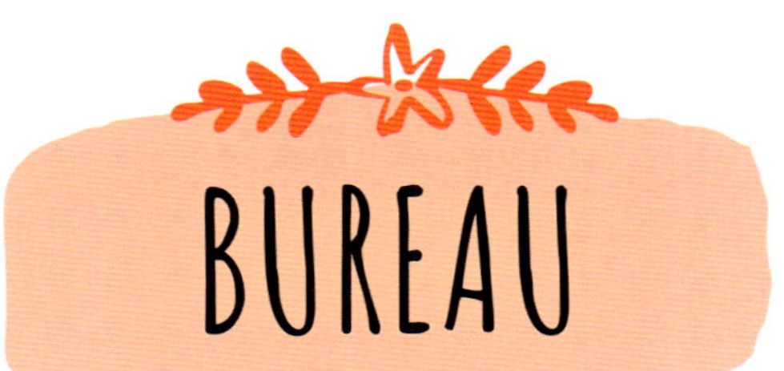

BUREAU

This fun project uses acrylic paint and colored pencils to create a bureau that would look right at home in a French villa.

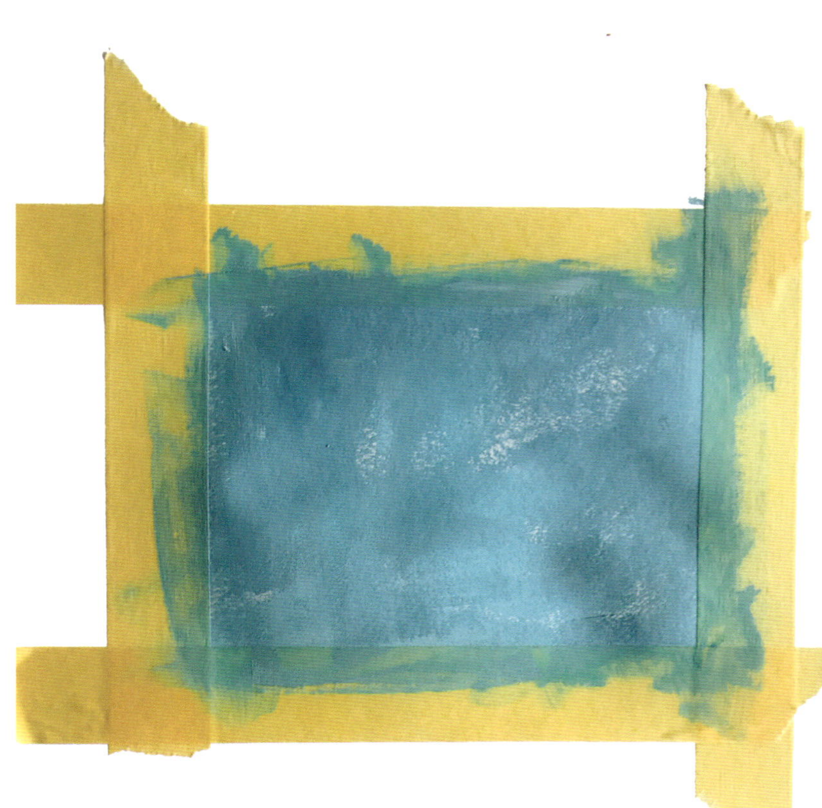

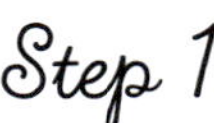

Step 1

Start by masking off a rectangle on your sheet of paper. Mix up blue and white, as well as green and white, for the main components. Don't use too much water when painting into the rectangle. Let this dry.

Step 2

Add your second color over the first layer with a dry brush. You don't need to fill in the whole rectangle here, as the blue undercoat is meant to show through for a pretty patina. Let this dry.

Tip

Anything goes here, but take a look at some French country furniture online for style inspiration.

Step 3

Add curved legs and a simple top using the remainder of your paint mixes. Take a colored pencil (any color you prefer; I've used turquoise) and make two drawers within the rectangular body.

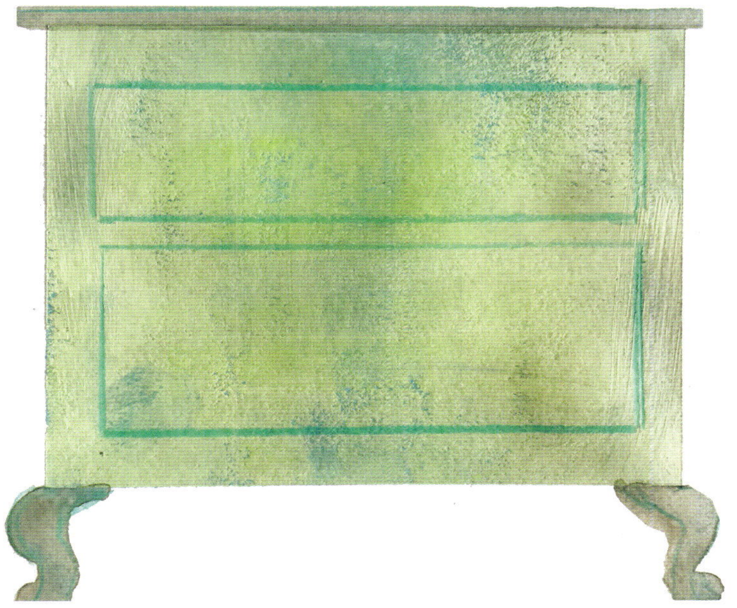

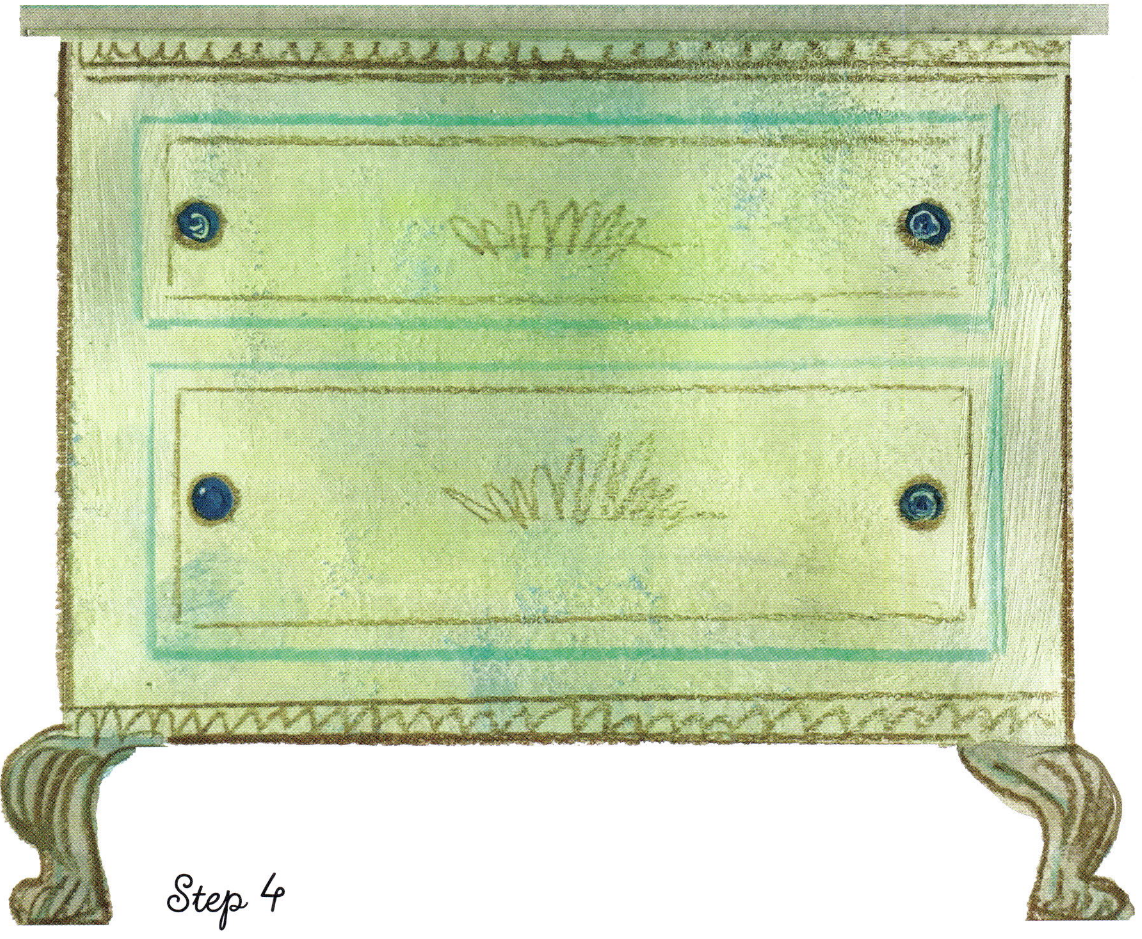

Step 4

Next, draw a second set of drawer lines within the first lines. Dip the end of one of your round brush into blue paint and create four knobs. Once dry, finish these off with a colored pencil. Then add decorative details.

RUSTIC BIRDHOUSE

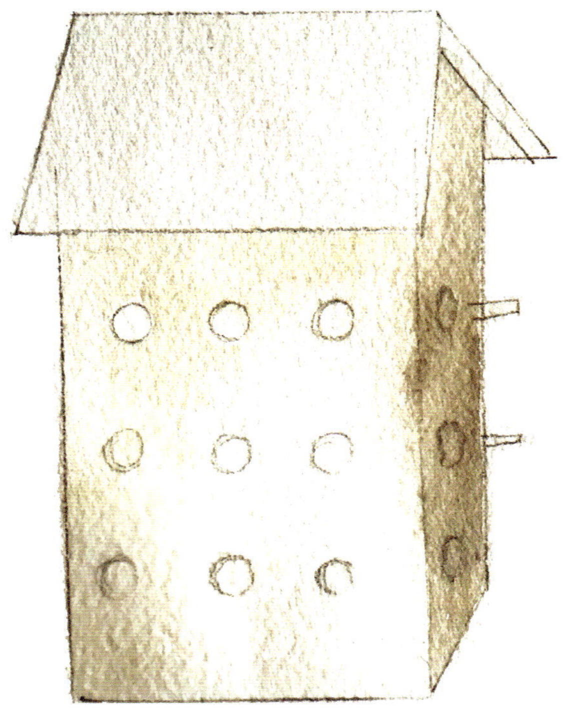

Step 1

Map out the basic shape of a birdhouse using a pencil. Then add a watercolor wash on top, with a darker value on the side of the birdhouse. Using a small Filbert brush, make choppy down strokes on the roof. These will form the shingles. Then use a darker value to give contrast. While wet, you can score with a toothpick to add some rough texture and grooves. Fill in the pegs on the side and in the front, and add perches for the birds.

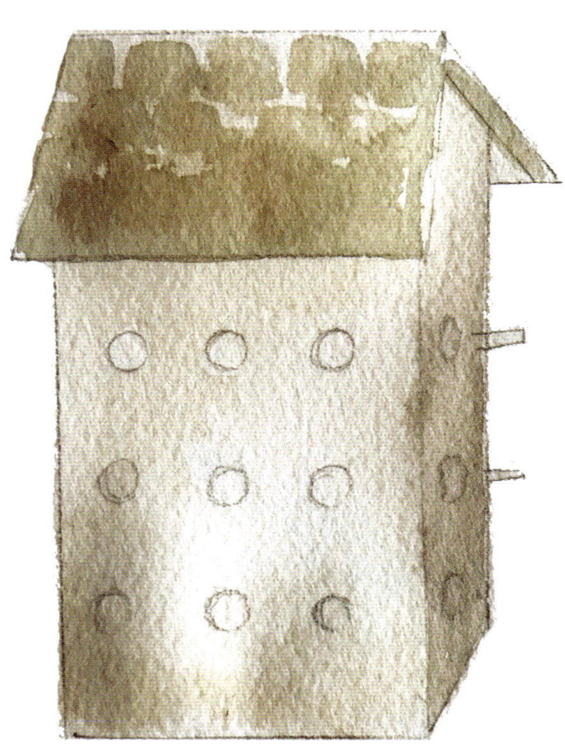

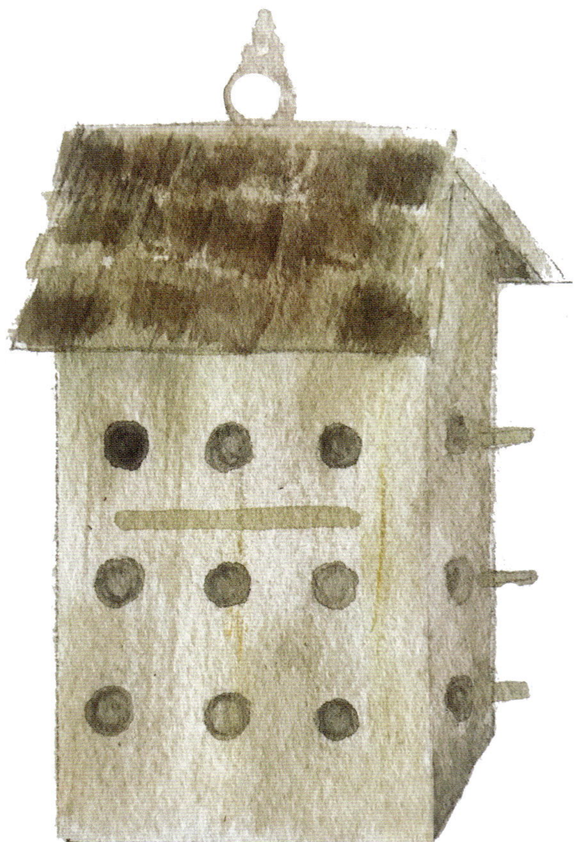

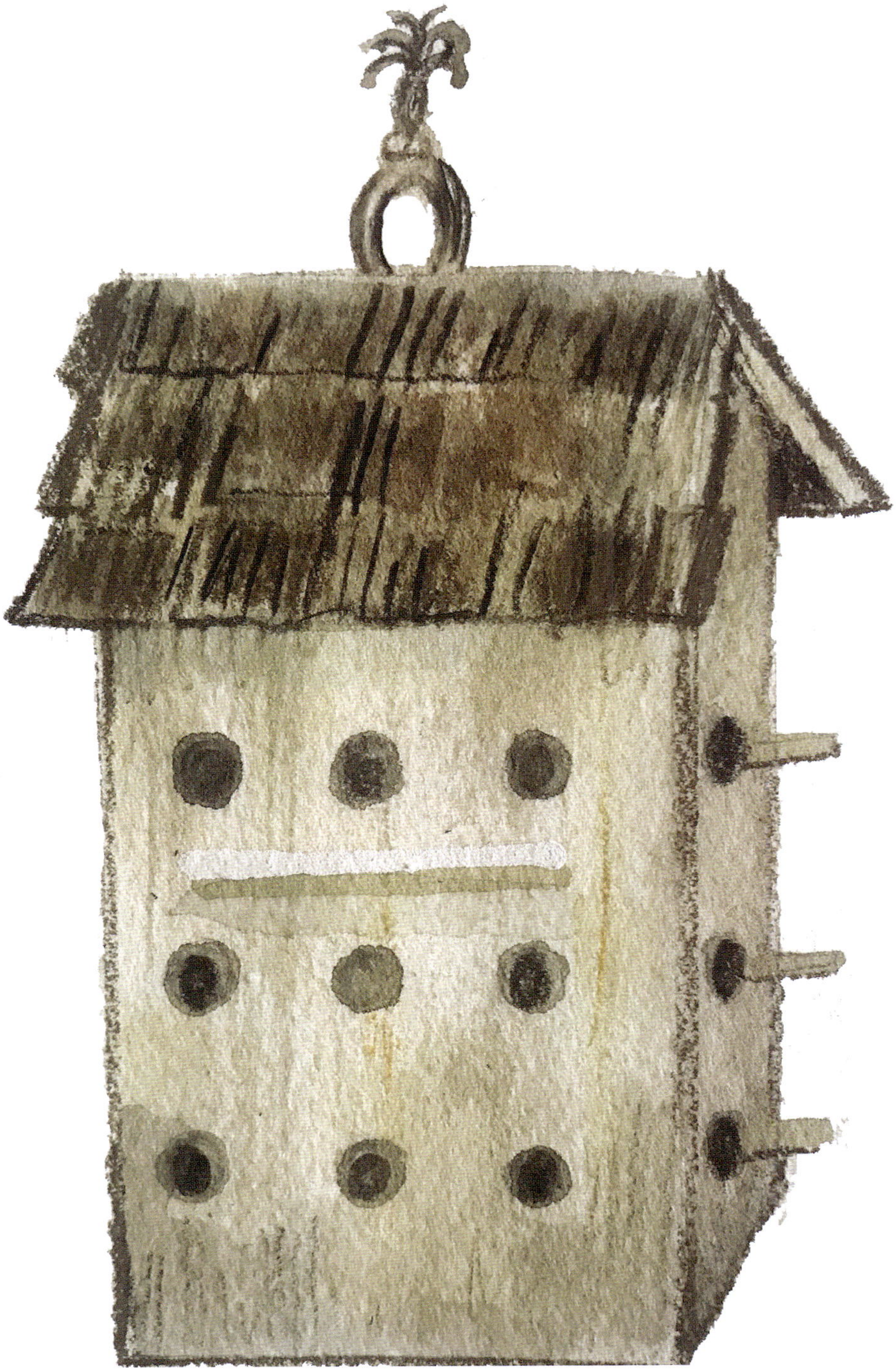

Step 2

Let the paint dry; then use a charcoal pencil to create short, vertical hatch marks on the roof for the shingles. Be careful not to overwork this step, as you don't want to be too heavy-handed with the charcoal.

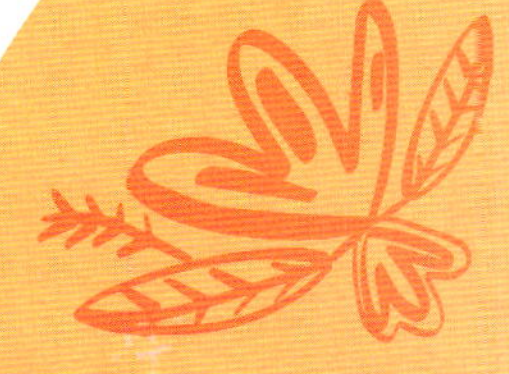

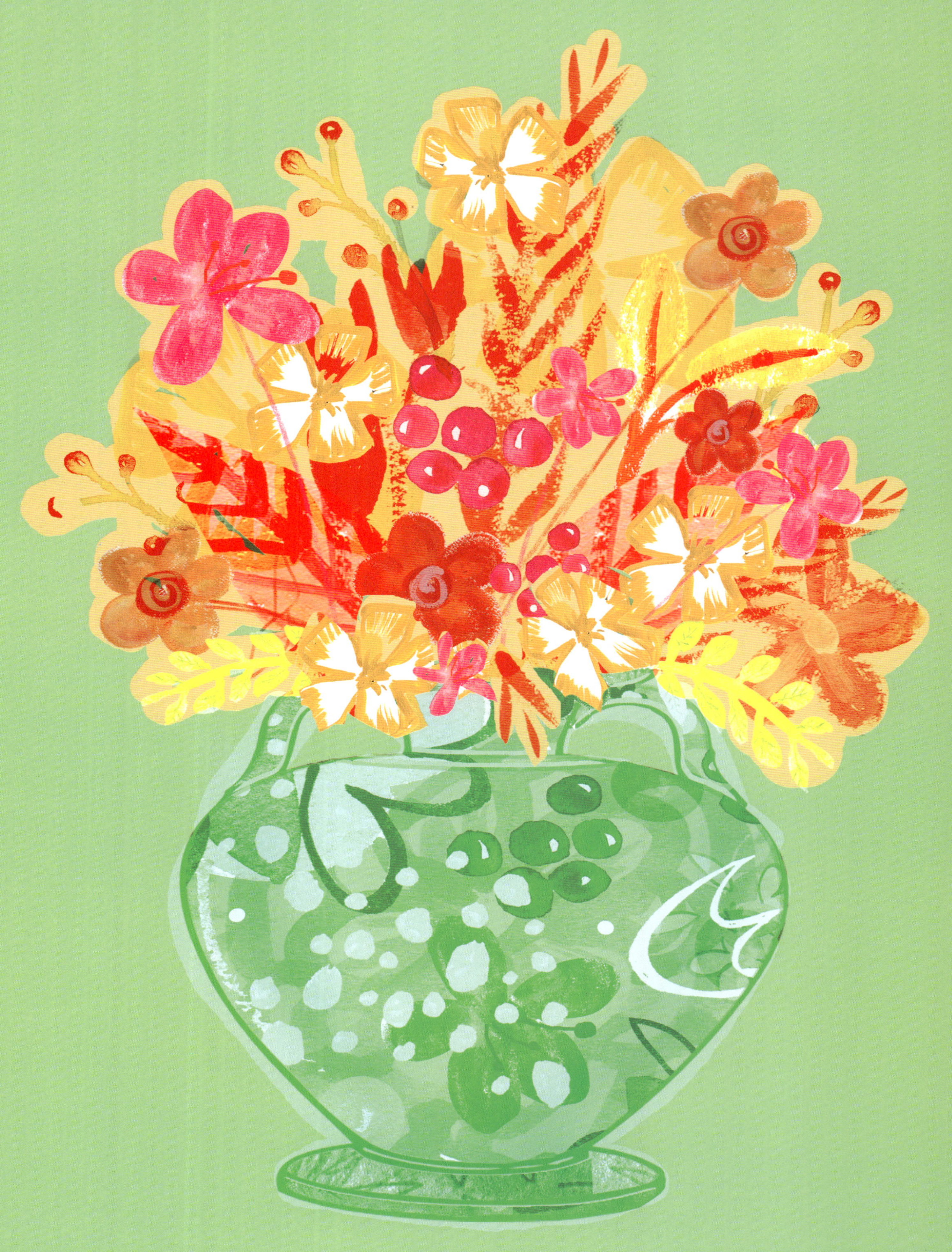

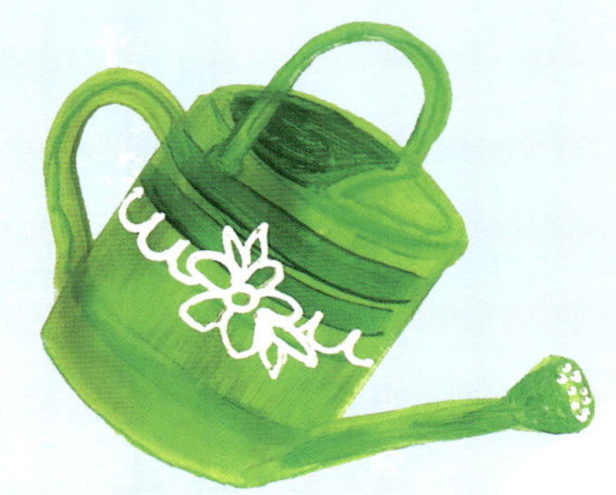
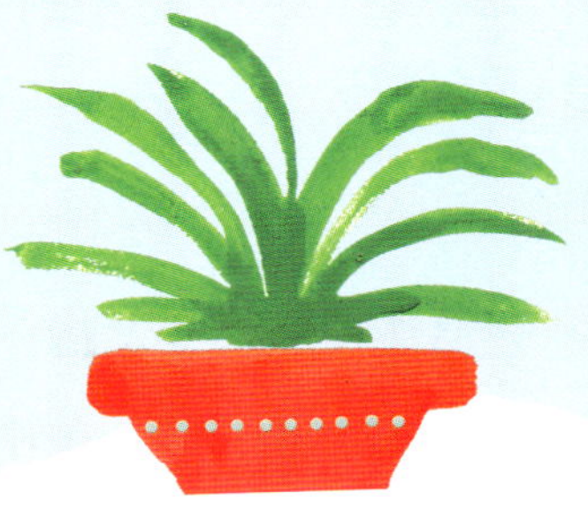
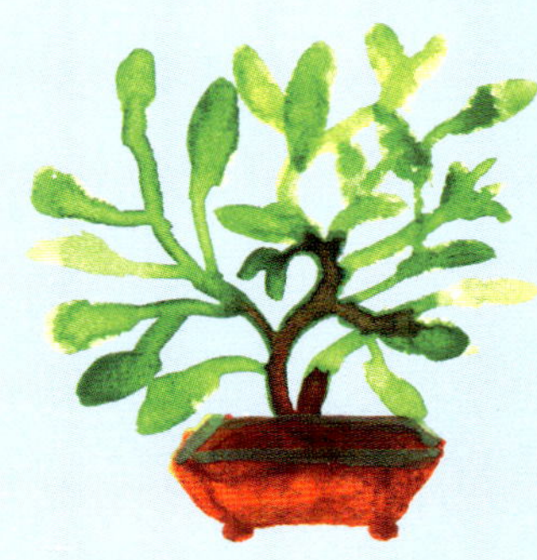
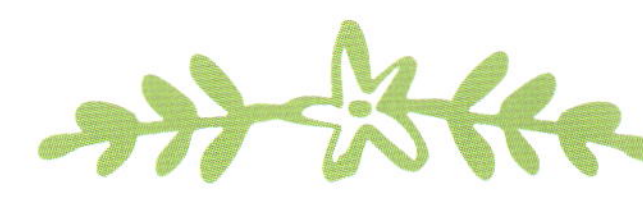

FEELIN' OUTDOORSY

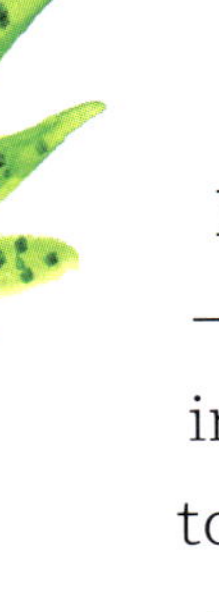
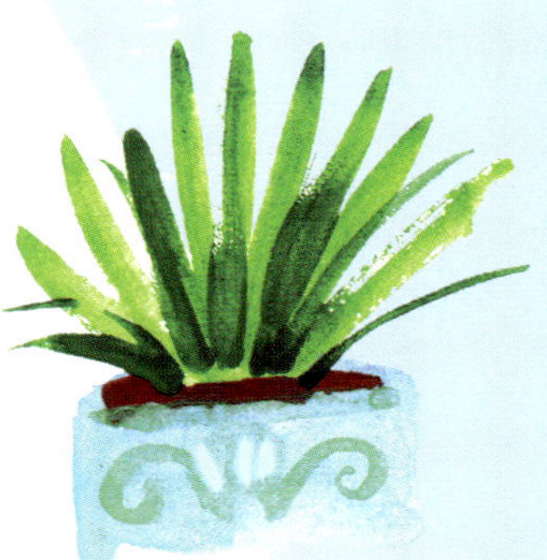

In this section, we will focus on the great outdoors—or more specifically, the items that you might find in your own backyard. There are so many fun objects to choose from outdoors: birdhouses, gardening tools, potting sheds, flowers, fences, deck furniture, beach umbrellas, and more!

If you can paint outside while working on this chapter, that's even better! It's always nice to hear the birds chirping and get some fresh air. We have some fun subjects to paint in this chapter, but as always, feel free to use the techniques I've described on any subject of your choice.

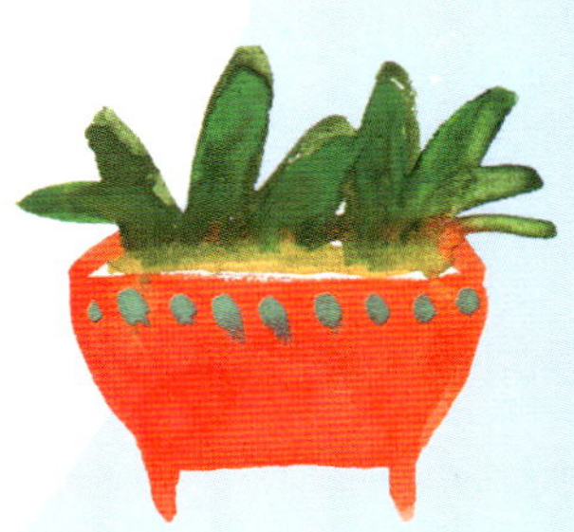
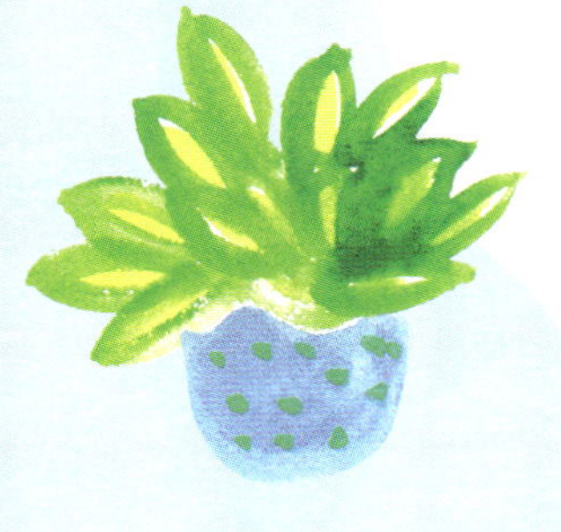
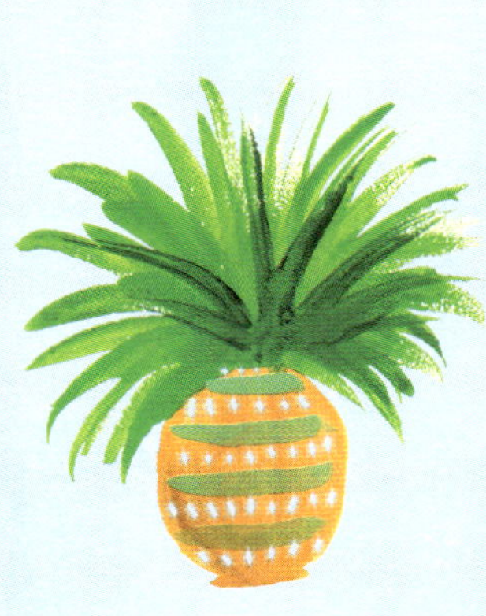
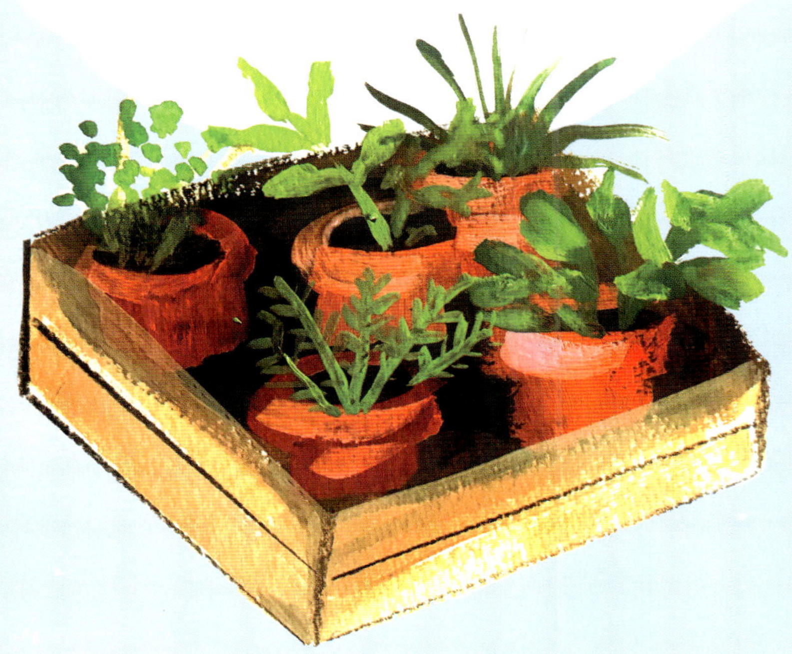
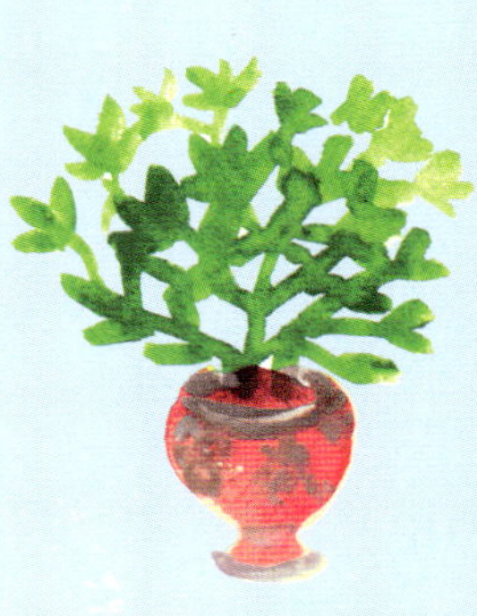

WATERING CAN & TROWEL

Gouache is the medium of choice for illustrating this classic green watering can. I've used light leaf-green and dark green, as well as a touch of white.

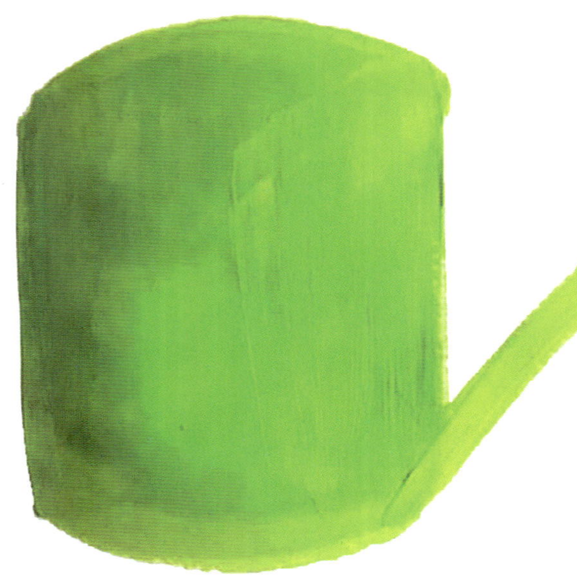

Step 1

Create the cylindrical shape of the container, and then add the neck at about a 45-degree angle, both using the lighter green.

Step 2

Add a handle and rounded spout at the top of the neck. Next, use the darker green paint to create two stripes near the top of the container and a half sphere at the top to form the opening.

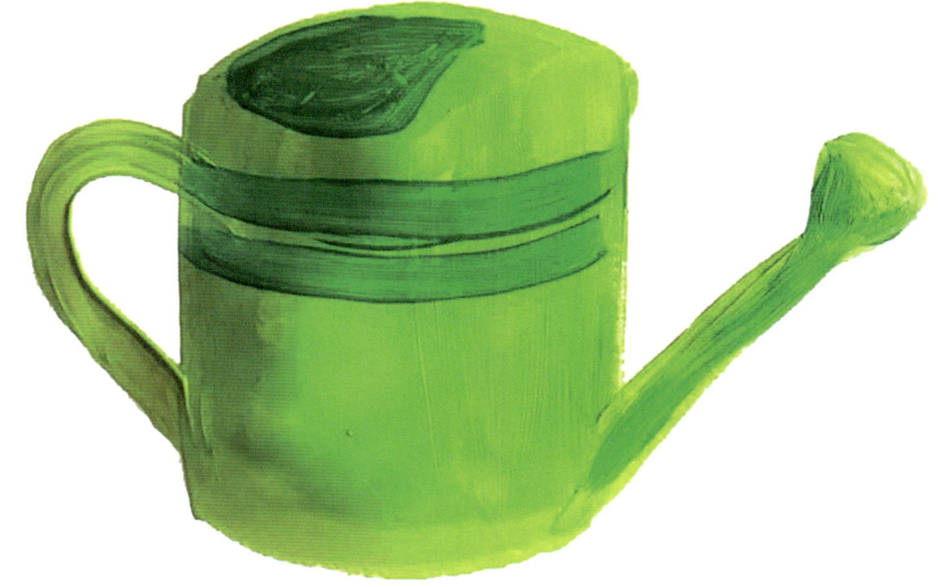

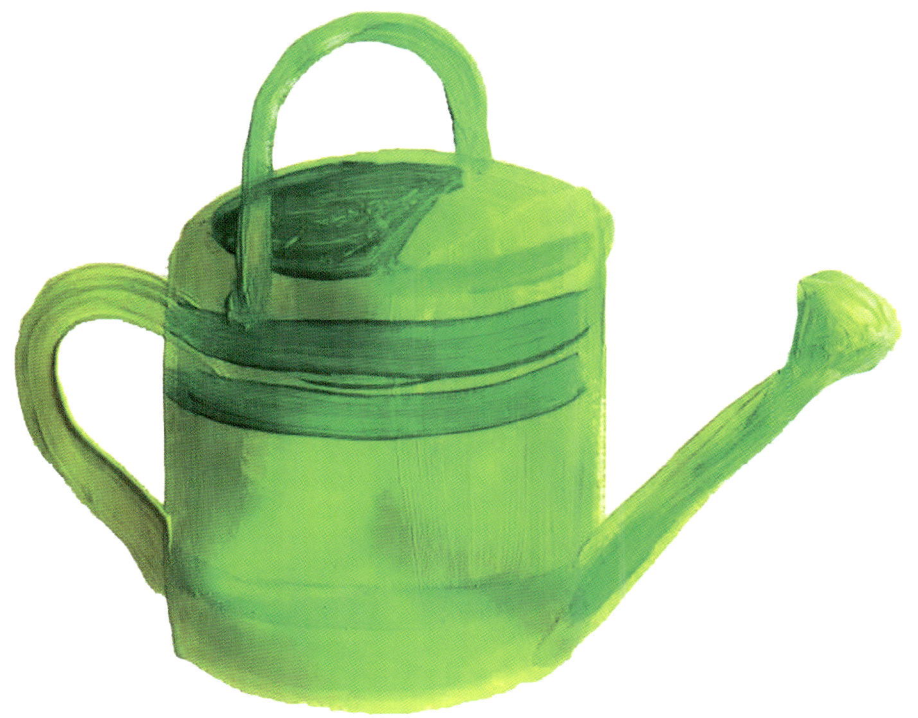

Step 3

Using the darker shade of green, form a handle over the top of the container. You can also add another stripe at the bottom if you wish.

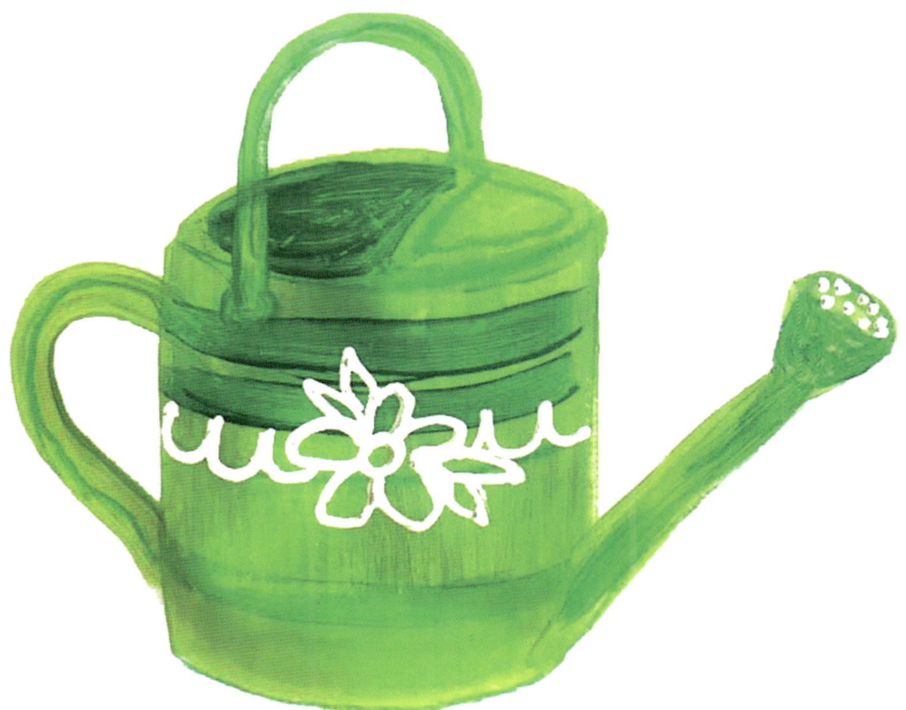

Step 4

With a liner brush and a small amount of white paint, create a decorative embellishment on the front of the can. Feel free to play here! You could paint your initials, a flower, or just decorative lines.

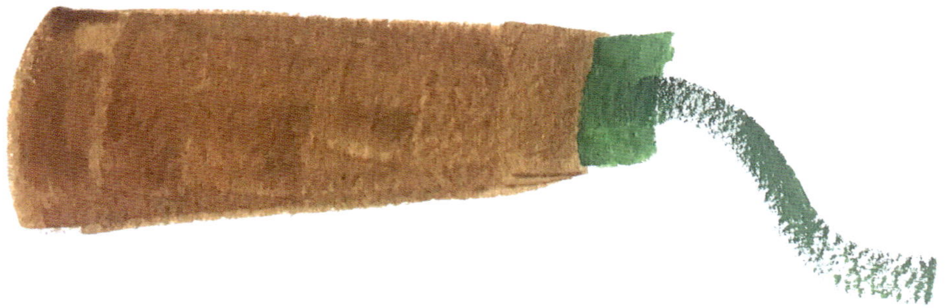

Step 1

Create a simple handle using warm brown, making sure to taper from left to right so that the narrow end is where the wood meets the metal part of the tool. Use a small, angled brush and medium green to create a downward curve, much like a slide.

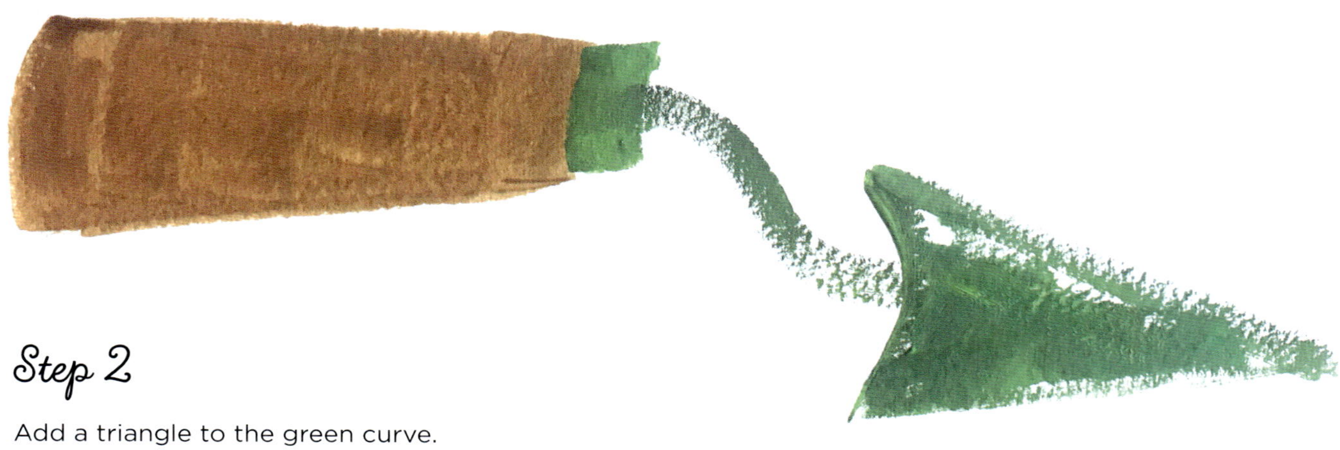

Step 2

Add a triangle to the green curve.

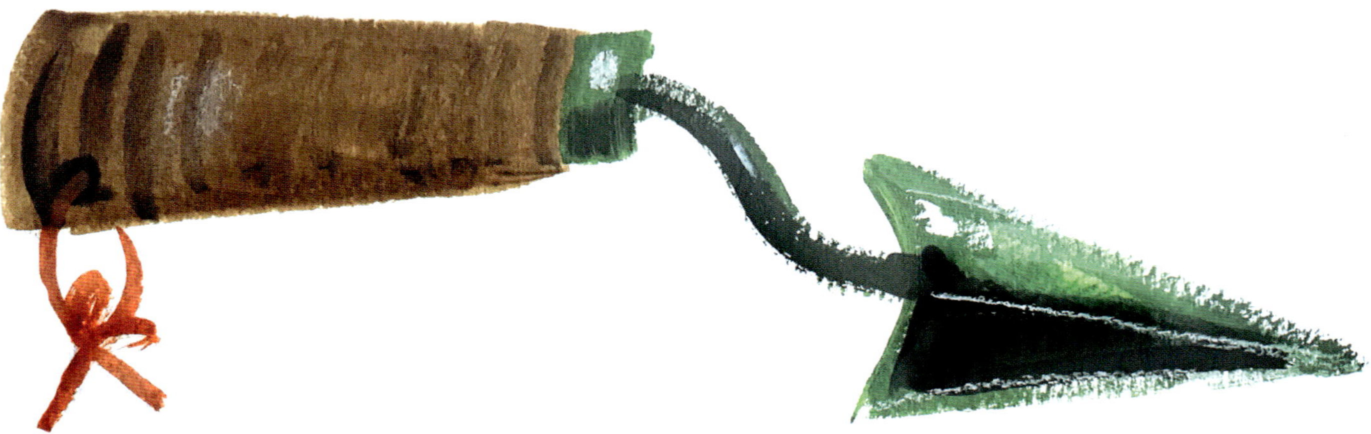

Step 3

Then use darker green to give the tool more depth. Add detail to the handle, using sepia and the drybrushing technique. Finish by adding a leather cord in the color of your choice.

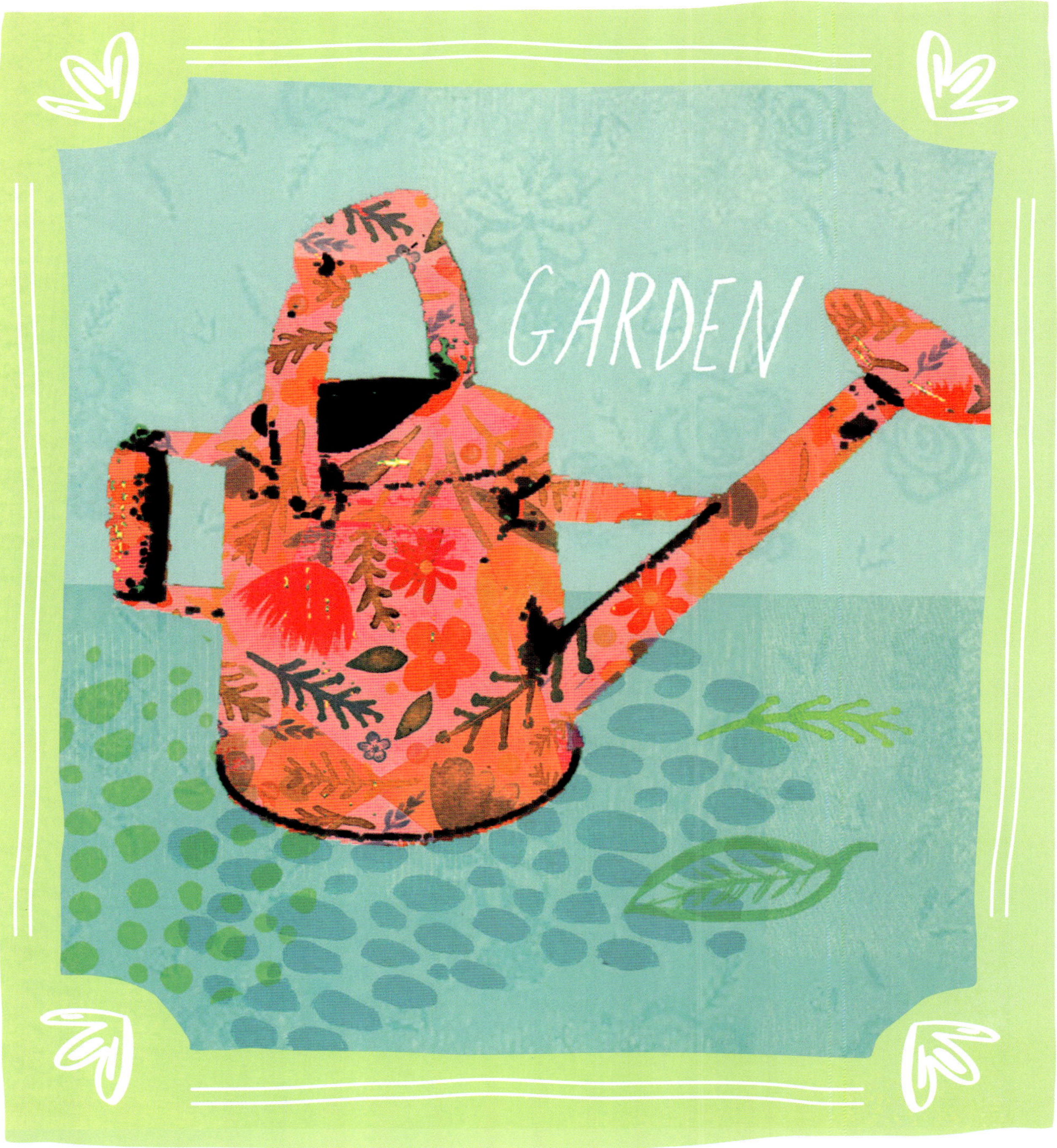

GARDEN

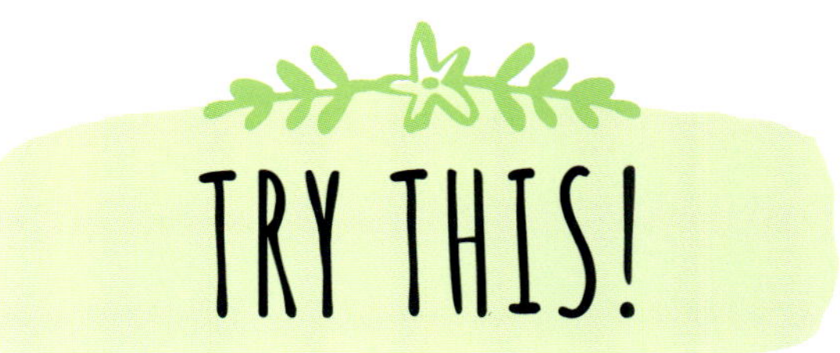

A quaint garden needs an equally rustic watering can.
Visit a local gardening store for ideas!

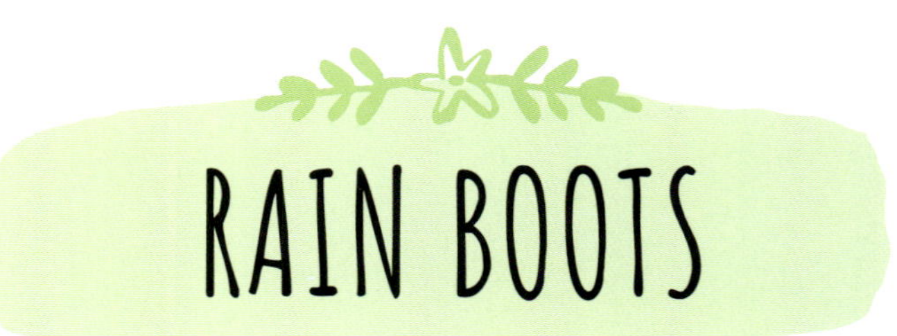

RAIN BOOTS

This is such a fun project that uses cut paper and acrylic. You can replace the acrylic with gouache if you prefer.

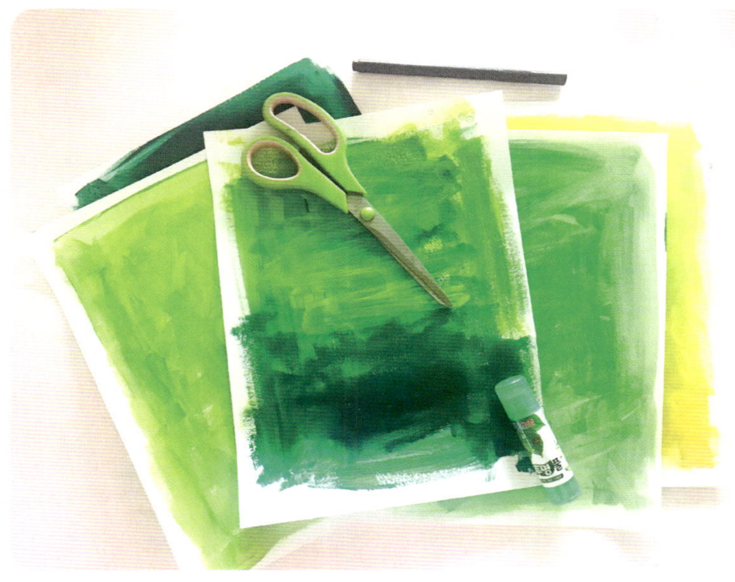

Step 1

Start by loading a generous amount of light and medium green paint onto a large brush, and make big sweeps of color onto your paper. Mix it up here! Alternate light and dark, drybrushing and full saturation, and so on.

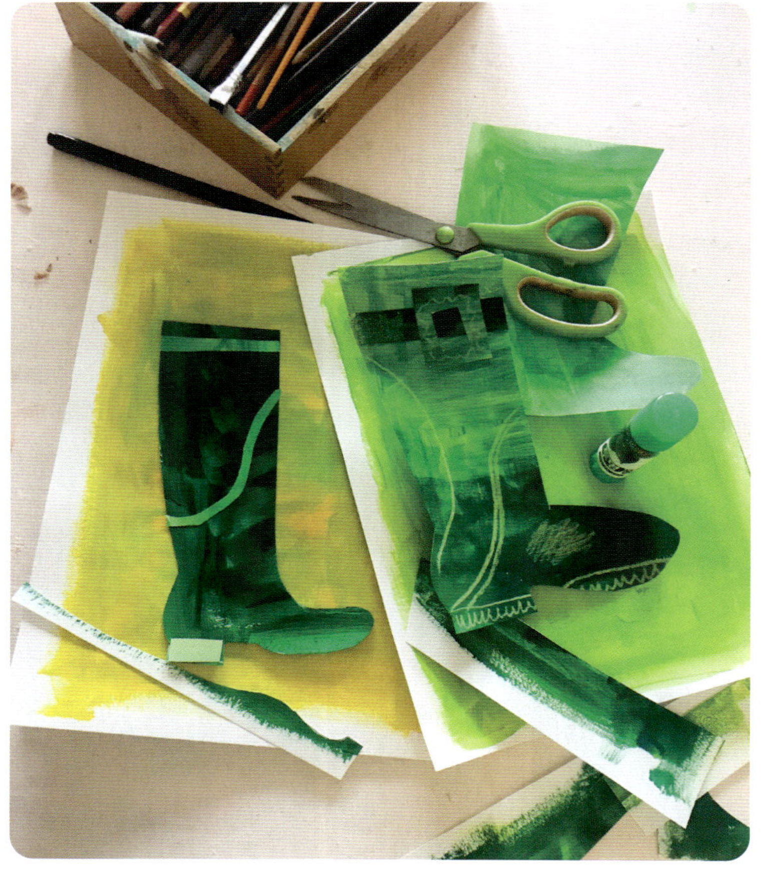

Step 2

Draw the basic shape of a rain boot (you can find one online and draw from that reference, or go by memory and experiment) and start cutting! Play with cutting heels, buckles, and other details. Mix dark with light. You can also use colored pencils to draw extra details like ridges.

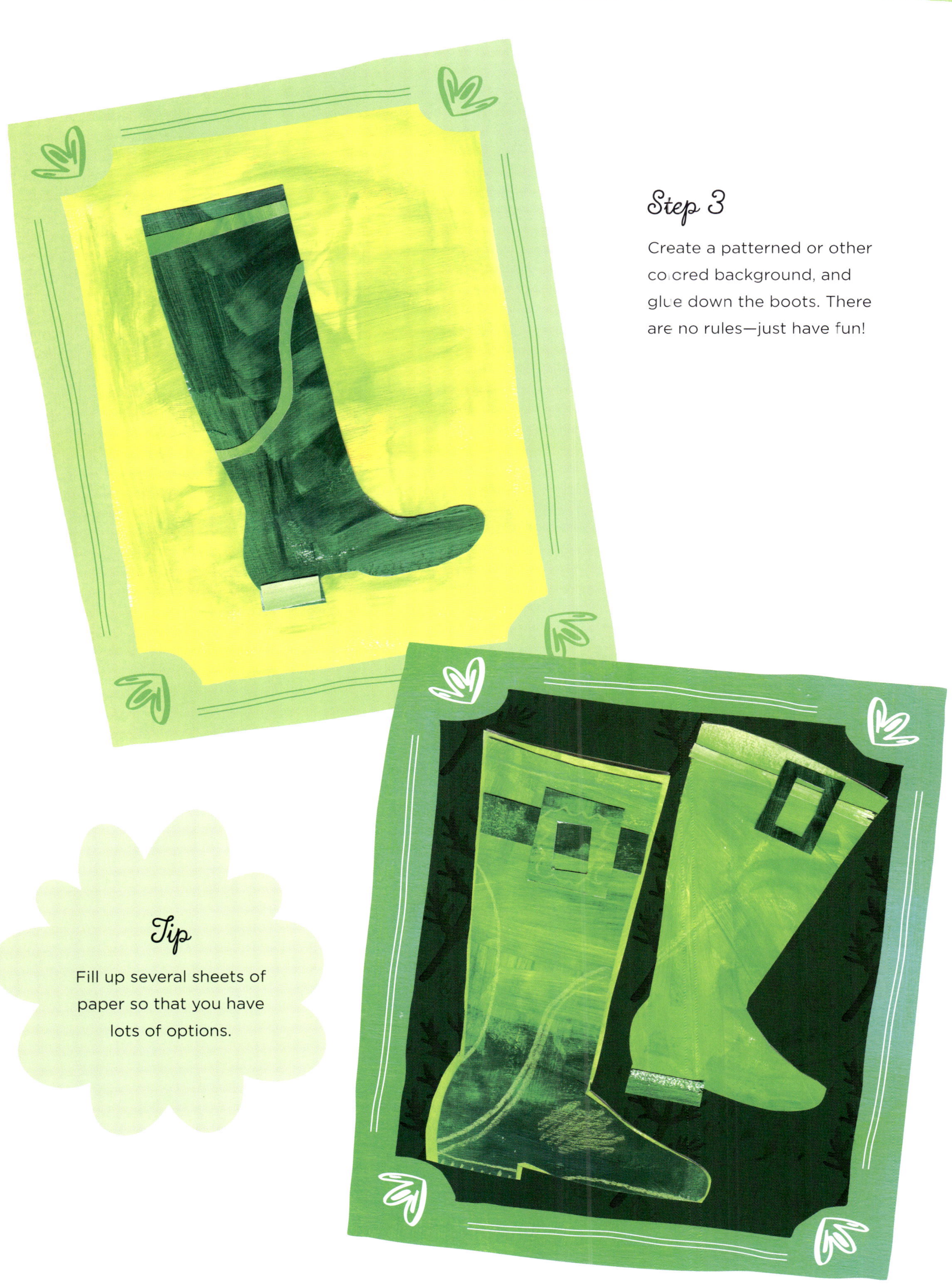

Step 3

Create a patterned or other colored background, and glue down the boots. There are no rules—just have fun!

Tip

Fill up several sheets of paper so that you have lots of options.

GARDENING GLOVES

Keep those scissors and glue sticks around from the previous project! Here we'll have even more fun cutting paper—this time creating a template for masking. Use gouache for this project.

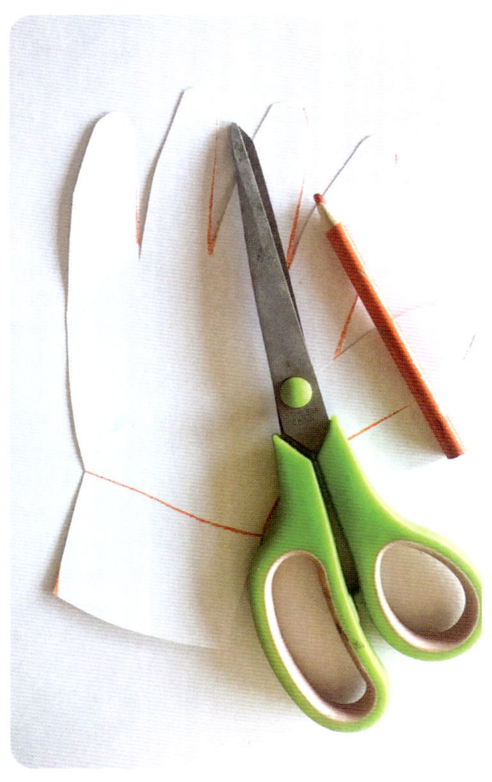

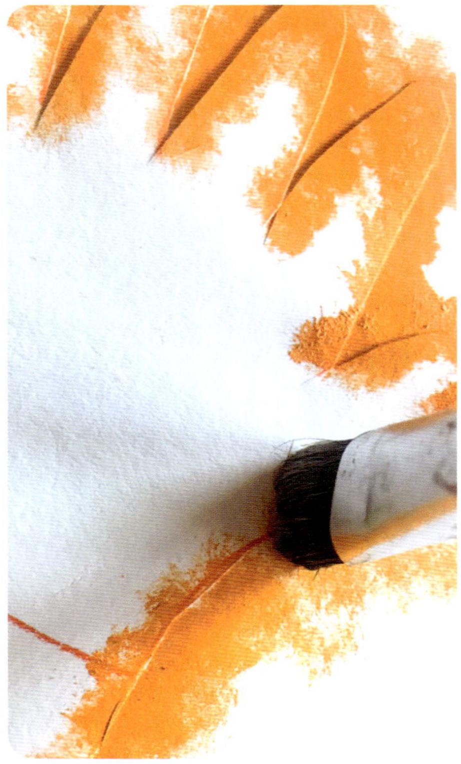

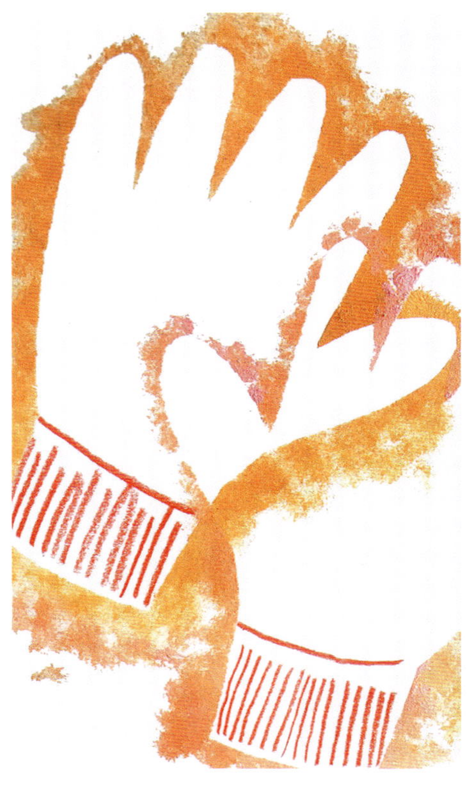

Step 1

Draw a simple glove shape onto sturdy white card stock and cut it out.

Step 2

Load a very stiff brush with the color of your choice, and stipple around the edges of the glove. Make sure to hold it down securely so that the paint doesn't get underneath the mask template. Let the paint dry.

Step 3

Once the paint is dry, flip over the glove to create another one, laying it slightly above the first glove. Now use a different paint color for the second glove, repeating step 2. Let the paint dry; then use colored pencil to draw in the grooves of the elastic wrists.

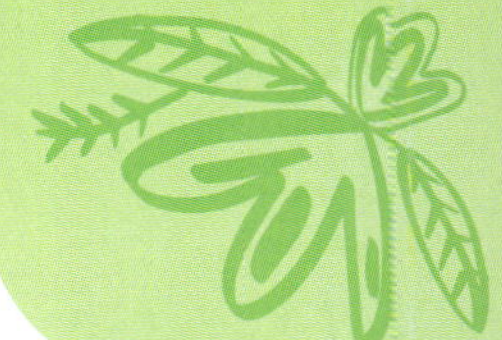

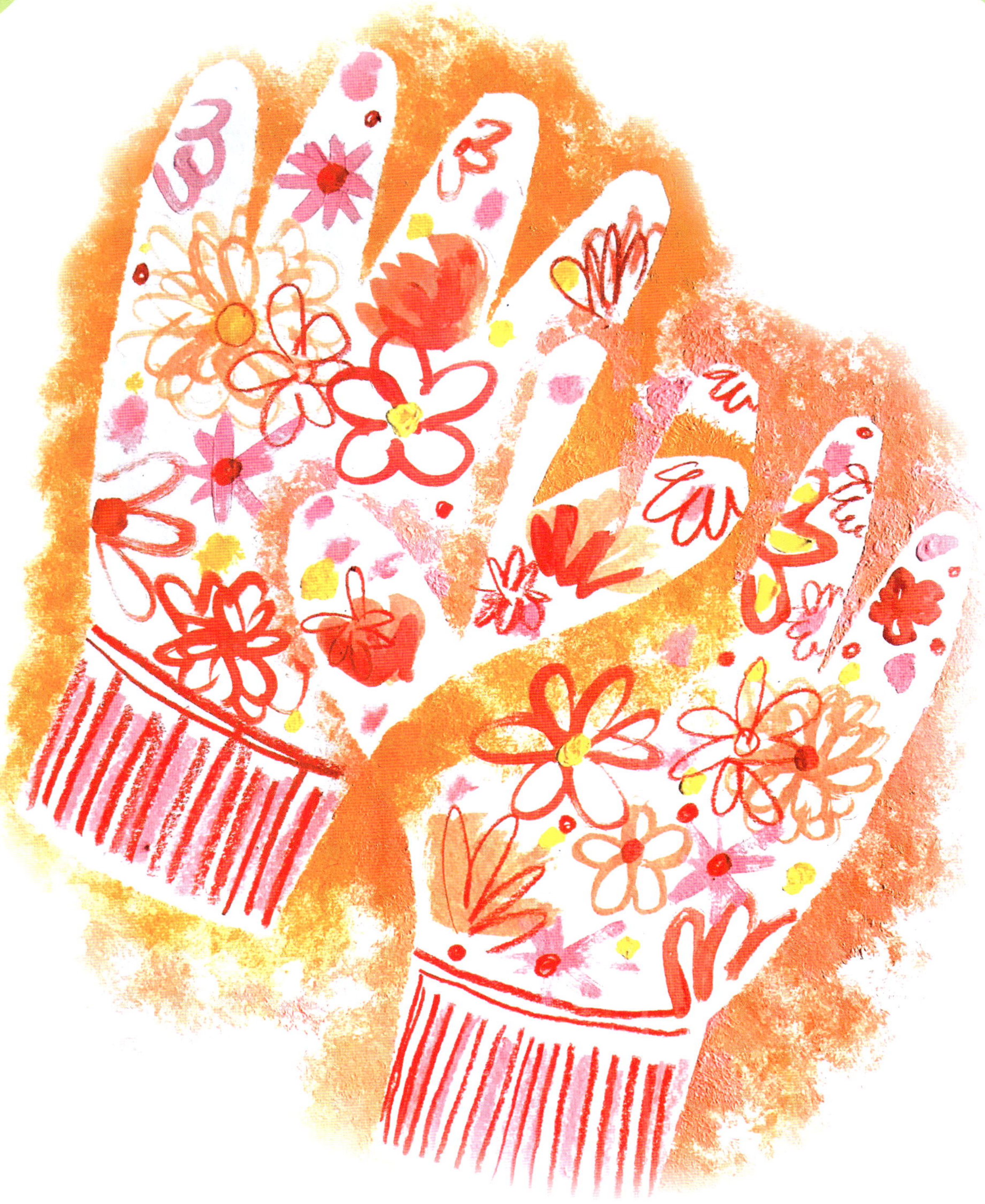

Step 4

It's time to give the gloves a pattern! I've painted free-form flowers here, using a liner brush dipped in assorted hues of pinks and oranges. Give the pattern additional contrast by using a darker hue (red in my case). You can also add more details in colored pencil once it all dries. Weeding is far more fun when wearing cute accessories!

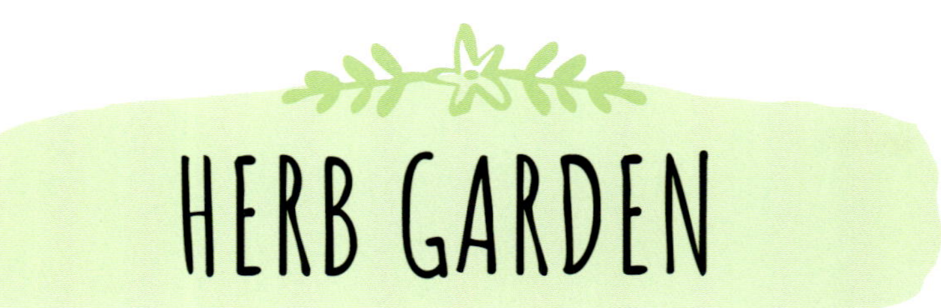

HERB GARDEN

This project also uses gouache to paint a cute little herb garden, perfect for a small patio or balcony!

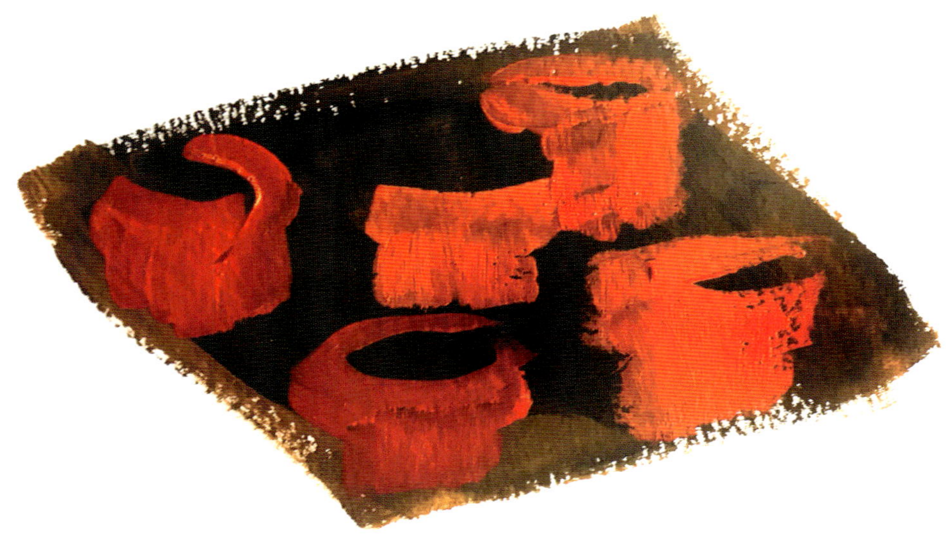

Step 1

Load an angled brush with brown paint and create an angled box. Using a smaller angled brush, create the impression of terra-cotta pots with a few simple swipes of red-orange.

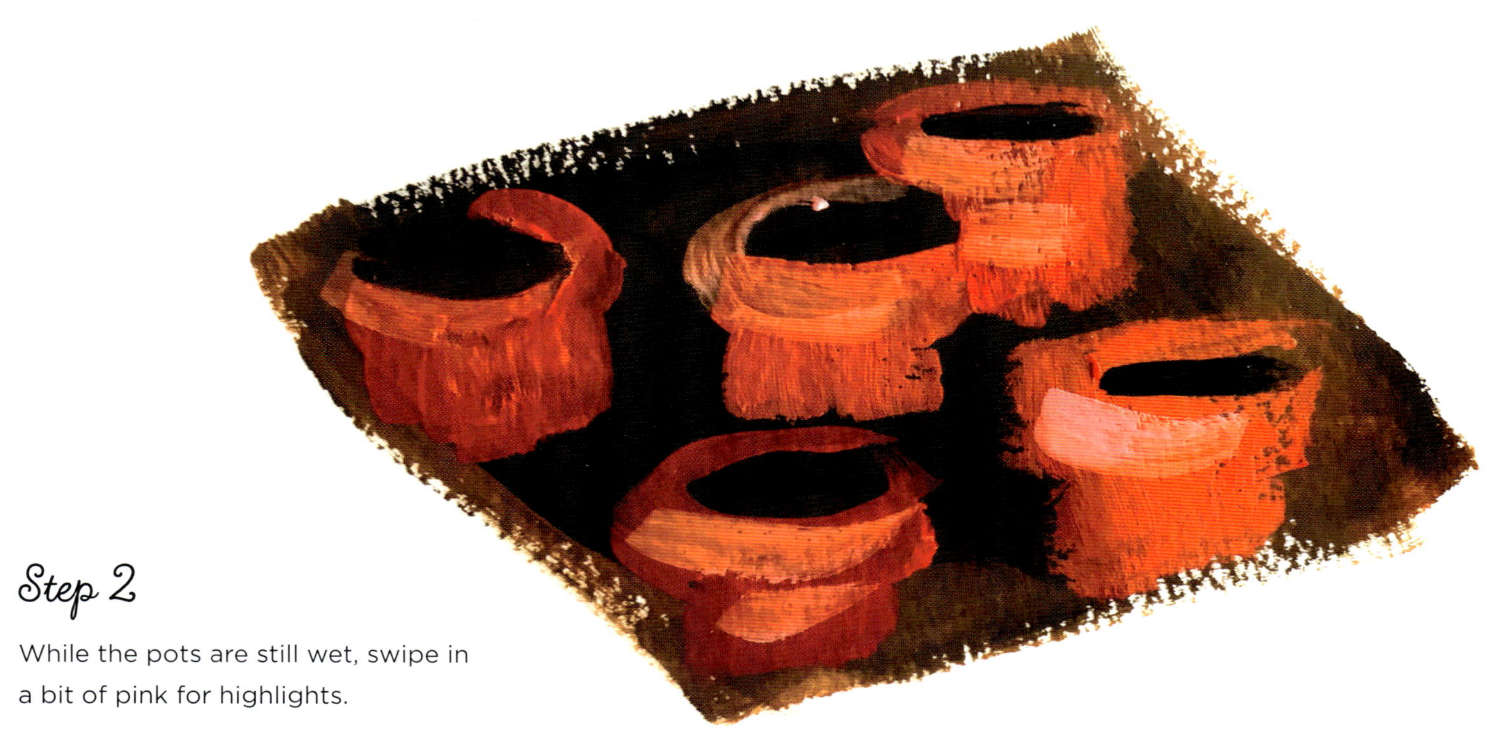

Step 2

While the pots are still wet, swipe in a bit of pink for highlights.

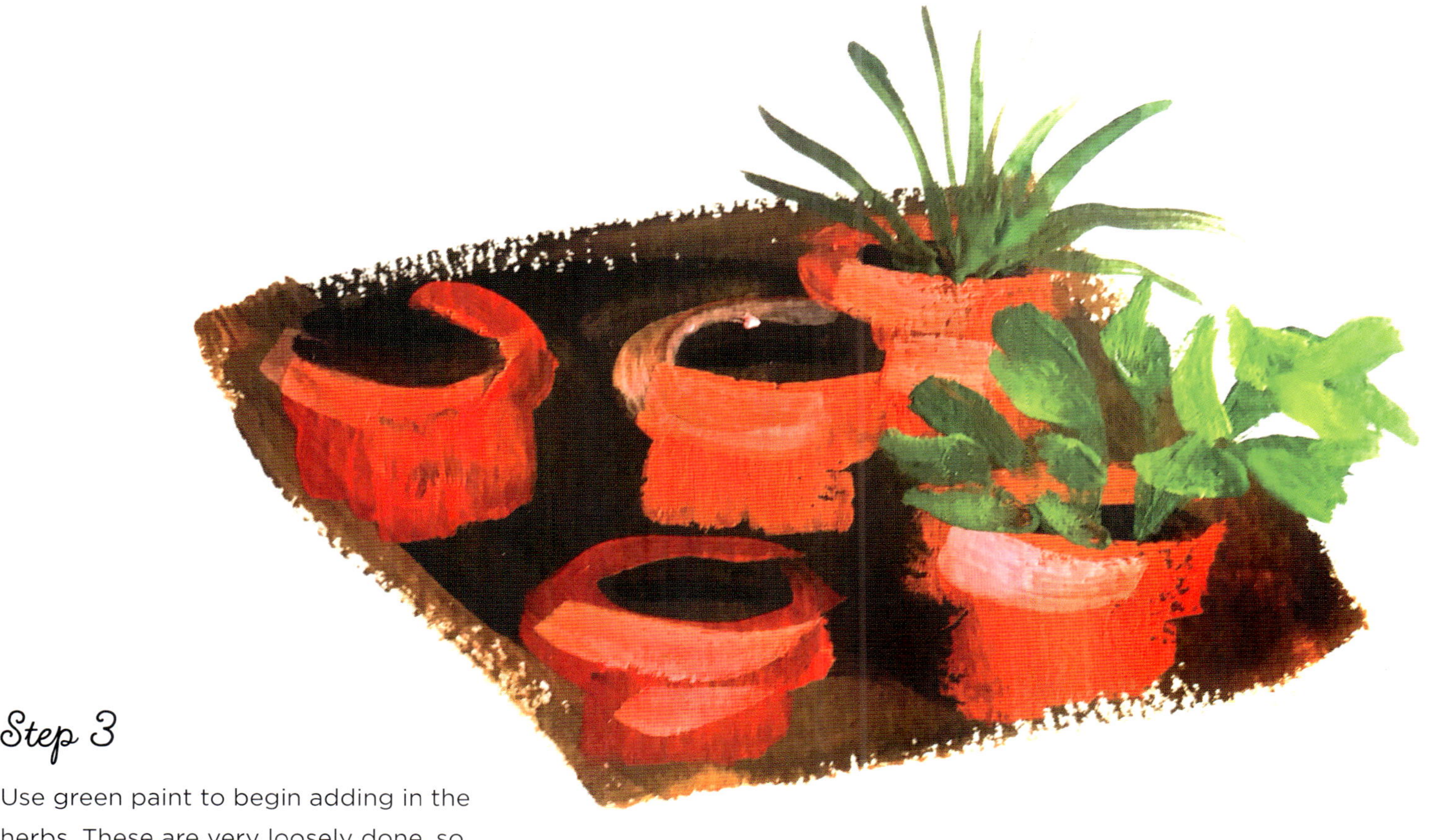

Step 3

Use green paint to begin adding in the herbs. These are very loosely done, so don't get too hung up on the details.

Step 4

Play with different hues and values of green, and continue adding various herb plants.

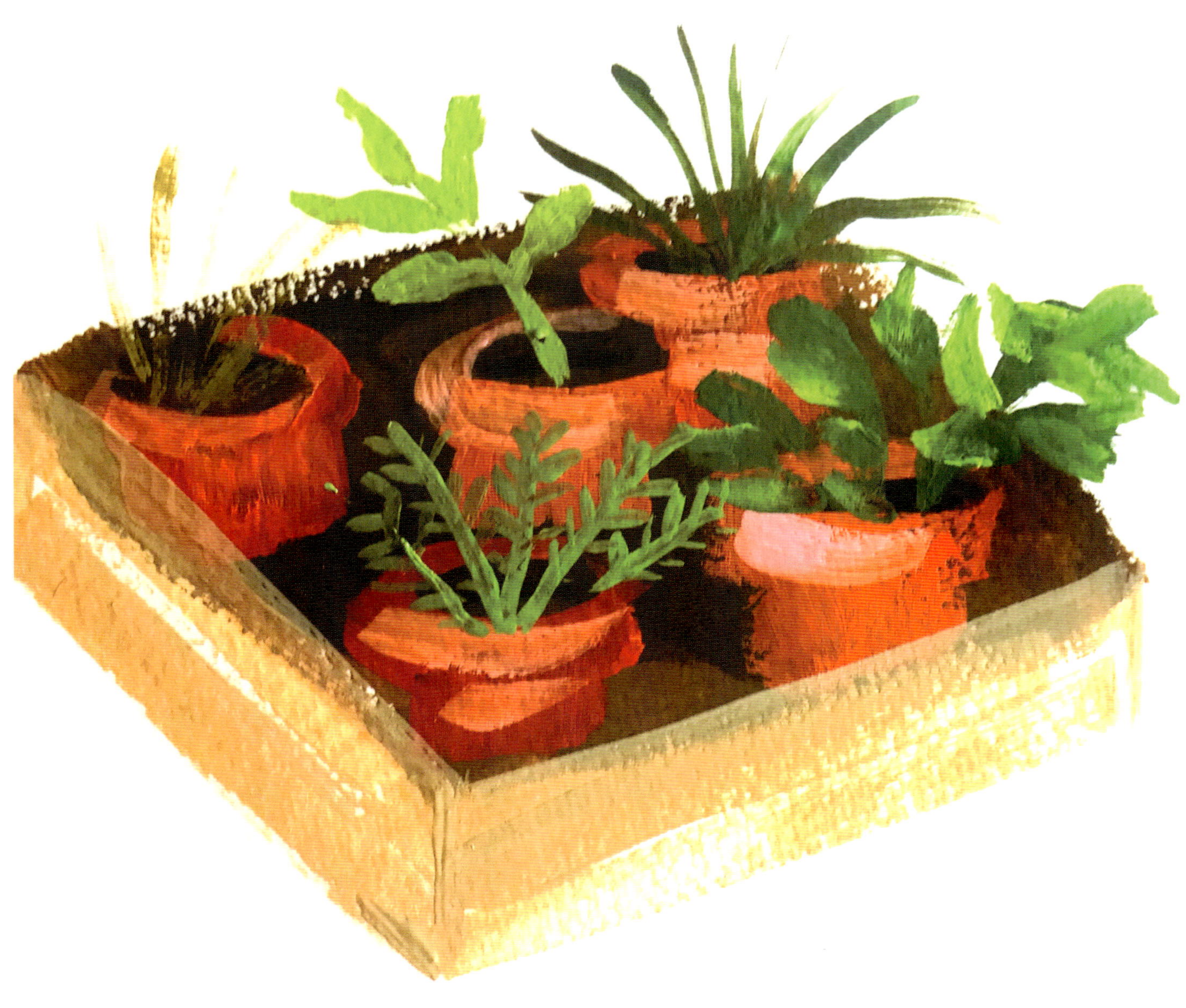

Step 5

It's time to frame the plants in a raised garden bed. Mix some raw sienna and white gouache, and grab your angled brush. Dip parts of it in lighter or darker browns. Blot the brush a bit on paper. You want to use the drybrushing technique here so that the wood appears a bit coarse, with the help of the paper's texture. Make one downward angled stroke for the side and one left-to-right angled stroke for the front.

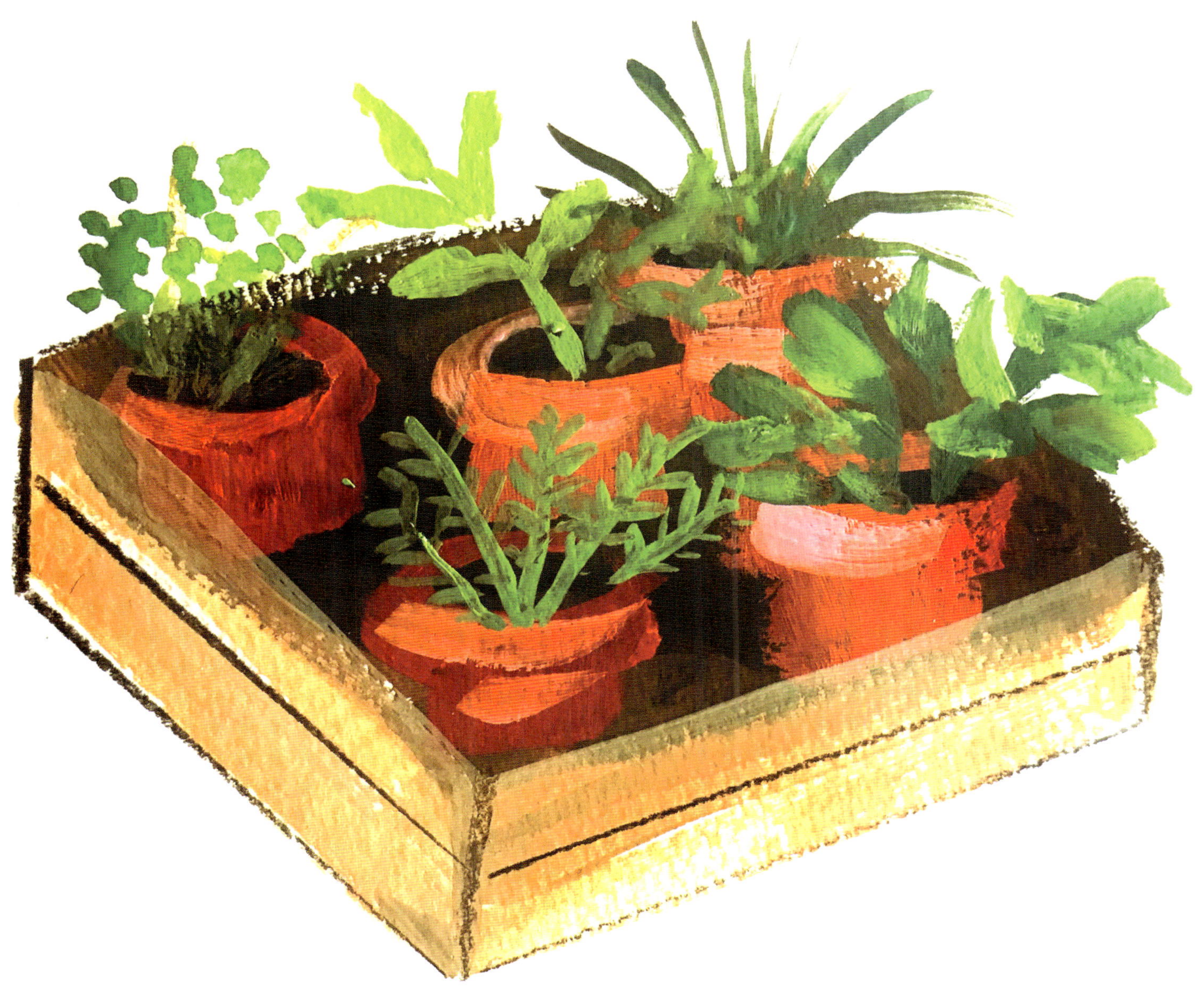

Step 6

Once the paint is fully dry, you can make a few strokes with a brown colored pencil to add details to the grooves of the bed. Use a ruler here and follow the lines of the painted bed.

Nine Different Ways

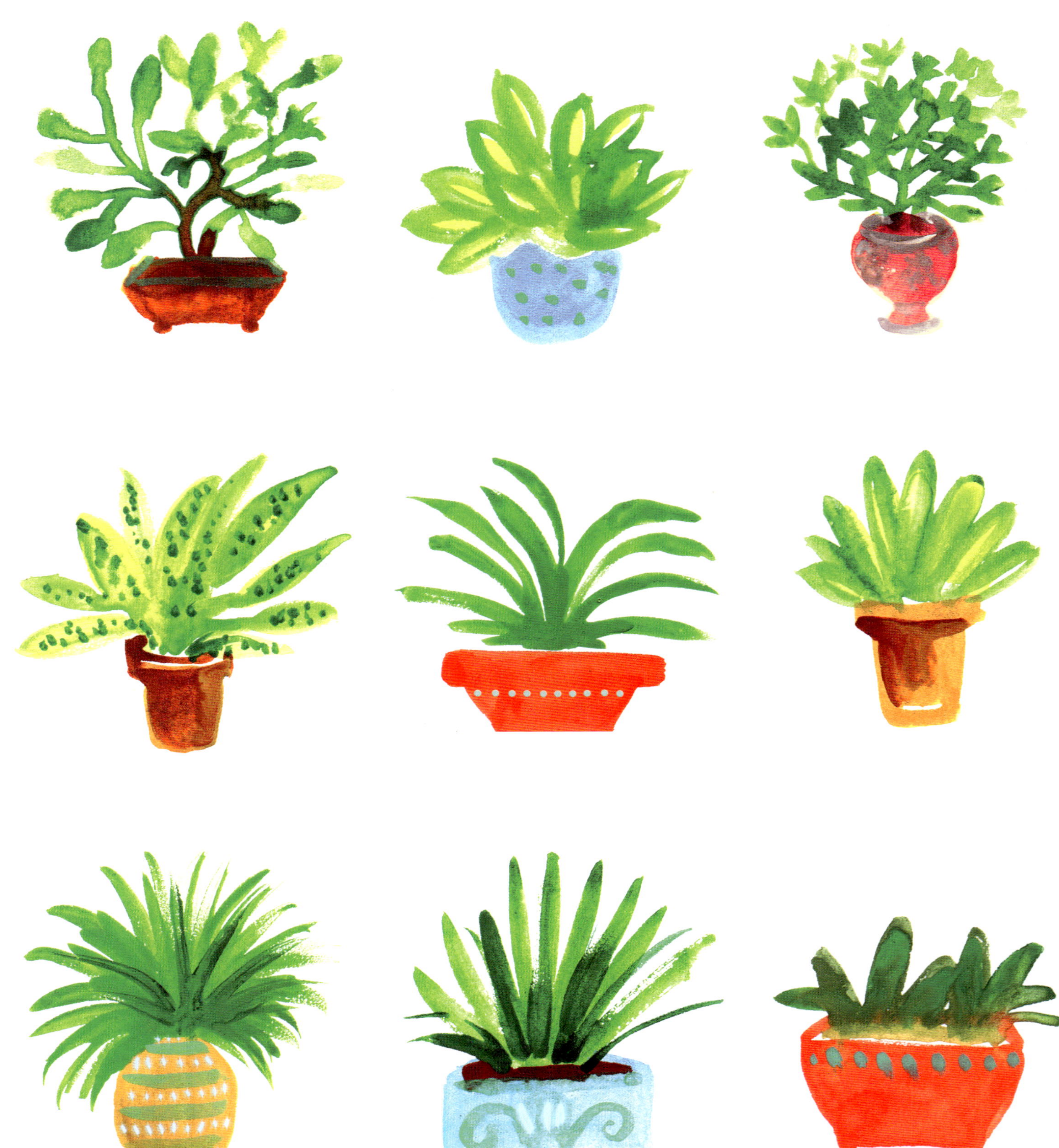

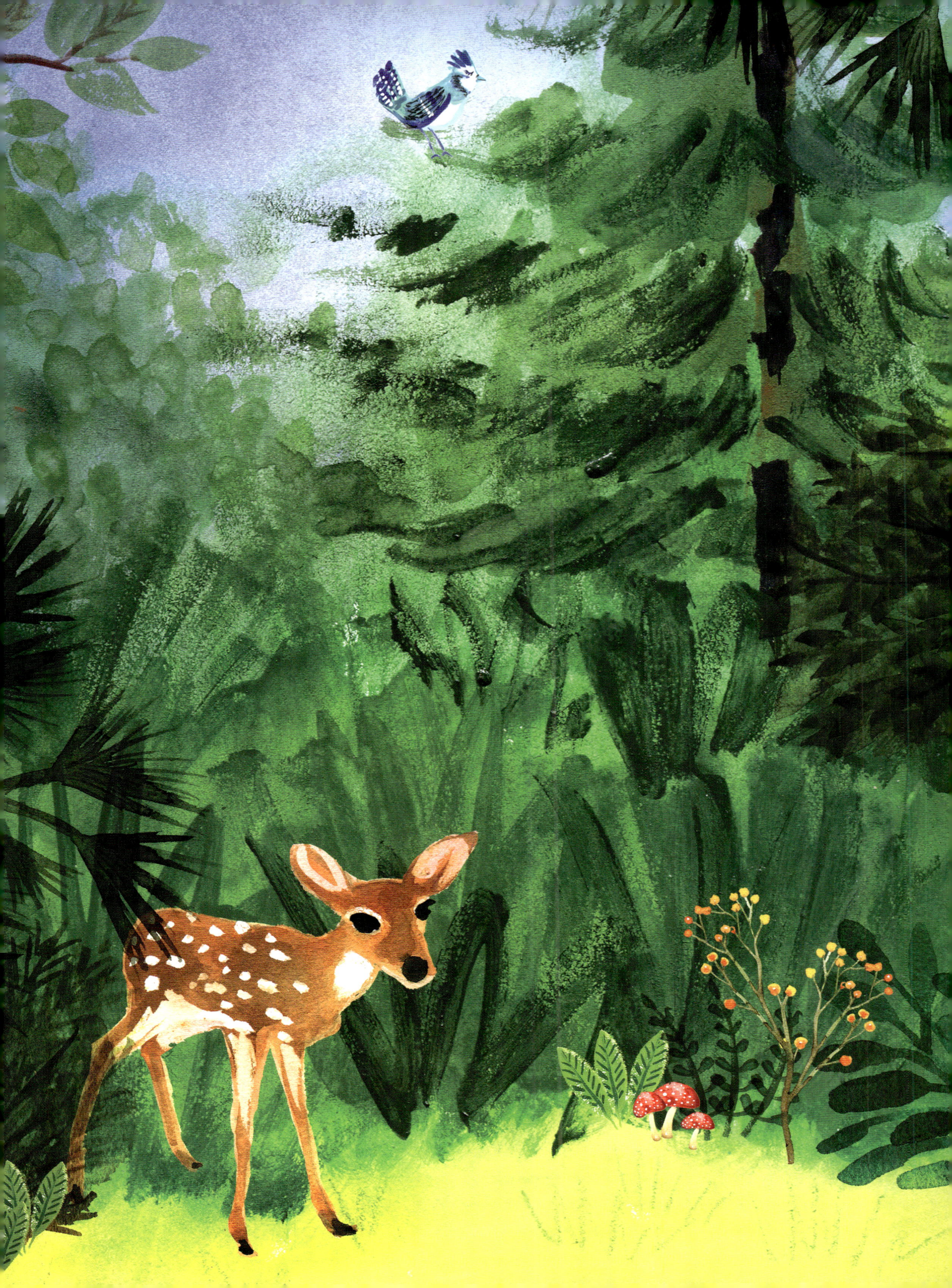

GARDEN BUNNY IN A LETTUCE PATCH

Now add a cute little bunny to your garden space! This project also uses gouache.

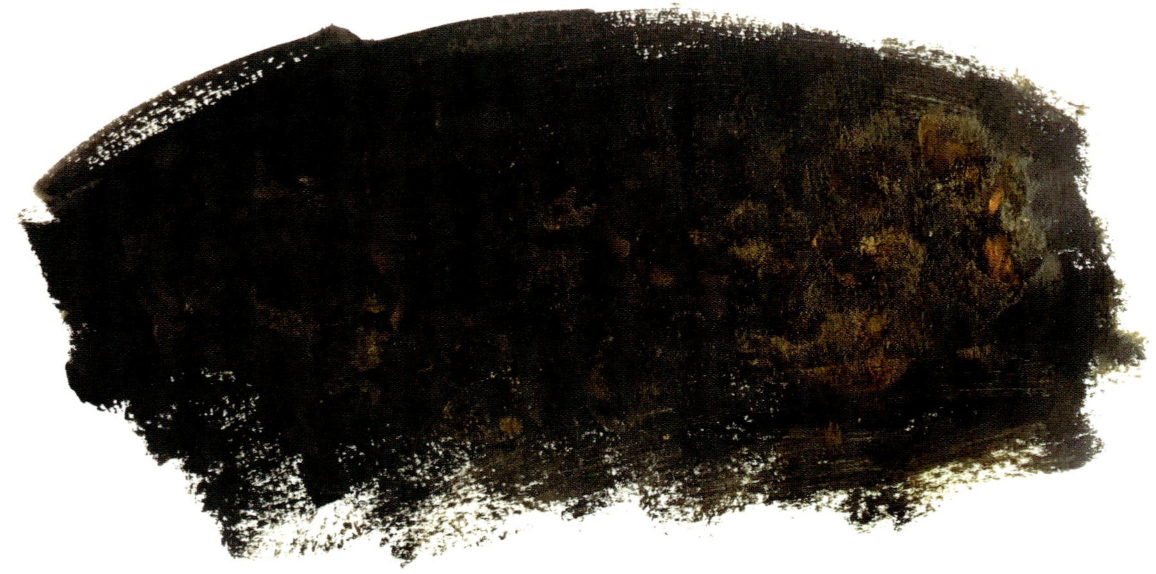

Step 1

Start with a very free-form swath of sepia, using a large, broad brush. You can stipple in some raw sienna too to give it a soil-like texture. Let the paint dry.

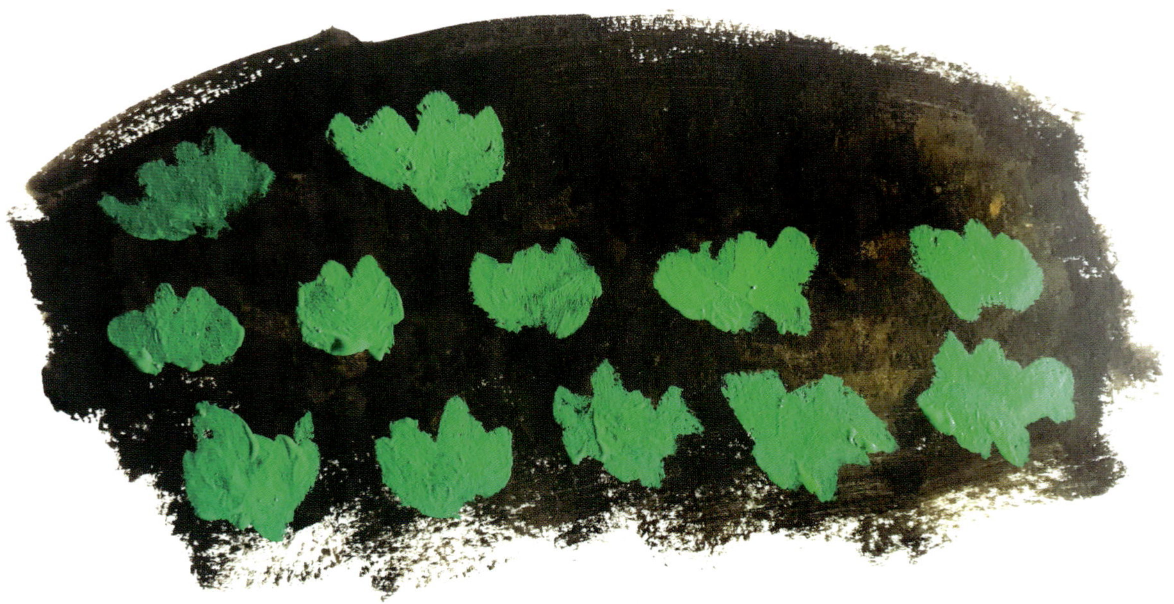

Step 2

Using wet cadmium green or any other medium green, create leafy little plants with your round brush.

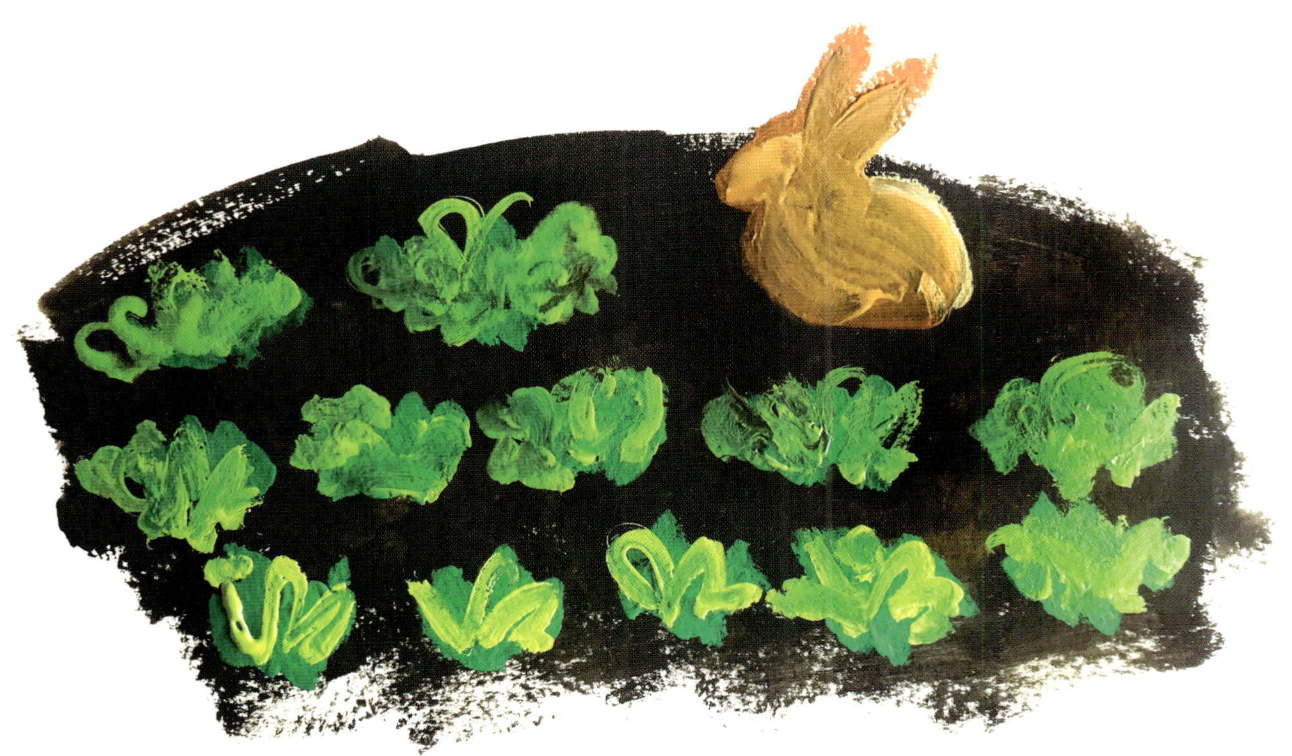

Step 3

Using a round brush and raw sienna mixed with a touch of white, form the basic shape of a bunny.

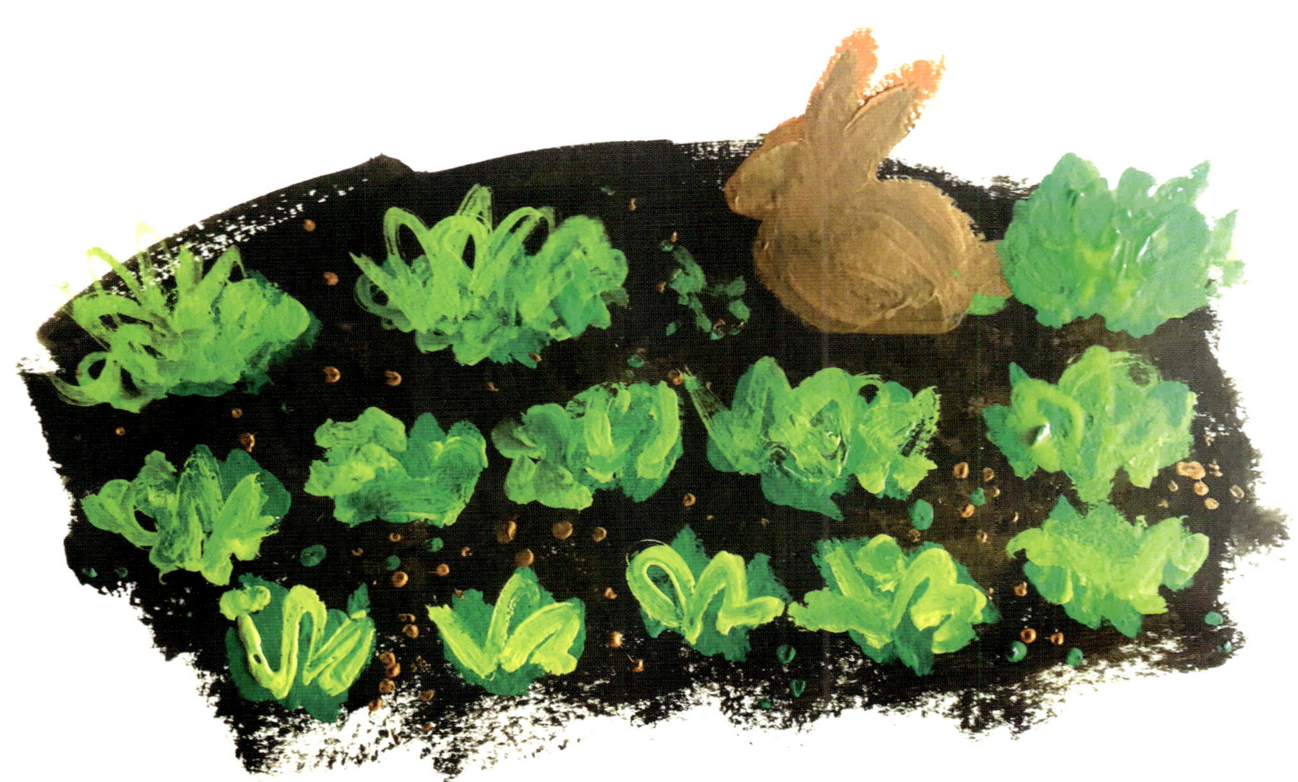

Step 4

Go over the plants with a lighter hue of green for contrast and that leafy-lettuce look. You can also use the tip of your brush to tap into the browns and greens to create the appearance of tiny budding plants.

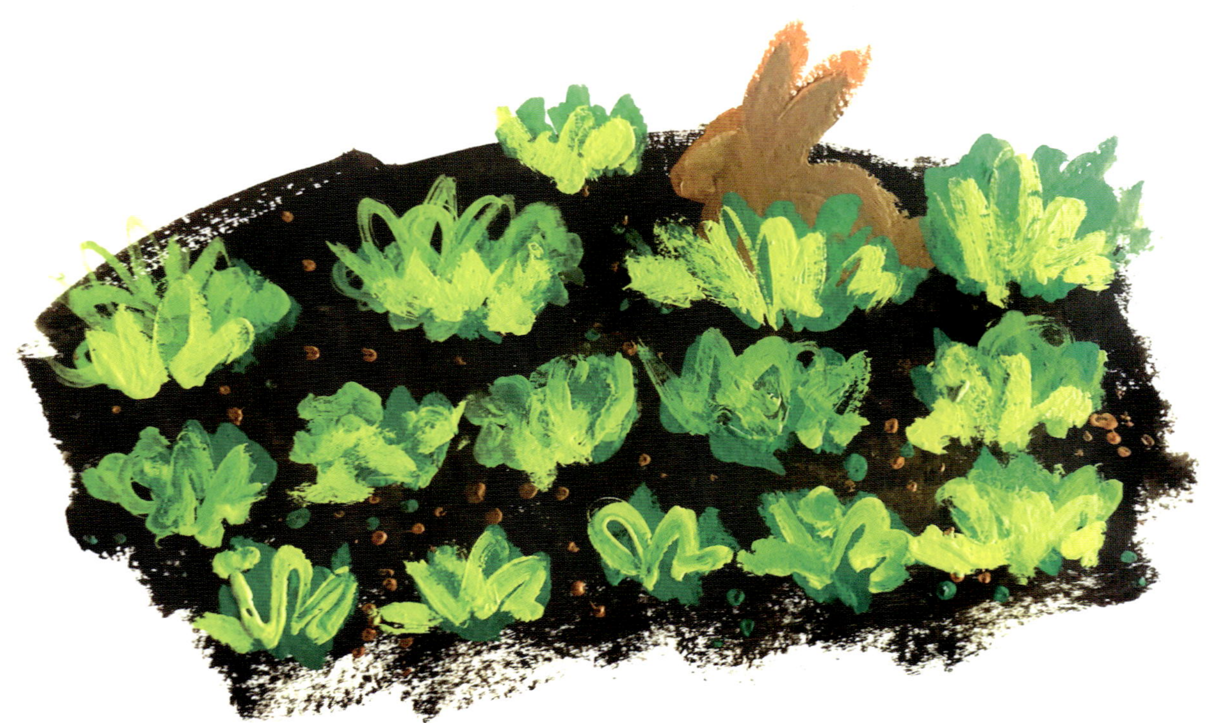

Step 5

Once the last step is dry, add a lettuce plant in front of the little bunny, as well as any other clusters where there may be empty space.

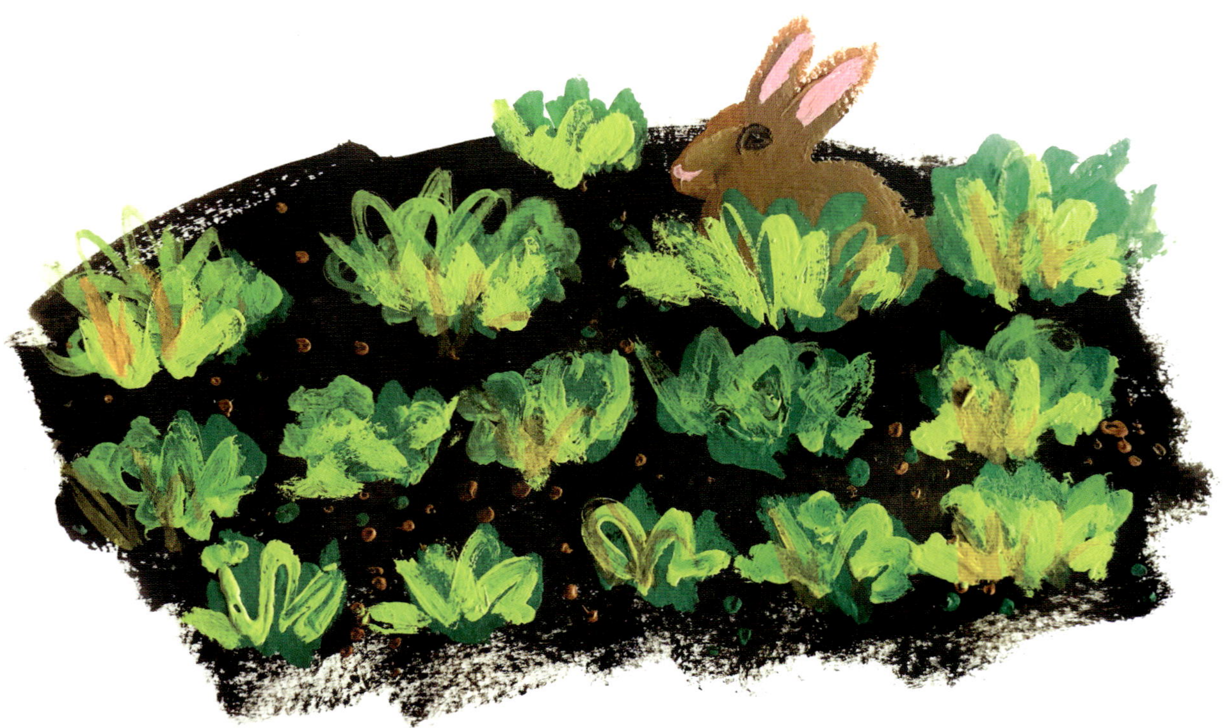

Step 6

Lastly, give the bunny some pink ear details and a tiny nose. Using the liner brush, create a small, almond-shaped eye. Add any other details as needed. I've lightly added a bit of raw sienna over the lettuce clusters.

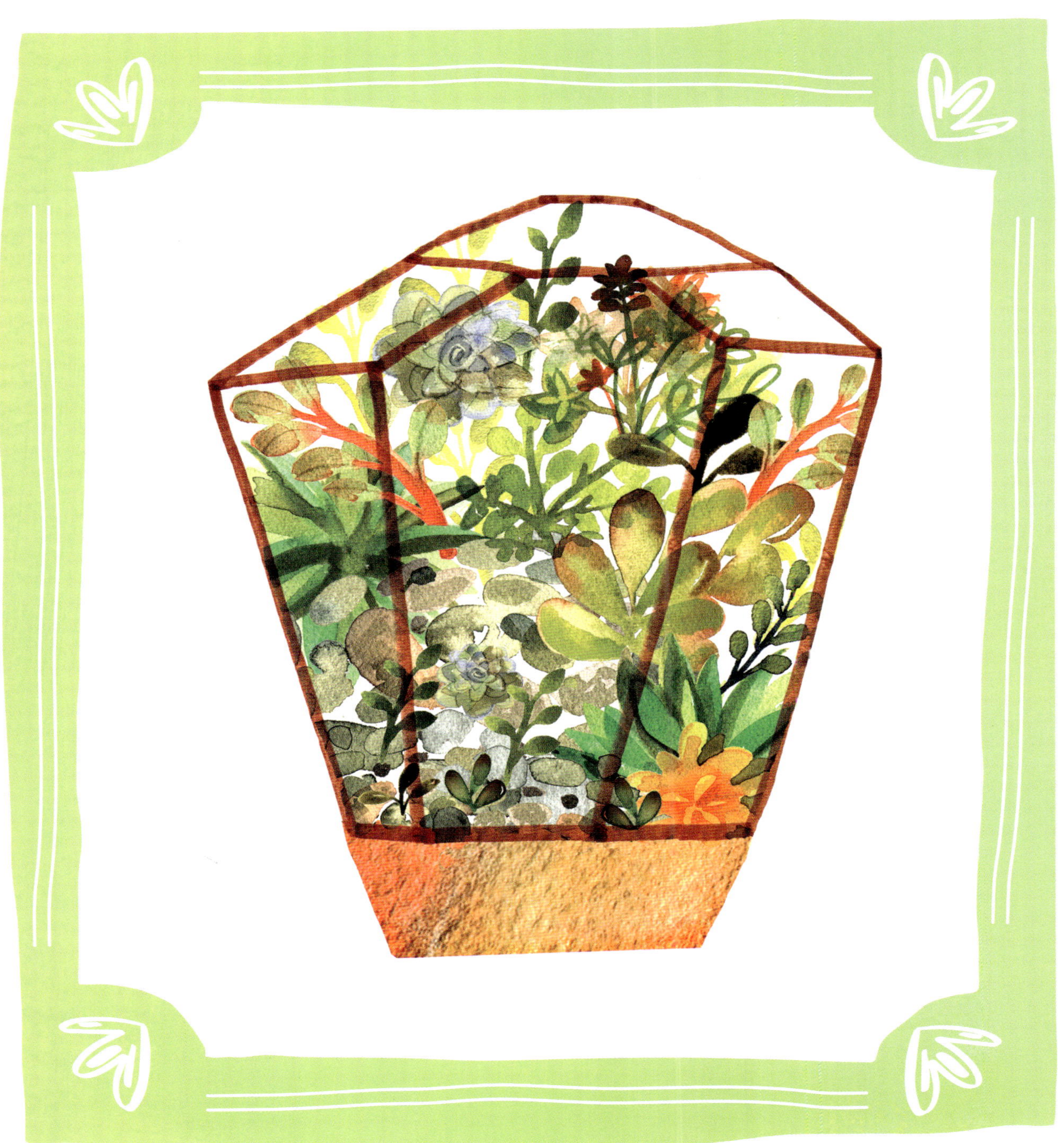

TRY THIS!

Terrariums are lots of fun to paint. Start by using masking tape to mask off a geometric shape, and then paint a variety of succulents inside. Let them dry; then remove the tape to paint the basic lines of the copper-fused glass and base. Now place in a sunny spot!

ADIRONDACK CHAIR

Sit back and put your feet in the grass...after painting this delightful-looking Adirondack chair using gouache.

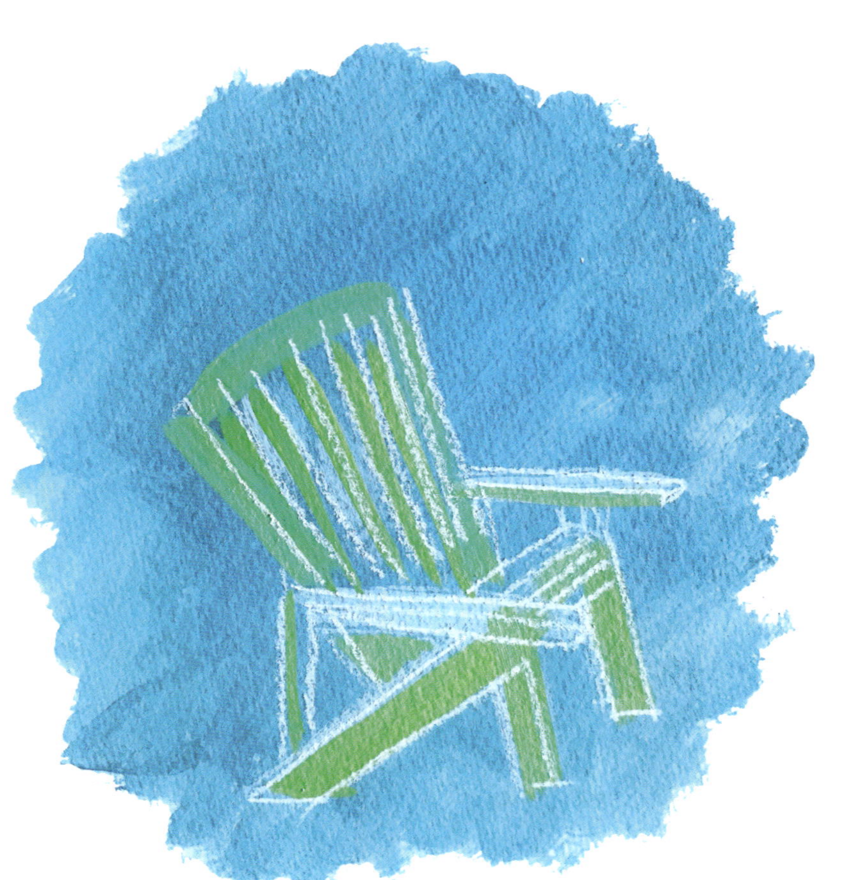

Step 1

Start by creating an irregular background using a large, angled brush. Let the paint dry. Then, with a white charcoal pencil, draw the basic shape of the chair until it looks about right. It's a complicated chair, but we're not aiming for perfection here—a more stylized version is great. Mix up some medium-green paint and thin it down with water. Begin filling in some of the drawn areas.

Step 2

Mix a warmer green and go over the already-green areas with thicker paint. Let the paint dry; then take a green pencil and draw in some grass at the base of the chair.

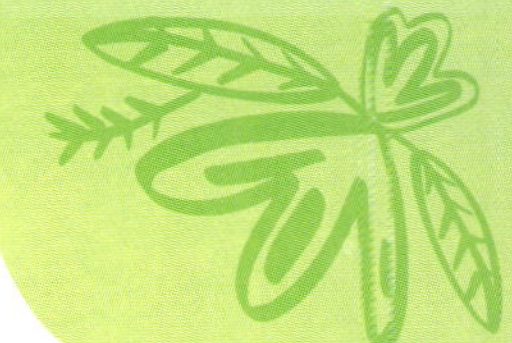

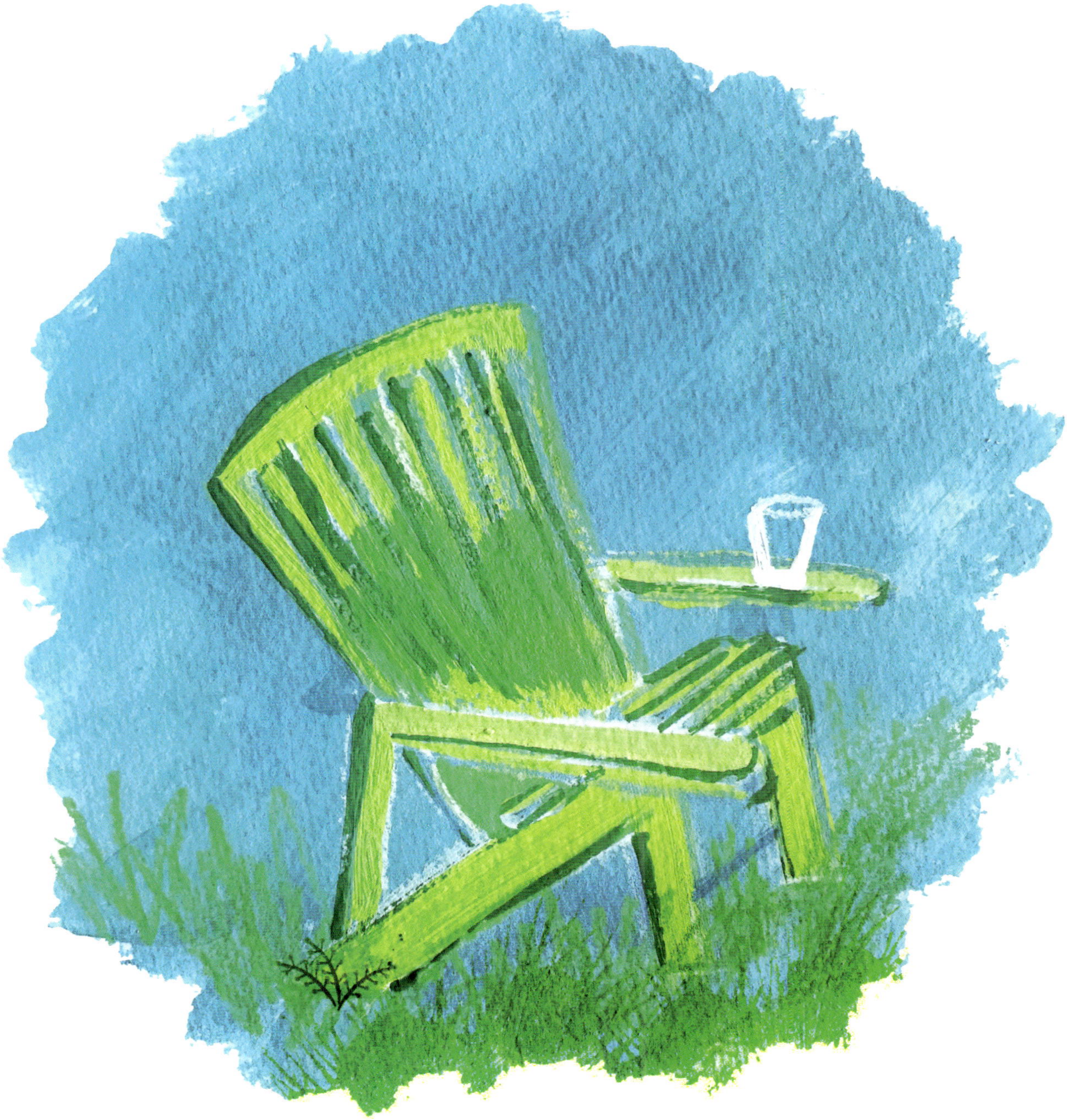

Step 3

Using dark green and a liner brush, add details in the areas where the light isn't hitting the chair. A lot of this is a back-and-forth process, so play with the different hues of green until the chair appears more dimensional. Add more detail to the grass, a glass on the left arm, and any other touches you'd like.

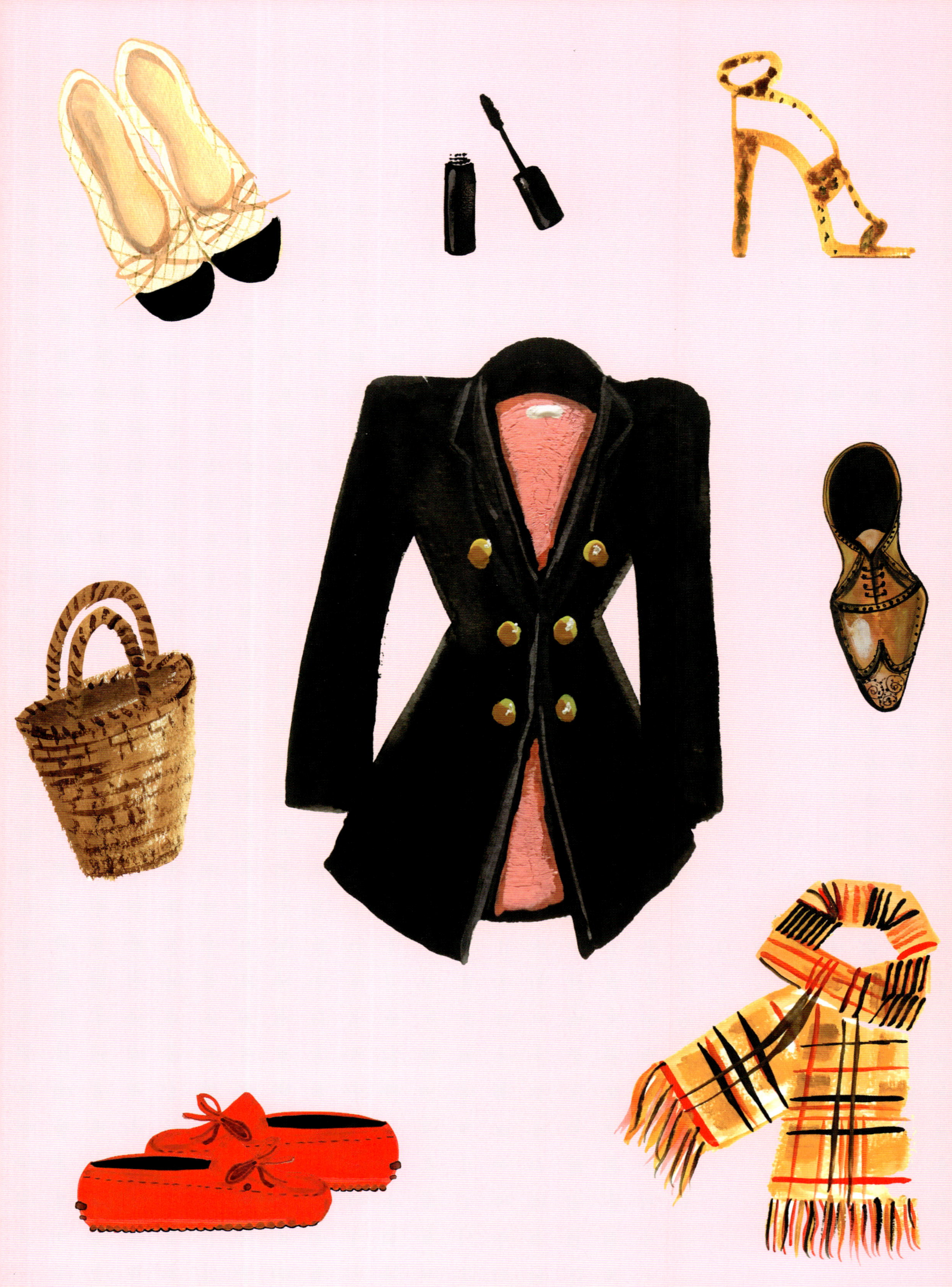

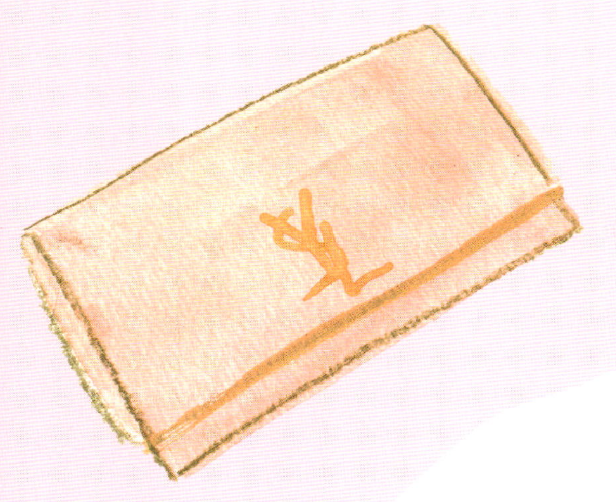

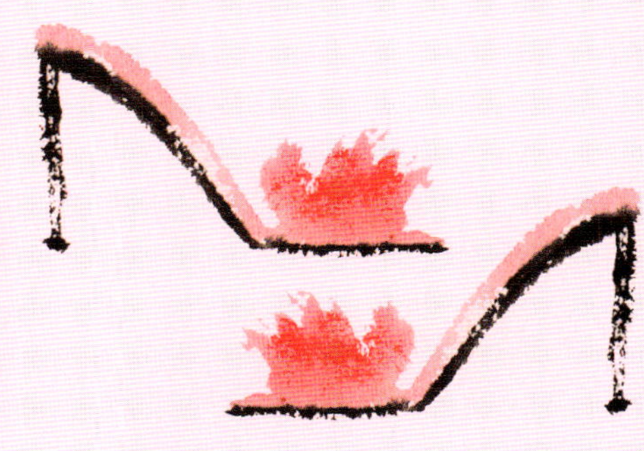

FASHION-FORWARD

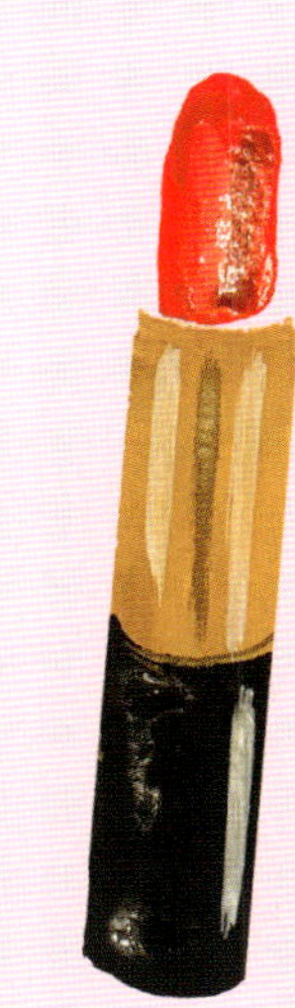

Who doesn't appreciate great style? In this section, inspiration is as close as your own closet! We will cover shoes, handbags, classic blazers, accessories, and more, but as always, feel free to branch out and use some of your own staples as subject matter here. Not inspired? Go out and grab the latest issue of your favorite fashion magazine and take a crack at some of the trendiest pieces on the runway.

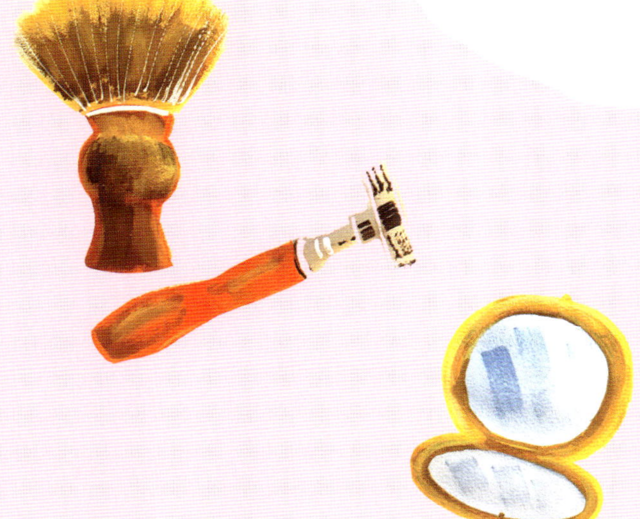

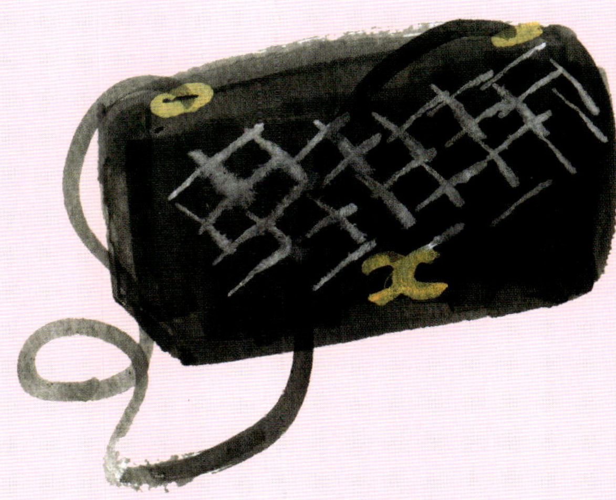

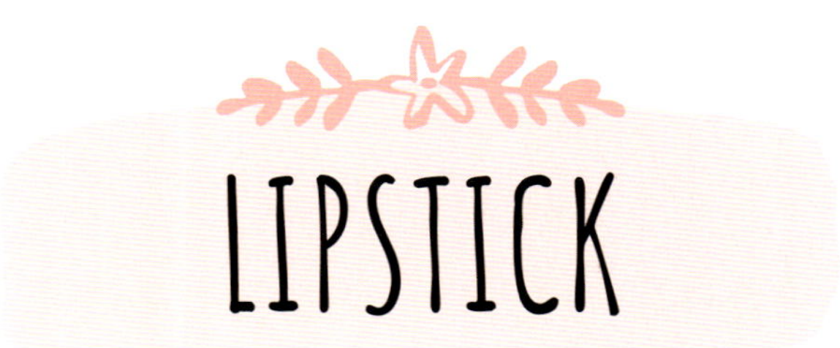

LIPSTICK

I've used gouache to illustrate this simple tube of lipstick. Any colors could be used here—maybe you prefer a darker shade of lipstick with a pastel-colored tube?

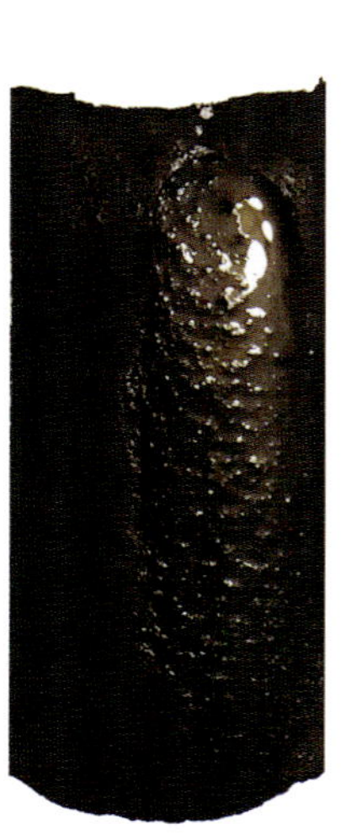

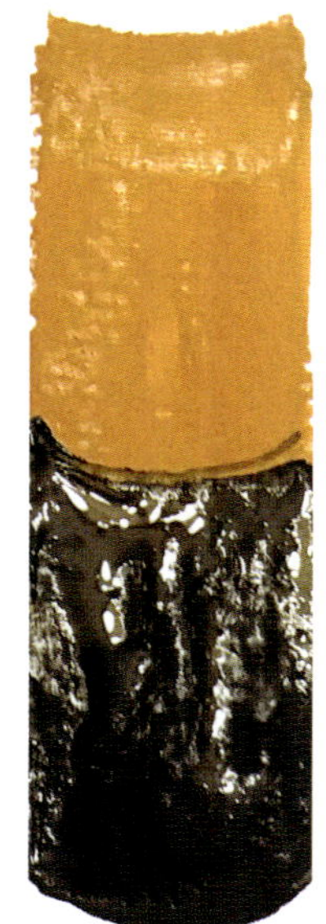

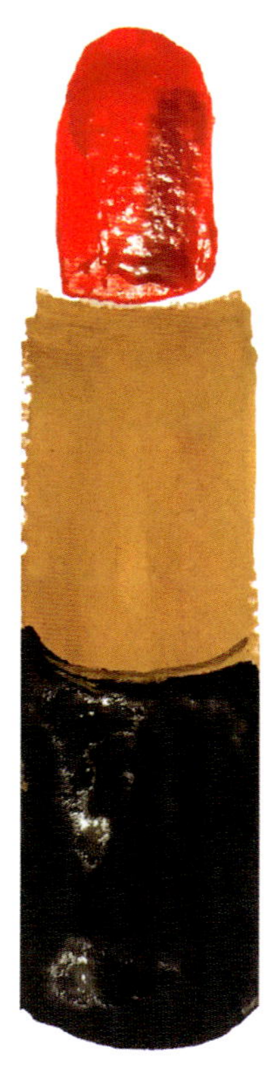

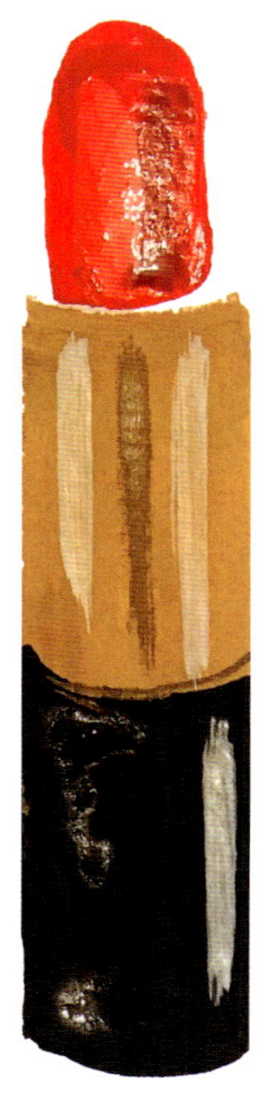

Step 1

Using an angled brush and black gouache, create a cylinder shape by dragging the brush straight down and then using its tip to curve the top and bottom. Let the paint dry.

Step 2

With raw sienna, create another cylinder on top of the black one.

Step 3

With red paint or any lipstick hue you like, create a small, domed cylinder shape above the others. I've used the drybrushing technique here to show a bit of a reflection on the paper.

Step 4

For the final step, mix white with raw sienna and use a liner brush to create two highlights on the metal part of the tube. Then mix white with black to create a highlight on the plastic bottom. Add a darker lowlight to the metal cylinder by mixing a tiny bit of black with raw sienna.

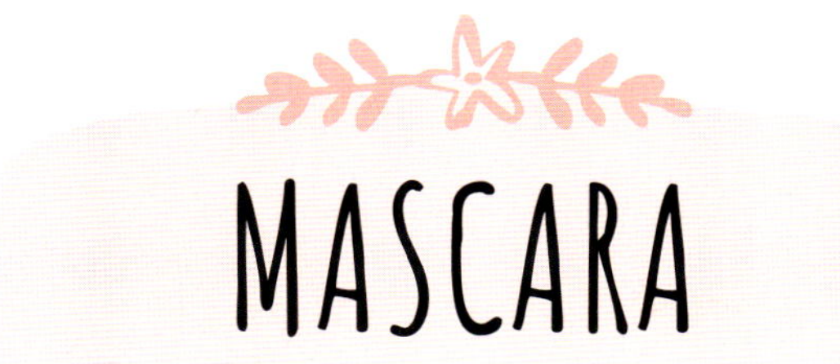

MASCARA

This super-easy project uses just black gouache and an angled brush.

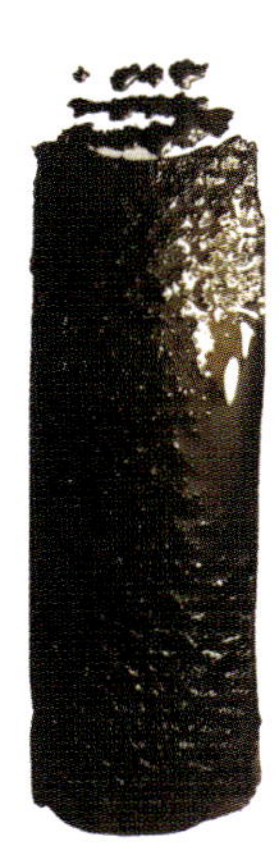

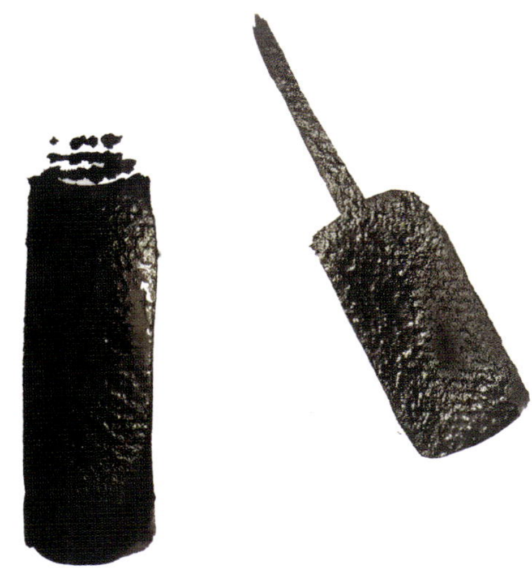

Step 1

Following the same technique as with the lipstick, use an angled brush to form a cylinder. With the tip of the angled brush, tap three curved lines at the top of the tube base to form the threaded area for the cap.

Step 2

Form the cap at an angle; then add a thin line with the tip of the brush to form the base of the mascara wand.

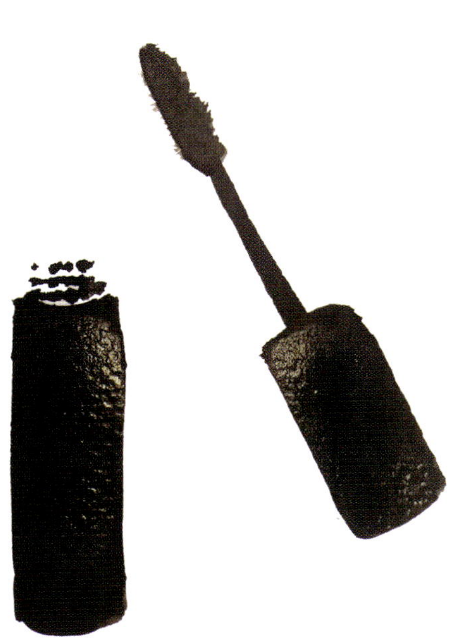

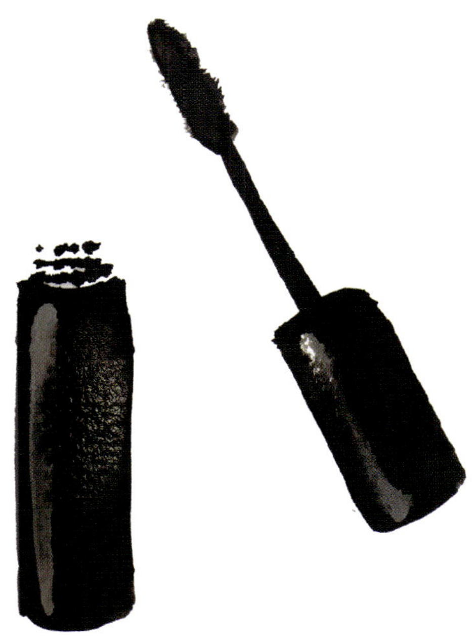

Step 3

Use the tip of the brush to form a conical shape and create the mascara applicator. Using the drybrushing technique, fly the brush slightly outward from the applicator to create the impression of fine bristles.

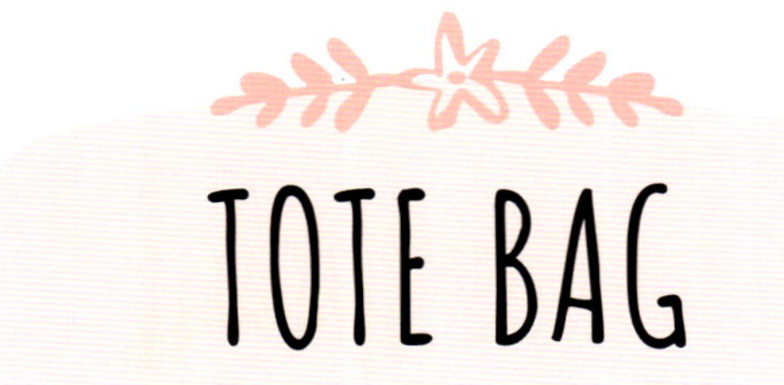

TOTE BAG

Follow the instructions to paint the tote bag seen here, and then try your hand at a variety of them, as shown on page 113.

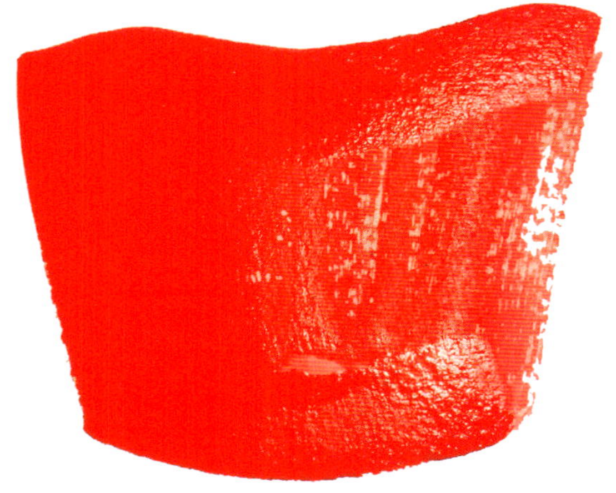

Step 1

Form a bucket shape with an angled brush and red paint, curving the bottom edge a bit and adding two small hills with a dip between them.

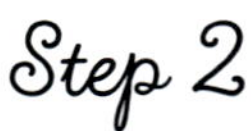

Step 2

Mix a bit of white with the red and using a small flat brush, create two straps that run down to the bottom of the bag.

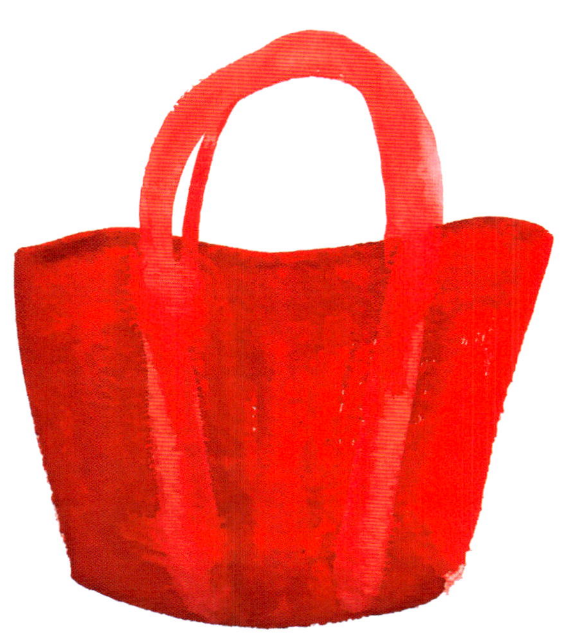

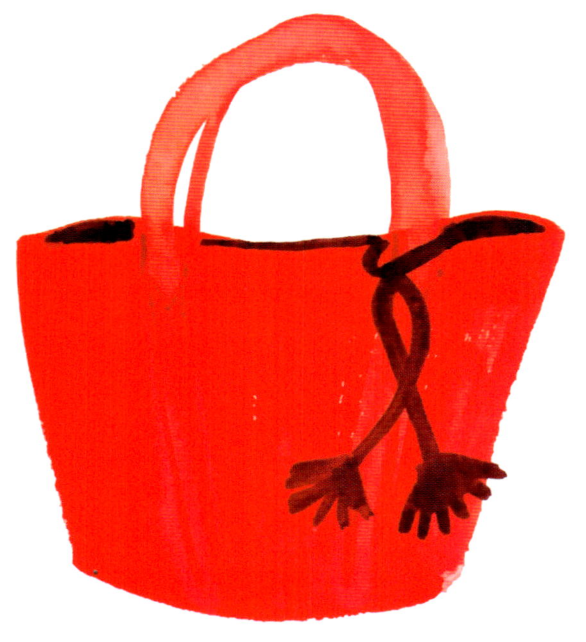

Step 3

Mix black into the red and use a liner brush to darken two small areas at the top to indicate the inside of the tote. Follow the curves of the top of the bag to guide the shape. Then add a simple leather cord around one of the straps, letting it twist a bit. Finish with a tassel by adding simple lines at the end of the cord. You can also add white highlights to the straps if you wish.

Nine Different Ways

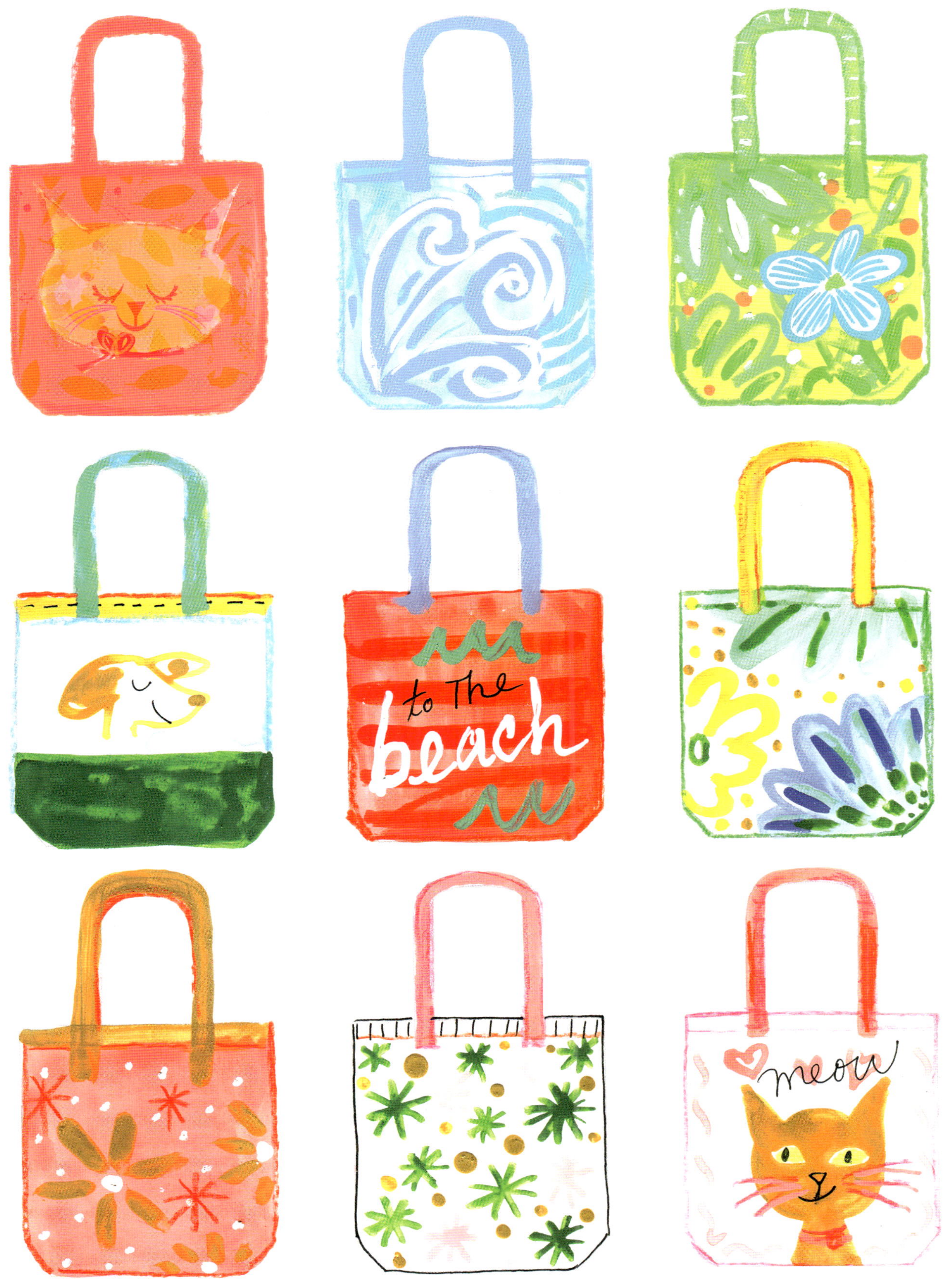

PERFUME BOTTLES

This project is a wild card! We'll use cut paper, gouache, and ink to create unique textures and shapes. Be prepared to go back-and-forth with the steps a bit until you arrive at a look that satisfies your vision.

Step 1

Start by painting a background using any two colors you like. I've created an ombré effect by blending the two colors from top to bottom. Let the paint dry.

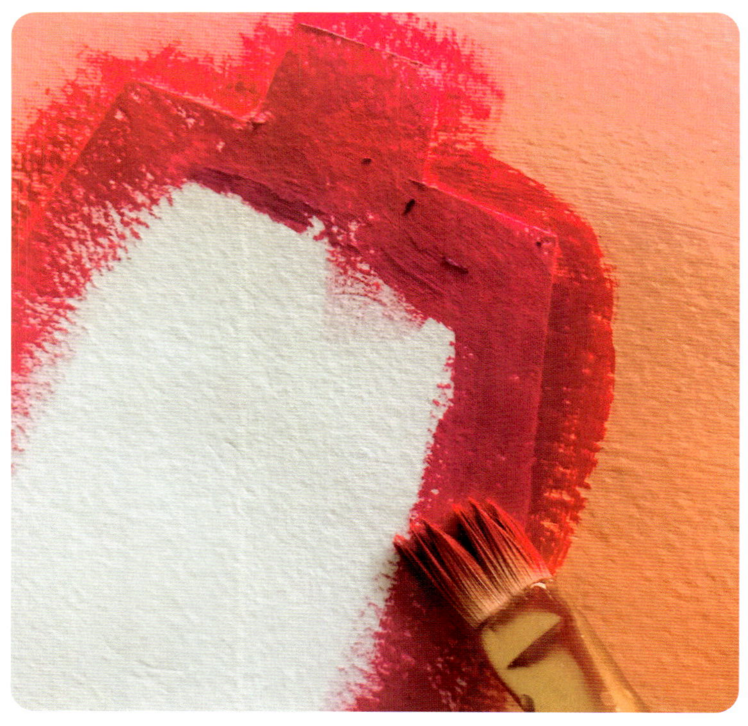

Step 2

Cut simple shapes from card stock. Snip the corners to create the facets of the bottle and curve the tops of any ovals you make to narrow the necks of the bottles. Holding down the card stock, grab a stiff brush and a contrasting color in a similar hue to blot along the edges. When you lift the card stock, you will have an irregular bottle shape.

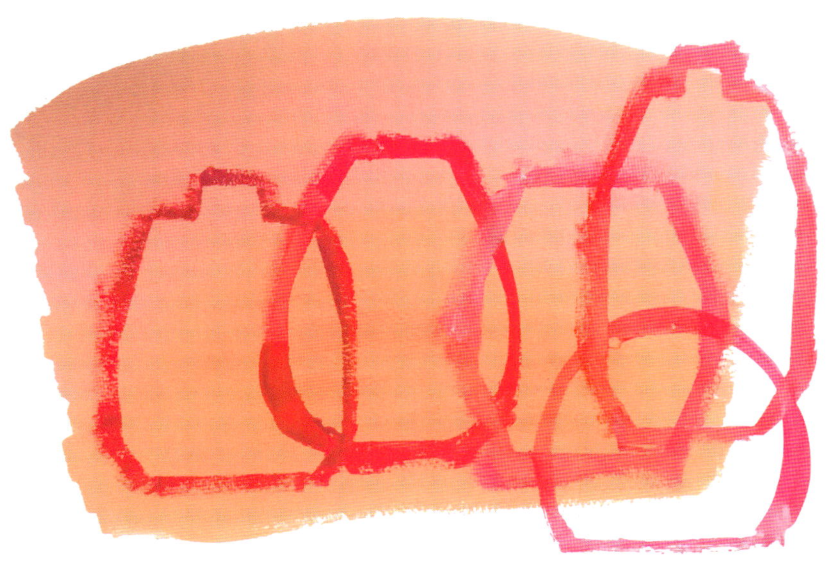

Step 3

Repeat step 2, placing the card stock shapes in different areas and making sure to overlap some shapes and even break out of the background if you wish.

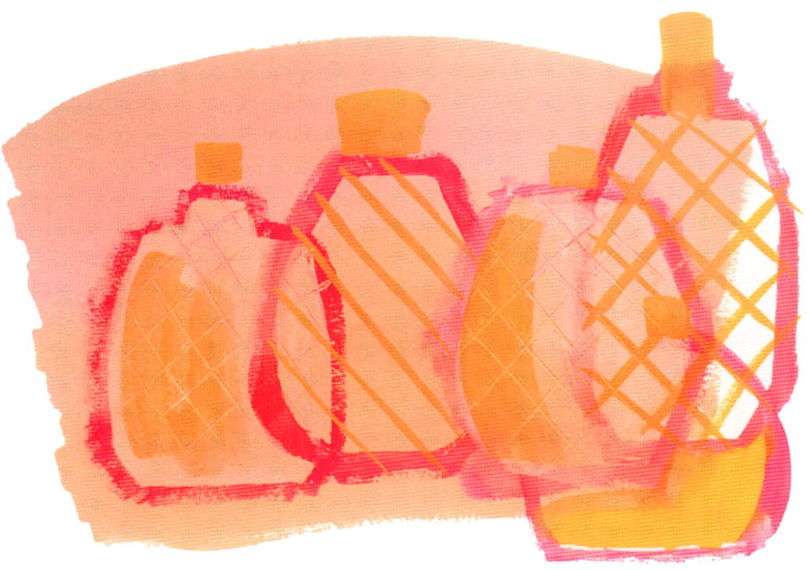

Step 4

Use a warm hue, such as gold, and a round brush to make a crosshatching pattern over some of the bottles to emulate cut glass. Also use this hue to add caps and labels and to fill in some areas of the bottles.

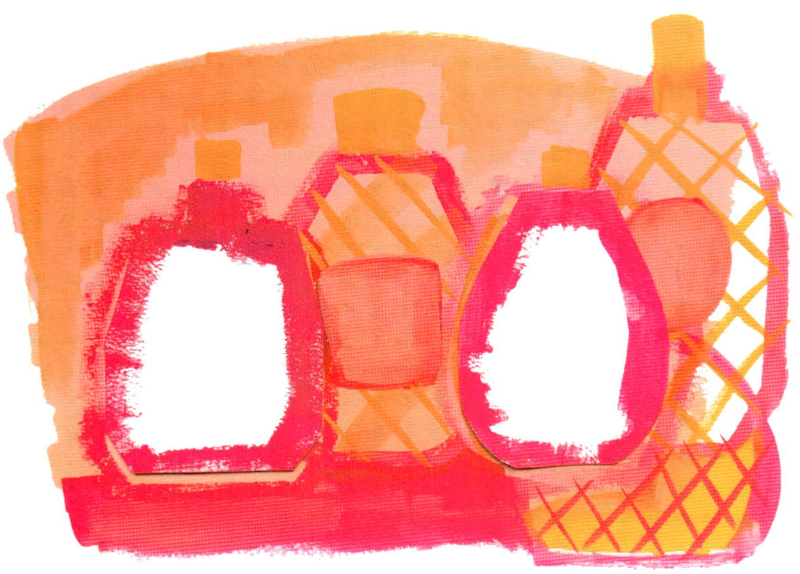

Step 5

If you want the bottles to "pop" more, this can be achieved a few ways. I've added a darker hue to the base of the bottles, and also glued some of the card stock bottle templates over the painting to lend a pop of white. You could also cut letters out of magazines to glue down and form labels, ransom-note style. The key is to experiment and have fun!

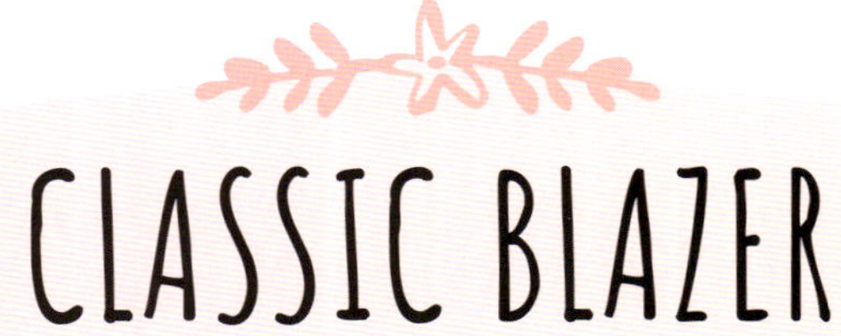

CLASSIC BLAZER

Use gouache to paint this stylish blazer with a surprising twist.

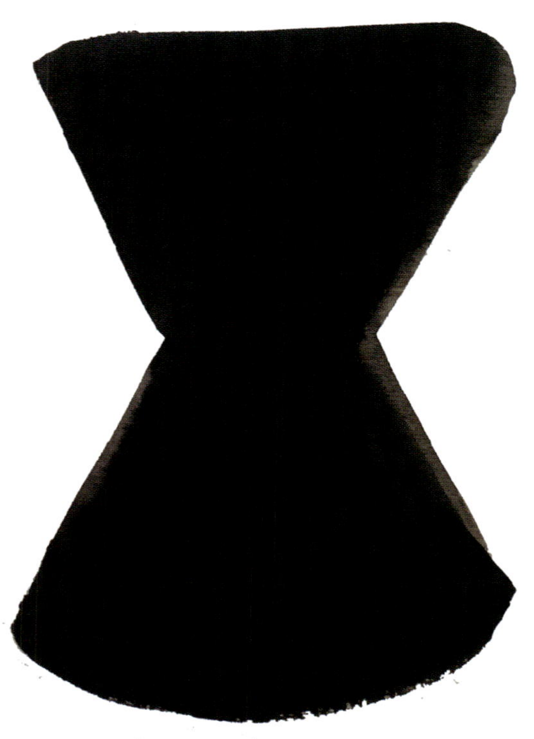

Step 1

Map out the basic shape of the blazer by creating an hourglass silhouette, using black paint and an angled brush.

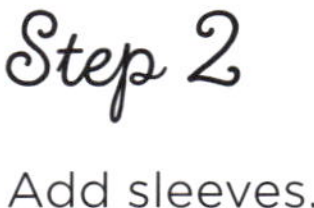

Step 2

Add sleeves.

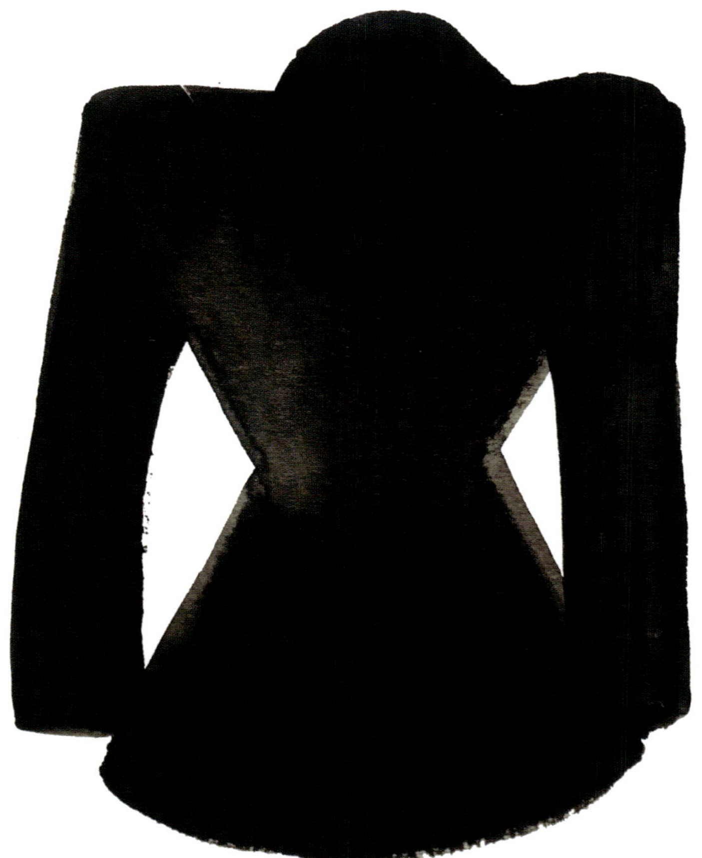

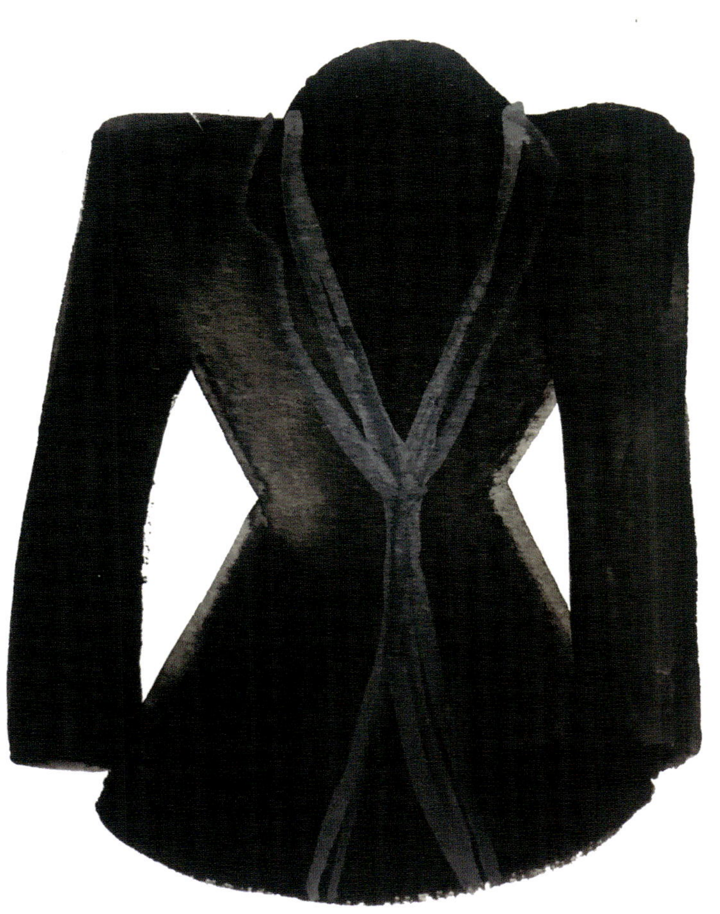

Step 3

While the paint is wet, add subtle shading to form the lapels and flaps of the blazer.

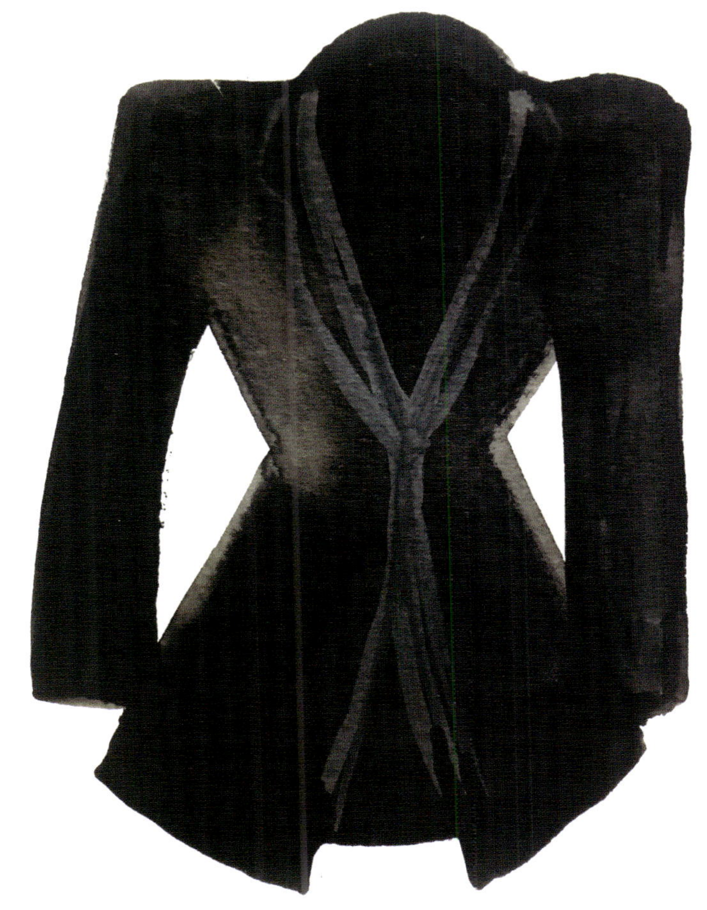

Step 4

Use more black paint to extend the flaps downward into two pointed ends.

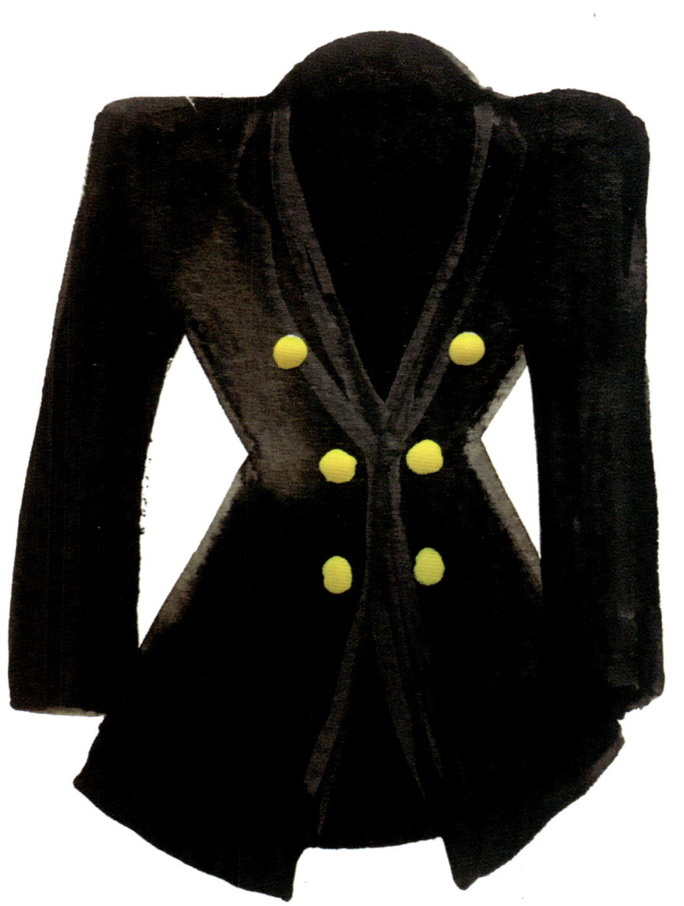

Step 5

With a small round brush and yellow paint, create six gold-toned buttons.

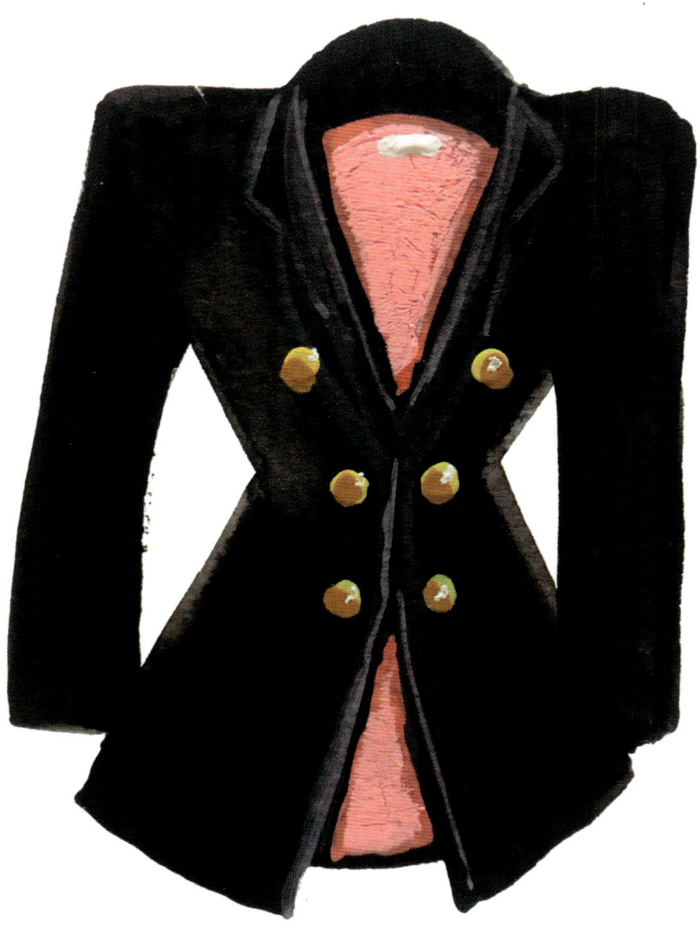

Step 6

Give the lining a pop of color by mixing up your favorite hue. Also, add white highlights to the buttons for additional shine. For an extra detail, use a liner brush to create a small label inside the jacket.

Nine Different Ways

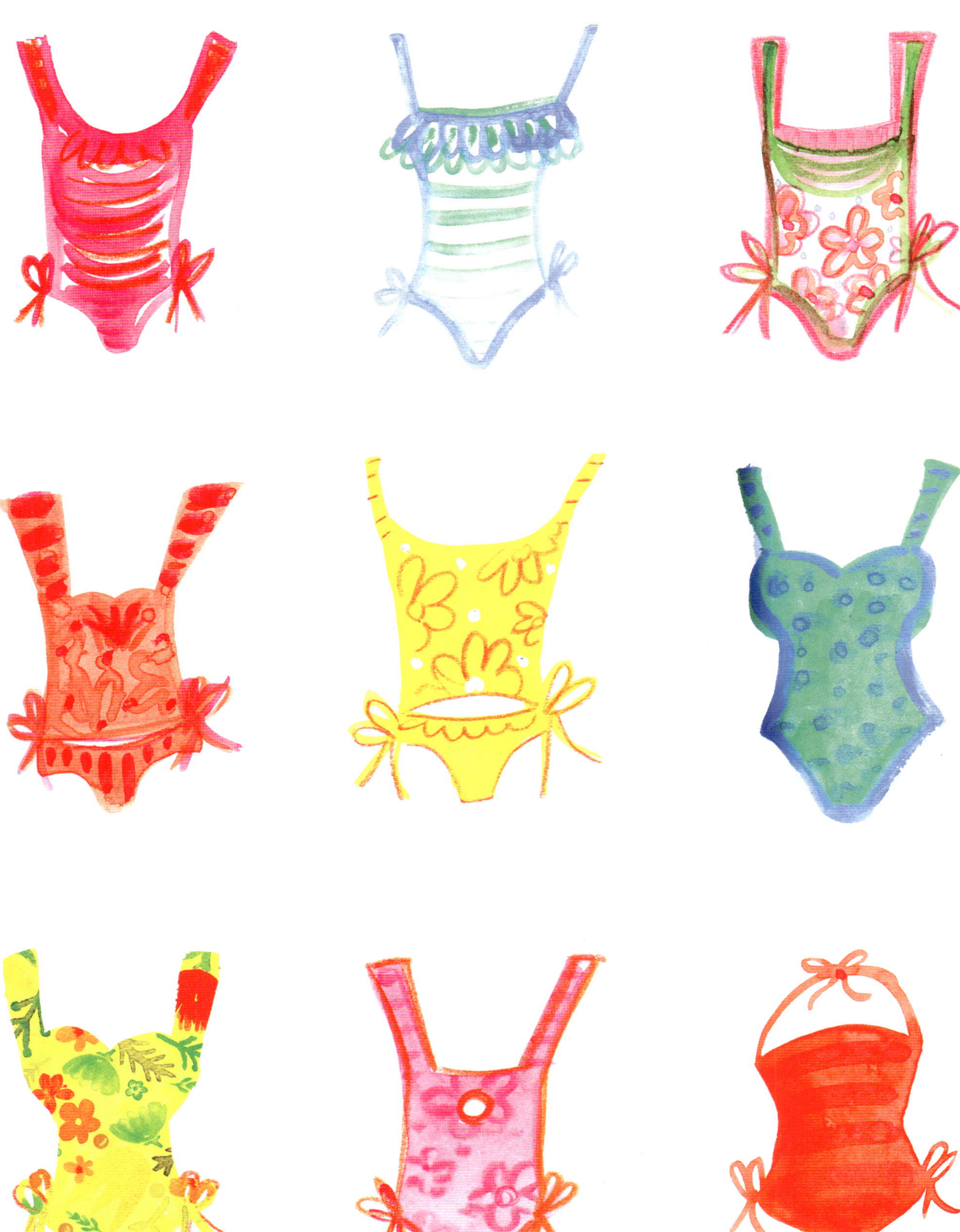

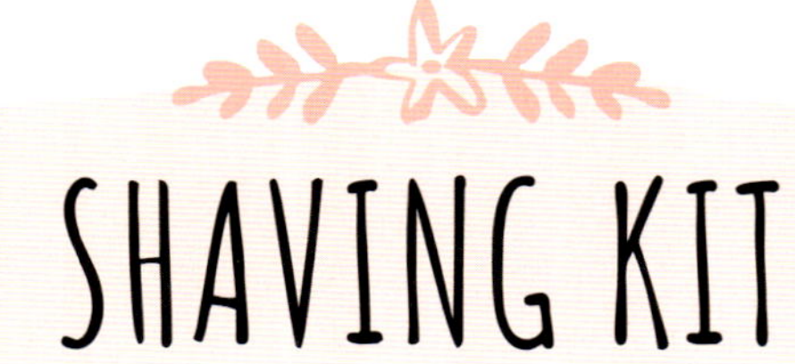

SHAVING KIT

Here I've used gouache to create a razor and a shaving brush. Don't forget the shaving cream!

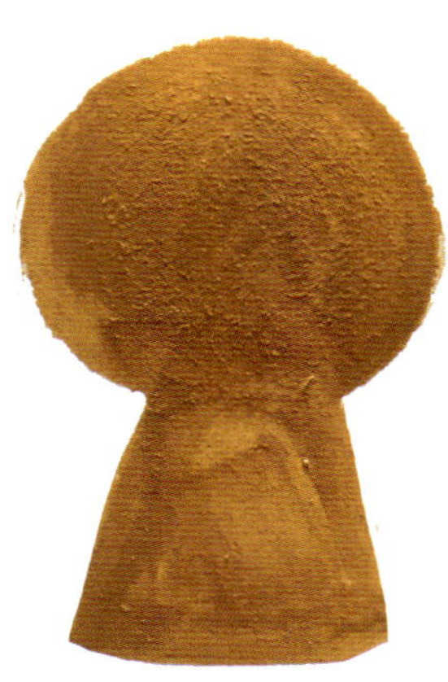

Step 1

Use raw sienna paint to form a circle atop a triangle to begin the base of the shaving brush.

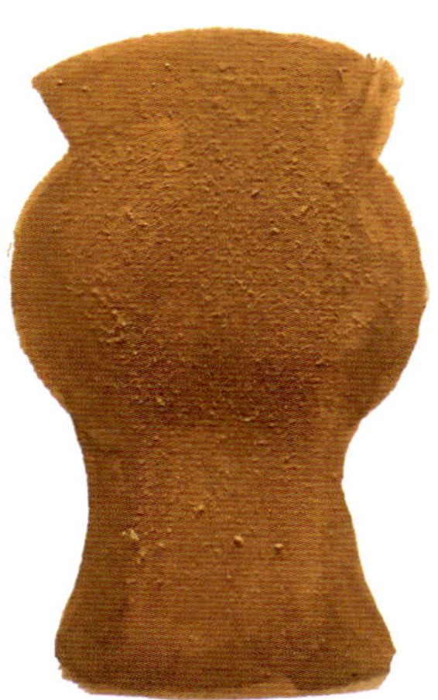

Step 2

Connect the two shapes by curving the sides, and add a dome at the top.

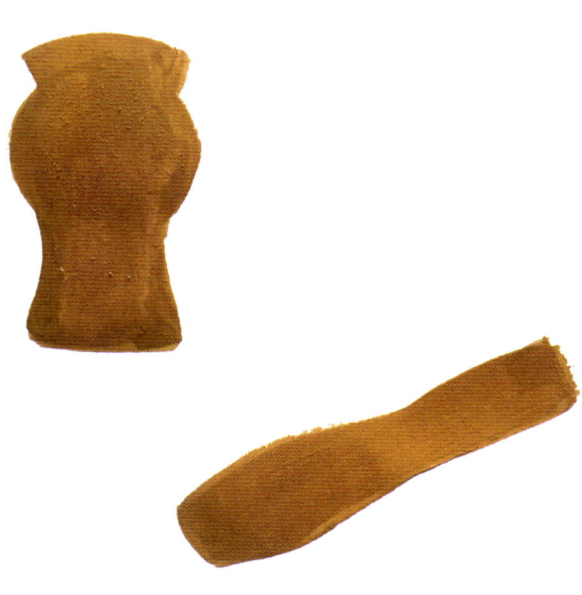

Step 3

Begin the shape of the razor using the same raw sienna and creating an oval morphing into a rectangle. Round each of these out.

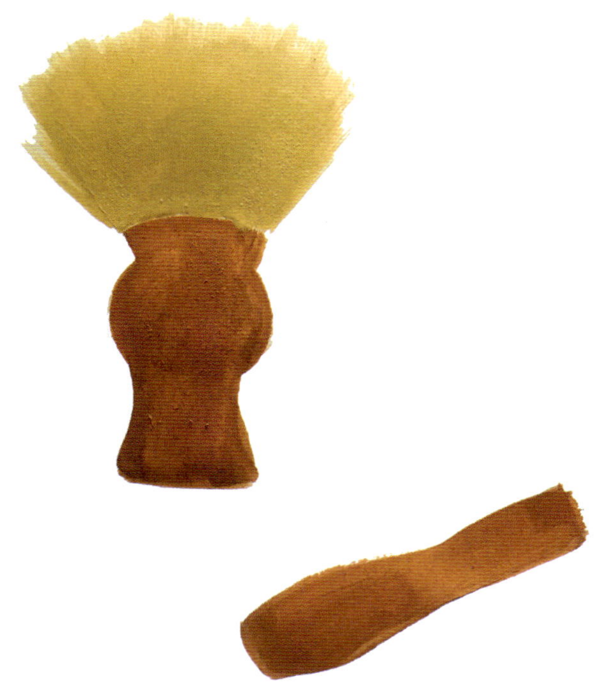

Step 4

Mix up yellow and white to form the base color of the brush. Fan this out using an angled brush and the drybrushing technique. Let the paint dry.

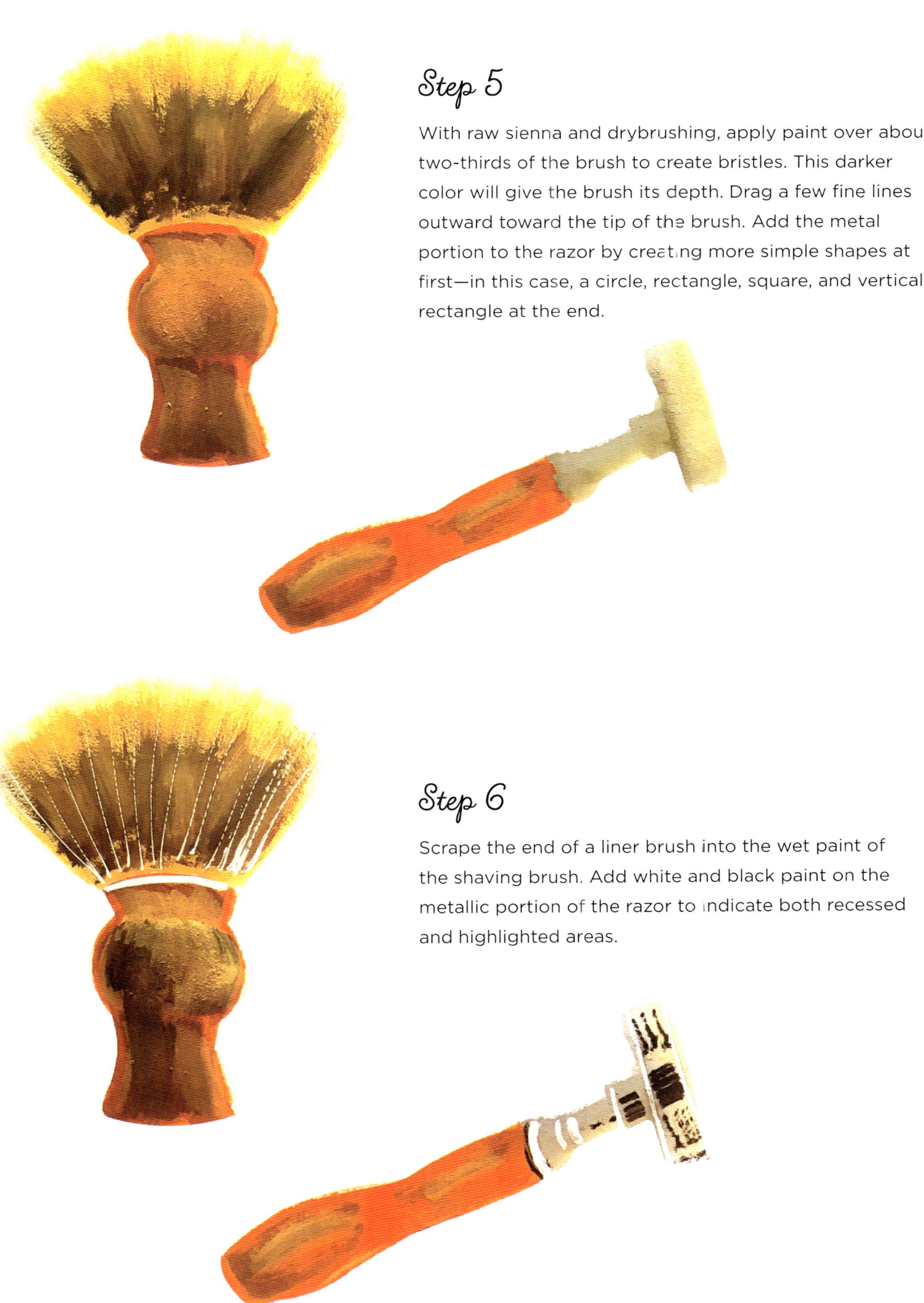

Step 5

With raw sienna and drybrushing, apply paint over about two-thirds of the brush to create bristles. This darker color will give the brush its depth. Drag a few fine lines outward toward the tip of the brush. Add the metal portion to the razor by creating more simple shapes at first—in this case, a circle, rectangle, square, and vertical rectangle at the end.

Step 6

Scrape the end of a liner brush into the wet paint of the shaving brush. Add white and black paint on the metallic portion of the razor to indicate both recessed and highlighted areas.

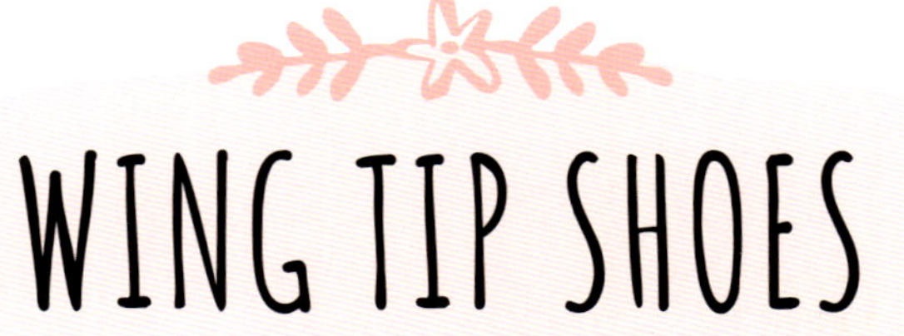

WING TIP SHOES

For more shoe inspiration, see page 125! I've painted these wing tips with gouache.

Step 1

Start by creating the basic shoe shape consisting of an oval over a rectangle over a triangle.

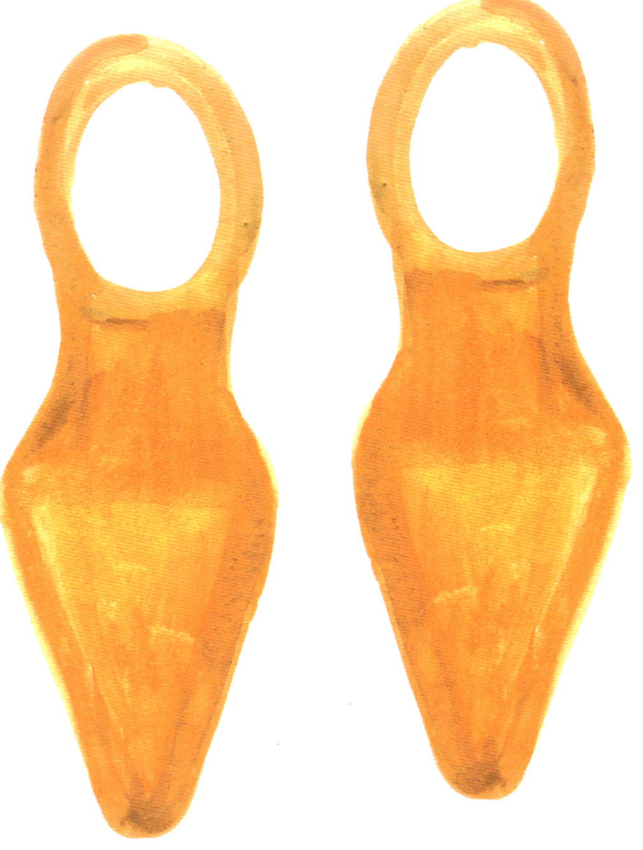

Step 2

Fill the rectangle and triangle with raw sienna.

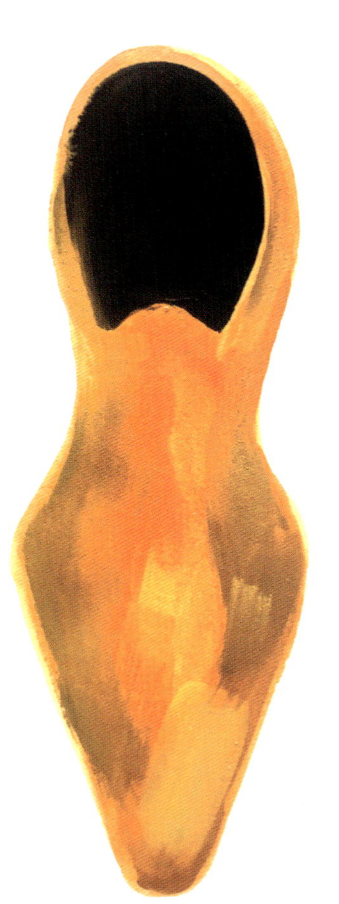

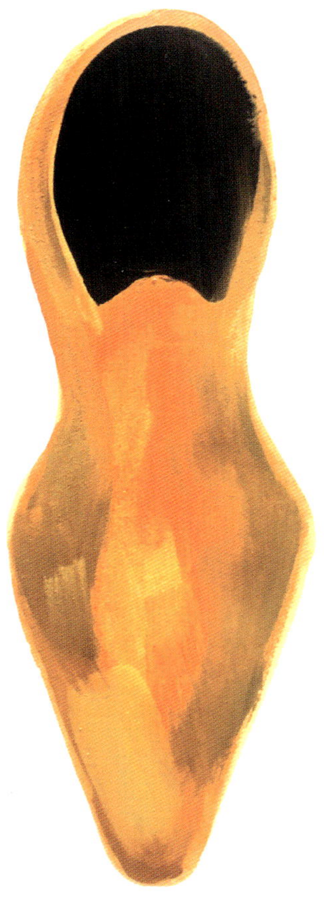

Step 3

Fill the heel with a darker mixture, such as black and brown. Add a touch of this mixture to the initial raw sienna hue and blend into the sides of the wing tip. Create a tongue for the shoe with raw sienna.

Step 4

Using the dark mixture and a liner brush, start drawing the outlines for the leather flaps, lace area, and stitched areas.

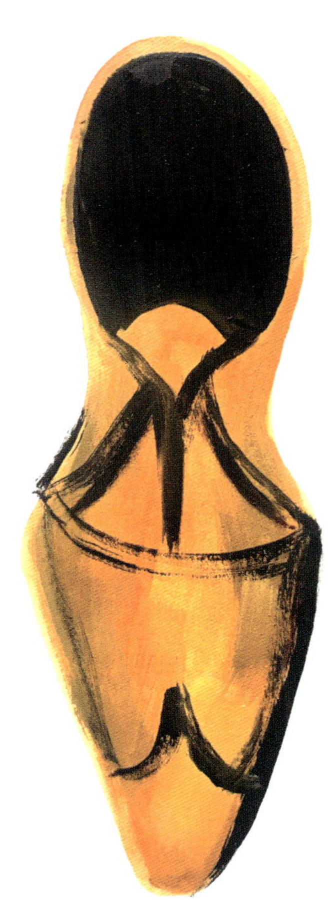

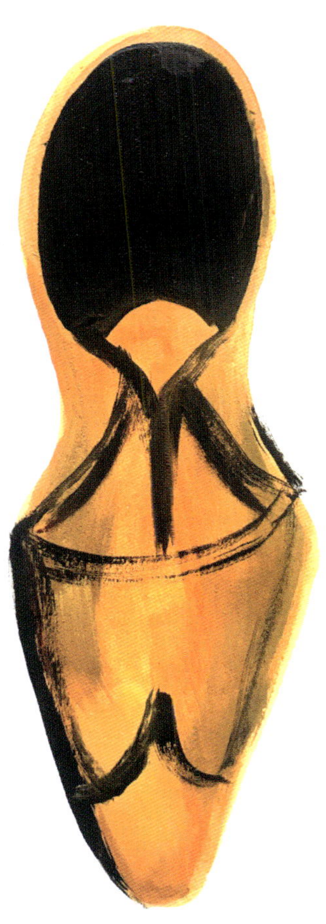

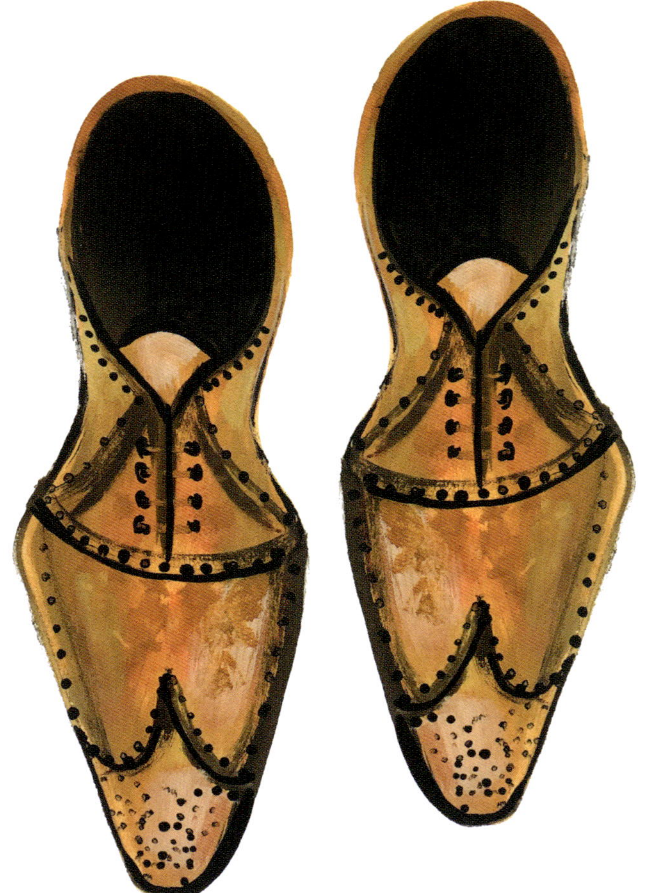

Step 5

Experiment with the base color of the shoe by alternating various hues of yellow and reddish-browns using the drybrushing technique with an angled brush. Take the liner brush and tap small dots around the flaps and stitched areas. Add these anywhere you want extra detail. The toe is a fun place to experiment; you can create swirls or other decorative patterns here.

Step 6

Paint straight lines to form the laces and connect to the dots. Add a highlight to the shoe with a quick swab of white mixed with a tiny bit of raw sienna.

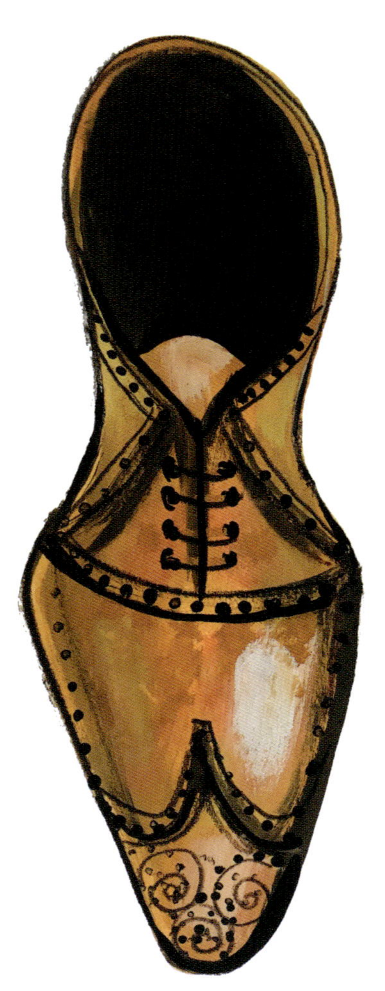

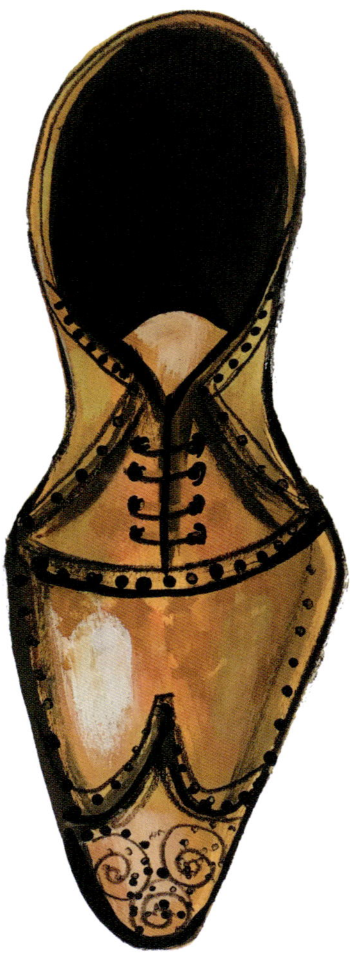

Nine Different Ways

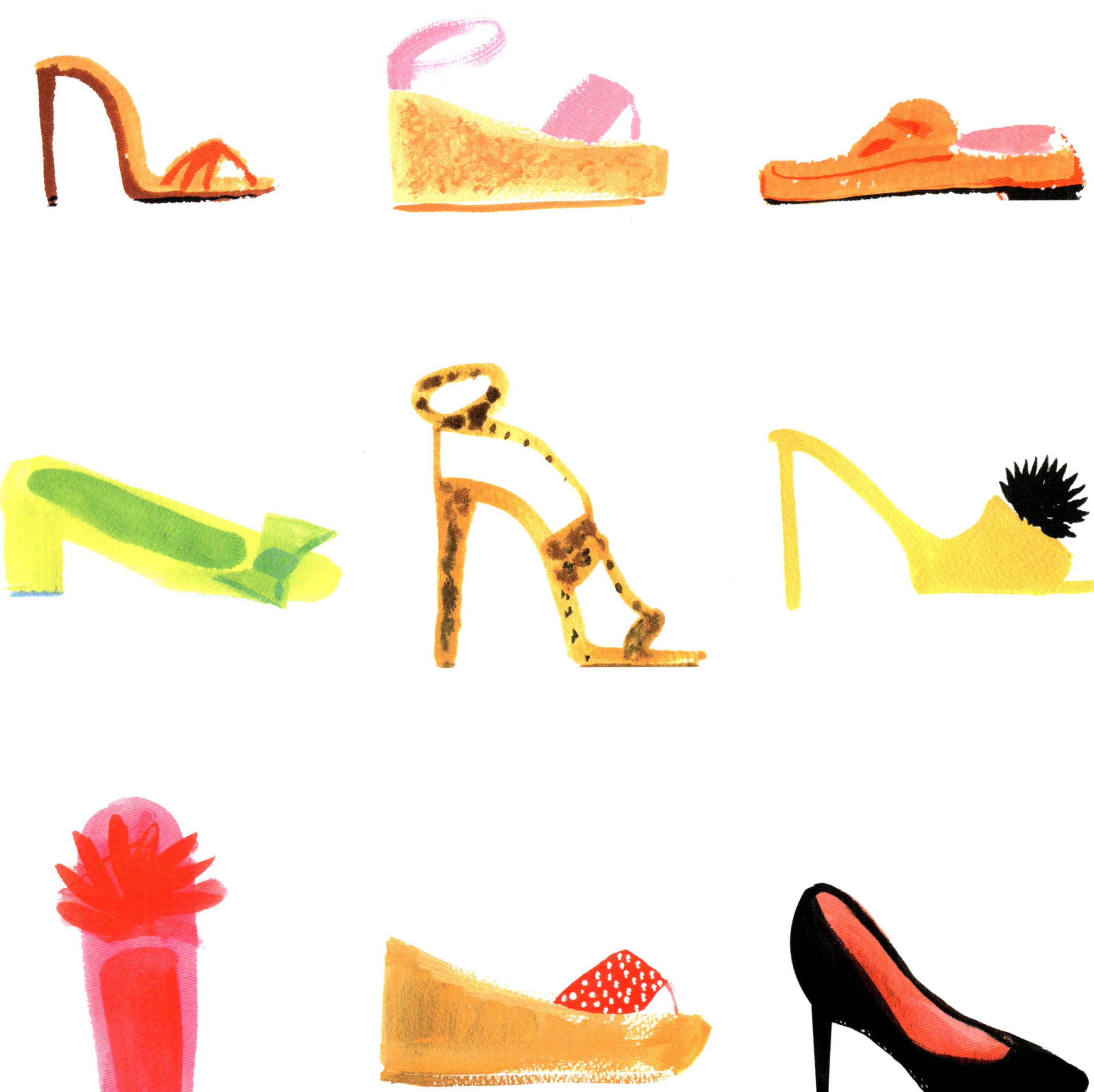

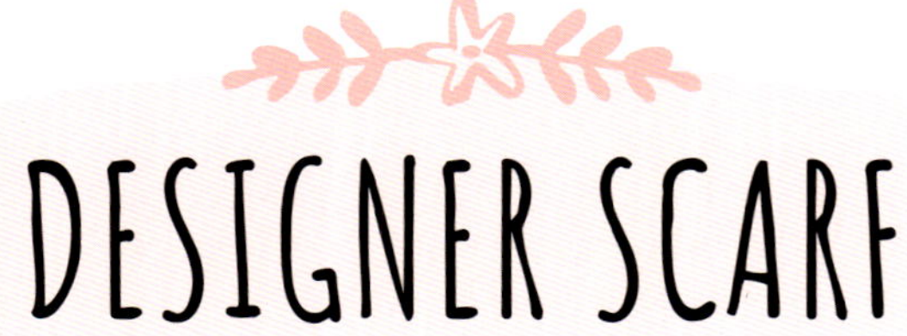

DESIGNER SCARF

This project uses just one angled brush to paint a scarf!

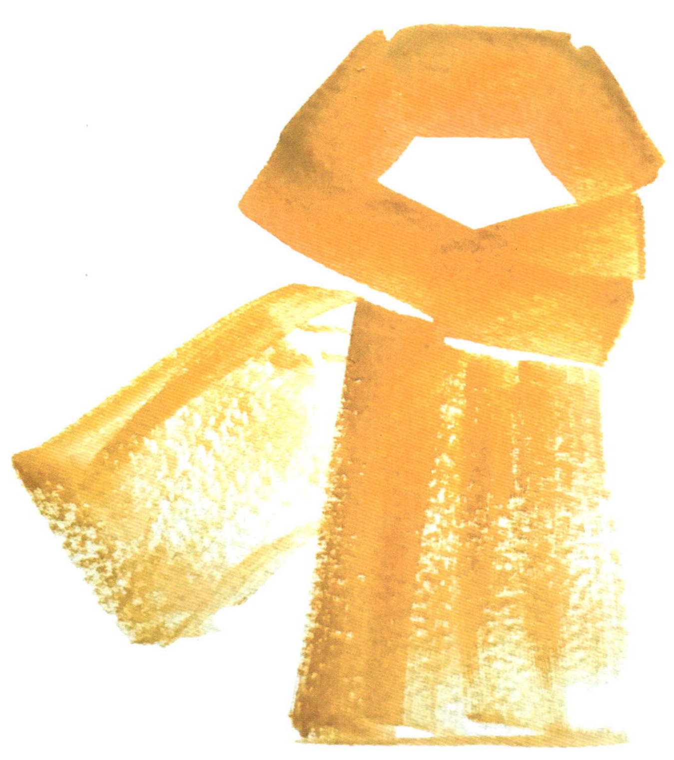

Step 1

Create a mix of raw sienna, yellow, and white to form the base color. Using an angled brush, make five quick strokes in a circular motion to form the neck of the scarf. Then drag the brush downward several times to form a slightly triangular shape for the portion that hangs down. With the brush nearly dry, form the piece that is folded behind by scraping right to left.

Step 2

Now go back into your paint and make short, deliberate brushstrokes along the neck, and down the tail and folded section on the side. This will begin to create the plaid motif. Let the paint dry.

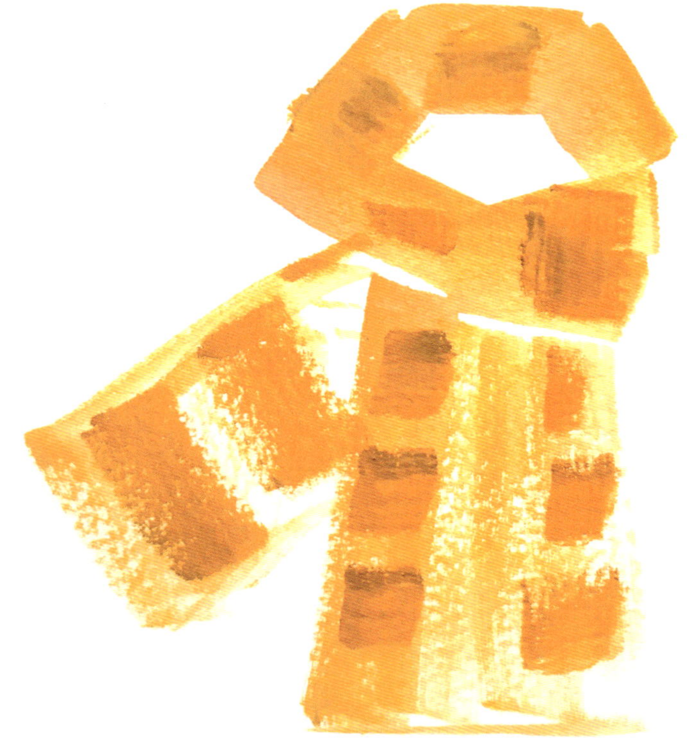

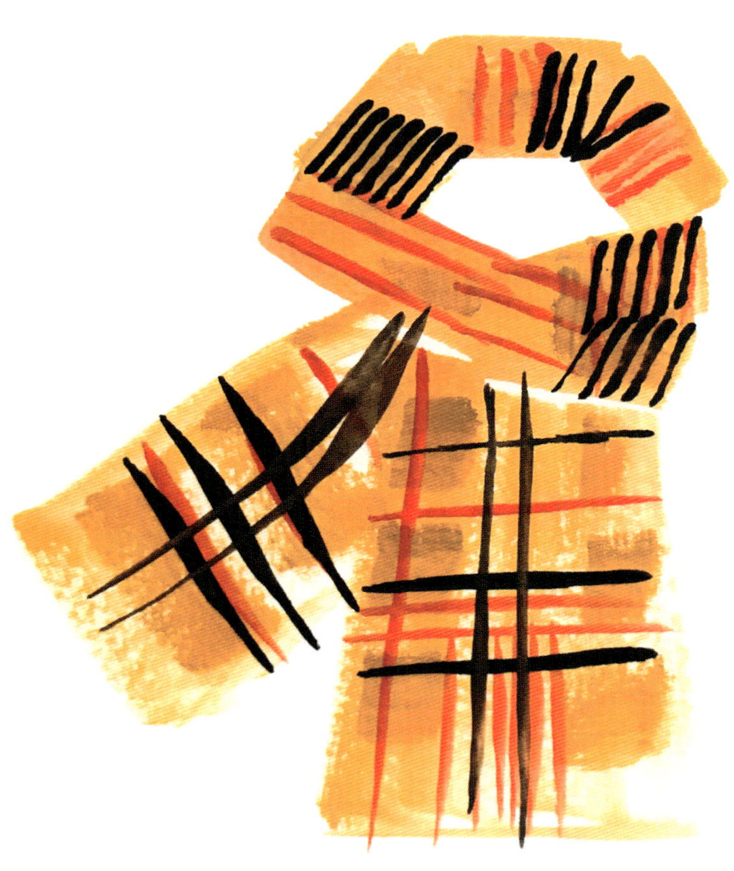

Step 3

Now dip the end of the brush into red paint and tap into the pattern along the neck and tails. Feel free to play here and add a variety of vertical and horizontal lines. Let this dry; then repeat with black paint.

Step 4

Add fringe using your liner brush and at least two colors. Lighten up on the strokes as you reach the end of the fringe to give it a wool-like texture.

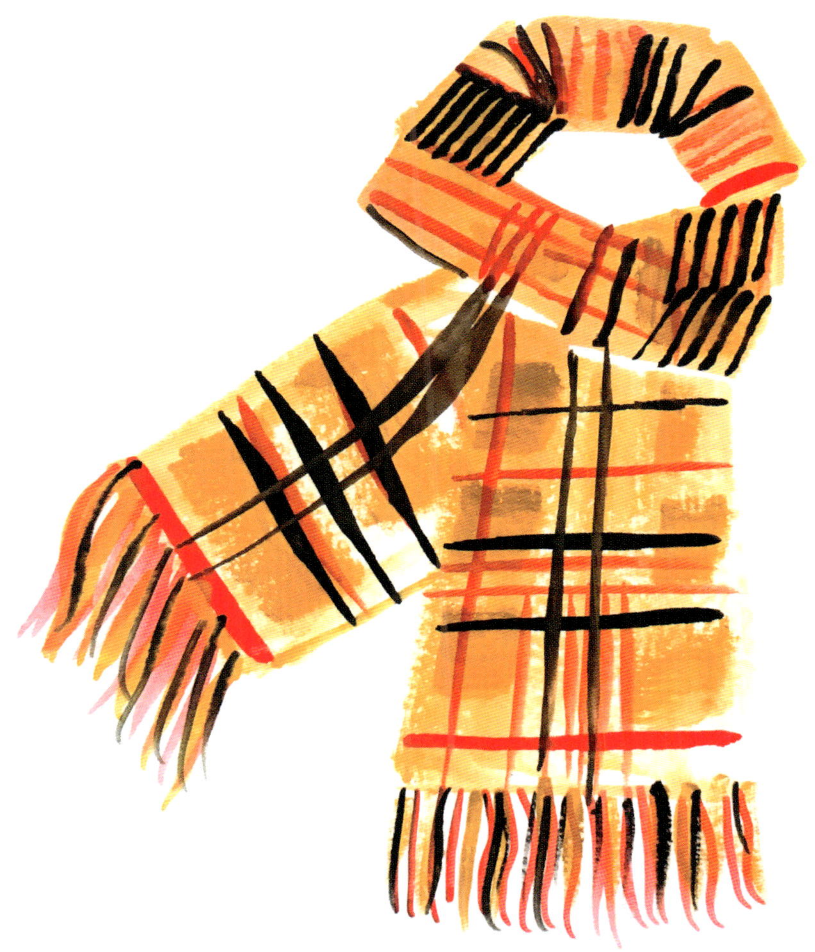

ABOUT THE ARTIST

Kristine Lombardi began her career in advertising and promotions, working on everything from Pepsi® and Conagra Brands to Orbitz® and Tanqueray®. In 2003, she left agency life to pursue both design and illustration, working with publishers, event planners, magazines, public-relations firms, corporate clients, and greeting-card companies.

In 2015, Kristine added author to her resume with the debut of her first picture book, ***Lovey Bunny*** (Harry N. Abrams). Her second book, ***The Grumpy Pets*** (also from Harry N. Abrams), received a glowing review in ***The New York Times*** and was named a "Children's Choices List" selection by the International Literacy Association. Her books have been translated into Romanian, Chinese, Korean, and Japanese. Kristine's work on ***Mr. Biddles*** (HarperCollins) was featured in "Ephemera" from ***UPPERCASE*** in 2019. She illustrated a timely picture book for Macmillan Publishers about inclusion and diversity, which released in 2020. Kristine is the author of ***Nature Painting in Watercolor***, from Walter Foster Publishing.

Kristine also teaches illustration classes for the Montclair Art Museum and community outreach programs, working with people of all ages, from 5 to 90. She creates artwork for the licensing industry and works on everything from greeting cards and gifts to decorative tableware, soft goods, and wall art. An early riser, Kristine can be found creating in her sunny studio while her sweet calico rescue, Boo, naps nearby.

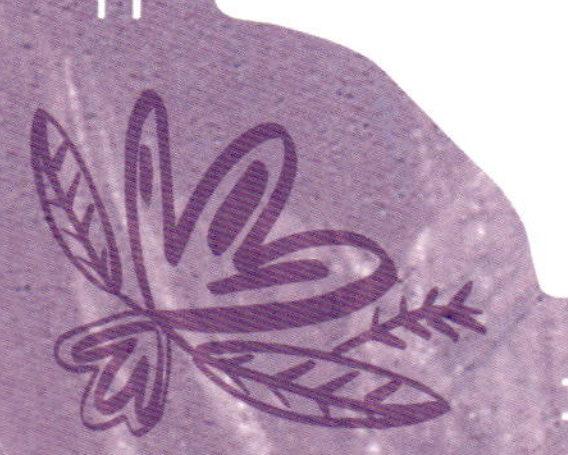